The Unconverted Self

The Unconverted Self

JEWS, INDIANS, AND
THE IDENTITY OF CHRISTIAN EUROPE

Jonathan Boyarin

The University of Chicago Press   CHICAGO & LONDON

JONATHAN BOYARIN is the Leonard and Tobee Kaplan Distinguished Professor of Modern Jewish Thought at the University of North Carolina at Chapel Hill. He is the editor or co-editor of five books, most recently of *Jews and Other Differences* (1997); the co-author (with Martin Land) of *Time and Human Language Now* (2008) and (with Daniel Boyarin) of *Powers of Diaspora* (2002); and the author of six books, most recently of *Jewishness and the Human Dimension* (2008) and *Thinking in Jewish* (1996), the latter published by the University of Chicago Press.

The University of Chicago Press, Chicago 60637
The University of Chicago Press, Ltd., London
© 2009 by The University of Chicago
All rights reserved. Published 2009
Printed in the United States of America

18 17 16 15 14 13 12 11 10 09   1 2 3 4 5

ISBN-13: 978-0-226-06919-7 (cloth)

ISBN-10: 0-226-06919-2 (cloth)

Library of Congress Cataloging-in-Publication Data

Boyarin, Jonathan.
The unconverted self : Jews, Indians, and the identity of
Christian Europe/Jonathan Boyarin.
p. cm.
Includes bibliographical references and index.
ISBN-13: 978-0-226-06919-7 (cloth: alk. paper)
ISBN-10: 0-226-06919-2 (cloth: alk. paper) 1. Christianity and other religions—
Judaism. 2. Christianity and other religions—Islam. 3. Indians of North America—
Religion. 4. Europe—Ethnic identity. I. Title.
BM535.B64 2009
261.2—dc22
20099016596

♾The paper used in this publication meets the minimum requirements of the
American National Standard for Information Sciences—Permanence of Paper for
Printed Library Materials, ANSI z39.48-1992.

CONTENTS

Christianity began as a movement among Jews, centered on narratives of redemption and election that were part and parcel of other Judaisms of the era. It
rapidly began to attract non-Jewish adherents, and at least one of its dominant
formulations, the Pauline one, richly elaborates the tension early Christians
faced between the Jewish origins of their faith and its universal aspirations.
Repeatedly and in many places since that time and place (if not constantly and
ubiquitously), Christian thought, rhetoric, symbolism, narrative, and doctrine
have all been profoundly shaped by the tension between the Church's assertion of itself as the true Israel and the desire to become at last fully Christian precisely by expunging the Jewish trace from each Christian body and
from the universal body of Christ whose members Christians are held to
be. Again, repeatedly and in many places, Christianity and its cultures have
been driven by the desire to incorporate all of humanity while remaining
confident of the lineaments and litmus tests of true Christian faith.

Jews, Judaism, and Jewishness thus constitute formations of difference
both anterior to Christianity (whose sacred history only makes sense in
the context of the earlier dispensation to the Jews) and present "inside" its
geography—both its sacred landscape in the Holy Land and, especially for the
Latin or European Christendom I study here, inside the Roman Empire whose
official religion Christianity became. As such, they provide a striking point of
comparison and contrast, and at some points a convenient or nagging rhetorical model, for forms of difference encountered by Christians after the Church
and its role were well established.

I have chosen to juxtapose here Jewishness, as a problematic difference in late-medieval Europe, to the difference presented to Spanish arrivals in sixteenth-century New Spain by the native peoples there. Huge that topic is, and this essay must fall short of making any kind of definitive statement rather than being the spur to further comparison and contrast that I hope to inspire. If I intend to privilege anything by my juxtaposition of the Jewish and Indian differences, it is not the relationship between those differences per se; this is not some allegorical revival of the "lost tribes" thesis. Rather, my aim is to help us move beyond rhetorics of domination and resistance in our studies of collective identity, and toward consideration of dimensionality itself—space and time—as rhetorical tools and matters for anxiety in identity discourses. Both of these dimensions of identity—the spatial and the temporal—are contested, material, and contingent, as is suggested by the Andrew Marvell poem that inspires this book's title: we need world, and we need time as well.

Muslims and Islam are key to this analysis, first because of their obvious salience to Christians and Christianity as interlocutors and adversaries throughout the period examined in this book, but also because they disrupt the neat contrast between Jews and Indians suggested by the paragraph above. Muslims were not before or after, not inside or outside the formation of Christian Europe, that discursive formation whose very contingency this book aims to bring into new relief. Surely, my primary focus on the way Jewish difference denaturalizes any idea of a preexisting Europe is not intended to reinforce the distinction between " 'Europe and the Jews' and 'Islam and the West,' "[1] both of which reify Europe as well as the West. On the contrary, even if my gaze here is turned primarily from the Eurasian headland toward the New World, I hope to contribute more generally toward undoing the divisions between "modern and nonmodern, West and non-West."[2] Like the hero of Edwin Abbott's *Flatland*, who had experienced a third dimension but had trouble articulating more than two, I know that a fuller incorporation of the people called Muslims and of Islamic difference would yield an infinitely richer account. But that account is one I cannot articulate myself—at least not yet.

*

Acknowledging the assistance I have received in a project this long in gestation is a particular honor. The first time I presented the outlines of this project, Louise Tilly called it "exciting," and I am grateful to her for that. Research for the first draft of this book was supported by a grant from the Center for Jewish Studies at the City University of New York, facilitated by Marshall Berman and Paul Ritterband. Further work was made possible by a generous fellowship from the Harry Frank Guggenheim Foundation, and the book's completion was assisted by the Lucius N. Littauer Foundation. I owe further debts to the Center for Studies of Social Change at the New School for Social Research, where much of the reading and writing was done and where I first broached the subject in seminar; to Warren Bargad at the University of Florida, Donald Pease at Dartmouth College, Kalman Bland at Duke University, Osvaldo Pardo at the University of Connecticut, Jeffrey Cohen at George Washington University, Malachi Hacohen and Yaakov Ariel of the Jewish Studies Colloquium of Duke University and the University of North Carolina, and especially the Jesuit-Jewish Dialogue Conference, for sponsoring productive discussions of various drafts; to Bob Singerman for bibliographic suggestions; to Bud Bynack for indispensable editorial assistance; and to Chava Boyarin, Daniel Boyarin, James Brundage, Bill Christian, Sarah Nalle, Jonathan Schorsch, Peter Antelyes, Jennifer Ottman, Arthur Steinberg, Steven Epstein, Osvaldo Pardo, Andrew Bush, Jean-Pierre Sonnet, James Brundage, and Talal Asad for vitally useful comments and corrections. Marc Shell, Talal Asad, Jeremy Cohen, Charles Tilly, Louise Tilly, and Caroline Walker Bynum have served as referees on grant applications too numerous to recount. Elissa Sampson encouraged me to keep going. I can only hope that this book repays their trust.

This book seeks to help move us beyond the notion of what all too frequently are still taken to be two separate histories of Europe—before and after its 1492 encounter with the majority of the earth's population—toward a unified understanding of the tenuous constitution of Christian Europe.[1] Postcolonial scholarship has illuminated the difficult project of sustaining Christian European identity; what follows here aims to reflect insights about that project back onto questions of earlier and continuing Jewish difference and to suggest that these stories are ultimately one. It also points to ways—one is tempted indeed to say *crucial* ways—in which the troubling instability of Jewish difference shaped both Christian Europeans' self-image and their reactions to those they encountered in the course of exploration and conquest beyond what became Europe's borders.[2]

Although I call on evidence, especially literary and polemical, from much of what we now call northern and western Europe, my primary focus is on the regions eventually known to us as Spain, and on their particular colonial venture in the New World. Indeed the notion of Spain was reinvoked, on the model of ancient Roman Hispania, by the married monarchs of the joined kingdoms of Aragon and Castile in the same era as that fateful conjuncture which saw the fall of Granada, the expulsion of the joint kingdom's subjects who still confessed Judaism, and the departure of Columbus for the Indies that he went on to believe he had found.[3] Certainly Spain was not simply a representative case of a Christian Europe that, while it was itself never achieved as a political reality, nevertheless received further impetus as an articulated idea in and through the colonial encounter of many Europeans—and not only the Spanish—with the world beyond its co-territorial boundaries.[4] Nor, precisely because of the rich Jewish and Muslim presence within Iberia, can we presume that these figures of difference were juxtaposed to native difference in the same way by other European Christian colonizers as by the Spanish. Indeed, what I will call the Spanish case is especially revealing because of the extraordinarily rich and vital presence of Jews and Muslims within Spain's Christian realms—hence the especially rich evidence of how the legacy of Jewish difference, my particular concern, both shaped and contrasted with the management of difference between the colonizers and the colonized in sixteenth-century New Spain.

More generally, for both scholarly and ordinary Christians in medieval Western Christendom, Jews were an especially spectral other—neither quite dead nor quite external.[5] The stubborn survival of Jewish otherness spoke constantly to the limits of the Catholic Church's effort to include all of humanity within the spiritual and juridical body of Christ. Difference as such was a theological challenge to medieval churchmen such as Alan of Lille, for whom God was the ideal unity, and for whom accordingly "plurality increases with the distance from God."[6] Reducing difference to unity was thus a process of conversion, aimed simultaneously or sequentially at the non-Christian other and the unconverted Christian self. Within Christian Europe during and after the Middle Ages, Judaism as the "elder sibling" of Christianity already had provided a testing ground for the limits of Christian tolerance and the duties of Christian missionizing. So when Christian Europeans were faced with fellow humans who by most accounts had never been exposed to the Gospel truth (as the Jews certainly had), but who also appeared to present no rival claim to a universal divine revelation (as the Jews appeared to do), their experience with Jews as one of their most intimate others profoundly influenced their behavior and their explanations of it.

The relation between Jews and figures of Jewishness on one hand and Christianity in its self-presentation and its stance toward the rest of the world on the other has hardly been ignored. Some critical accounts of the colonial mindset see Jews—or at any rate ancient Israelites—as key figures in the rhetorical evolution of what became European imperialism. Thus, Frederick Turner sees a direct line of succession from Old Testament Israelite exclusivism and triumphalism to the devastating chauvinism of the early modern Europeans.[7] He does, therefore, relate Jews and American Indians, but in a way that obviates the subaltern status of European Jews, absorbed as they are (along with all other difference and distinctions within Europe) into a monolithic Western identity whose members are said to "shar[e] the same religious symbols" and that simplistically assumes that "monotheism" is at the root of both Israelite and modern European genocidal impulses. Following Turner, Peter Hulme sees a contradiction in European colonialism "between the 'restlessness' implicit in the Judaeo-Christian search for salvation (embedded in the 'mobile' imagery of pastoralism) and the classical ideal of the civic institutions of the polis: the city of this world."[8] It is not clear why Hulme should imagine that it is possible to describe Christianity, here subsuming its "Judaeo" component, in global terms opposed to the shaping influence of Greek and Roman culture, except that the rhetorical appeal of the dichotomy between Jerusalem and Athens seems to be irresistible.[9]

Failure to integrate the question of Jewishness in a dynamic history of difference that helps to constitute the very notion of Europe facilitates a different claim: that Jews suffered at certain times and places precisely because they were more "advanced"—that is, because they had already proceeded further along the predestined line of progress culminating in modern values and forms of knowing and inquiry. Thus José Faur's account of *conversos* and modernity asserts a stark contrast between backward, repressive, authoritarian Spanish Christianity and enlightened, individualistic, tolerant Judaism as exemplified by Maimonides.[10] In Faur's account the Iberian *conversos*, on acquiring Christian identity, were shocked at the loss of the individual autonomy they had enjoyed as Jews.

In this implicit scheme of cultural criticism there is a certain "stage of individuation" that different societies reach at different times, and some abstraction called "the Jew" reached that stage before "the West" did. Even within the latter, Iberia was a latecomer. Faur elaborates on the consequent distinction, providing a brief genealogy of Western notions of difference. Here he equates the ill treatment of both Jews and Indians, attributing it to concepts "deeply rooted in all Indo-European languages, in which the notions 'alien,' 'enemy,' and 'guest' are semantically and legally connected. These notions continued to linger throughout Europe. Spain never advanced beyond this initial stage."[11] As in the cases of Hulme and Turner, an analysis supposedly motivated by interest in the critique of racist and colonialist prejudice here relies on the most hoary constructions of nineteenth-century cultural philologies and higher criticism. Faur's epistemology, too, is exactly parallel to those of Hulme and Turner. Where they find the roots of imperial intolerance in Hebrew monotheism, Faur finds the antithesis of that intolerance, and its only antidote, in that very same place: "The discovery of the 'other' is the source of Hebrew morality and religion: it leads to the recognition of human subjectivity and monotheism."[12]

With Hulme and Turner we have a direct lineage from supposed Hebrew Bible chauvinism to Christian imperial exclusivism; with Faur we have a direct lineage from other-oriented Hebrew ethical monotheism, transmitted through the "elite" of the Jewish community, into the only voice protesting against Christian imperial exclusivism. Either of these master narratives can be sustained only through the most patently evident elisions and distortions of the record.[13]

What is the alternative? For some time now, critics of colonialism and literature have begun to question a somewhat conventionalized scholarly identification with the colonized, at least insofar as such critical examination of the colonial encounter is considered to be liberating or decolonizing in itself. Rolena Adorno, for example, has suggested that the very use of the term "colonial discourse"—with its overarching emphasis on the characteristics shared by every moment in the colonial encounter between modern(izing) Europe and what became "the Third World"—may be unhelpful when considering relations between the Spanish and indigenous Americans in the sixteenth and seventeenth centuries.[14] More abruptly, Stephen Greenblatt summarized what he called the academic left's belief that " 'difference' and 'otherness' are more progressive, more hopeful, than 'the illusory goal of wholeness'" and asked: "But why should we believe any of this?"[15]

Part of the answer is that we need not assume so rapidly that a positive valuation of difference depends on linking it to progress or hope. Much is at stake that has to do precisely with a reevaluation of progress. Sensitivity to difference need not be coupled with adherence to any fixed notion of progressive enlightenment.

Imagining people in history (especially those we do not see as our genealogical, moral, or intellectual ancestors) as we see ourselves may leave us more open to the moral contingencies of different choices made in the past, and less tempted to indulge in "progressive" triumph or demonization. At the same time I do not propose a return to an aesthetic of history as either sequentially ordered cultural determinism or an attempt to escape from the concerns of the present. Attempting to chart moments in the past and calibrate them with our own situation in the present as a way to understand our trajectory into the future is not the only way to conceive the link between our own situation and the situation we study. It is also possible to inquire into our limitations, the hopes and anxieties that move and hinder us, the received ideas whose contingency we recognize even as we hold onto them in desperation—and then to look for analogous formations, obsessive or inarticulate as they might be: articles of faith or reckless heresies that shaped the discourses and lives of

Jews, *conversos*, Muslims, *Moriscos*, Indians, friars, conquistadors and others, all centuries ago.

DOMINANCE AND DIFFERENCE

For some decades now, scholars have learned to question the nature and techniques of dominance in the production of Western subjectivity and the political and social modes of organizing and employing power. Problematizing dominance in medieval Europe helps especially in our attempts to understand the troubled and productive place of Jews and Jewishness. Thinking of dominance and difference as produced, not given, is one way for us to get beyond the older theory of anti-Semitism as scapegoating—beyond, that is, the simple assumption of cynical recourse to anti-Jewish rhetoric by various social groups in conflict. Moving the debate beyond the question of whether more or less anti-Judaism is found among non-Jews at a given time and place,[16] or even throughout that vast timespace called later medieval Europe, likewise opens up the question of the dynamics of anti-Christianity in medieval Jewish texts and demands that this issue be conceived more dynamically.[17]

This critical effort shifts our picture of the European past and the colonization of the New World considerably from an older consensus that was both Eurocentric and, sometimes less obviously, Christocentric. As late as the mid-1960s, for example, a respected historian of the New World, Lesley Bird Simpson, could introduce a new translation of a pathbreaking Spanish historical work with assurance that "the reader will confidently share" its author's "frank admiration of the first missionaries."[18] In the study introduced by Simpson, *The Spiritual Conquest of Mexico* (originally published in 1931), its author Robert Ricard calls evangelization "one of the glories of the sixteenth century."[19] In retrospect, of course, what is interesting is not whether sixteenth-century missionizing was or wasn't glorious, but that early in the twentieth century a scholarly author could so unquestioningly presume a reader who viewed the missionary heritage in this light.

Still, Ricard's book was itself pathbreaking in its carefully researched and detailed character. Ricard admitted that the missionaries "considered their Indians to be a little like children" and that some of them had "a secret and at times unconscious will to dominate." He attended to topics that have become fashionable only in the last decade, such as the ethnographic and linguistic training of the missionaries. He acknowledged that the form of his account was imposed by his own design, not simply by the facts of the history he studied.[20] Still, his book is entirely predicated on the assumption that the Spanish missionaries' endeavor to bring about mass conversion to Christianity was worthy and reasonable.

Thanks in part to detailed critiques of the techniques of domination and differentiation in medieval and early modern Europe and the New World, that assumption is no longer part of the scholarly consensus on European colonialism. This change has come through work by historians, anthropologists, and other scholars both within the "Western" academy and in universities and other settings in the decolonizing world. Their accomplishment now makes it possible for scholars to combine generous human interest in the missionaries' conceptions with full awareness of their often blinding arrogance, along with an understanding that they were as determined and sometimes "as ruthless as any conquistador."[21]

MAKING THE DOMINANT

At the same time, historians of European Christianity now understand that much Christian polemical literature that has been aimed explicitly at the demonization of non-Christians has served first and foremost to reinforce an anxious Christian identity.[22] There is little to be learned from assuming that ethnocentrism and demonization of difference are "natural" in human history, or from then proceeding to the further assumption that those with greater power will manifest proportionately greater ethnocentrism and demonization, for such assumptions preclude any possibility of historicizing and comprehending specific dynamics that link power, identity, generosity and anxiety. In particular, the very process of separating out orthodox Christianity from rabbinic Judaism shaped not only Christian rhetoric and attitudes toward Jews ever after, but also dominant European stances toward difference more generally.[23] My focus is on the centuries closer to the beginning of the New World encounter, a period of both internal expansion and renewed tensions at the boundaries—whether geographical or symbolic—of Christendom, Judaism, and Islam. Beginning in that era, the often complex and contradictory efforts to produce (or purify) a Christian Europe and then a Christian globe on that European model began to be articulated and to take recognizable and analyzable form. Key to that effort were articulations of the nature of non-Christians that made the efforts to unify Europe and the world seem simultaneously necessary, possible, and open to serious and persistent doubts. In that same era, treatment of Europe's Jews also began to be systematized in ways that would sometimes serve as templates for the subsequent treatment of other forms of difference.

A signal moment during that period was certainly the Fourth Lateran Council in 1215, which reflected, crystallized and further stimulated the broad process of rationalization and surveillance. Fourth Lateran was notable also for the emphasis in several of its decrees on tensions and balances between church and crown.[24] By the thirteenth century, the church bureaucracy had become sufficiently well ordered and ramified that the Holy See could pass regulations relating to Jews in Christendom and expect them to be carried out—although sometimes it was disappointed. Archbishop Rodrigo of Toledo, for example, avoided implementation within his diocese of Fourth Lateran's regulations aimed at the segregation and degradation of Jews in lands where the Roman church held sway.[25]

In any case, neither the church in general nor the papacy in particular was always on the side of intolerance. On the contrary, virtually the only parts of western Europe from which Jews were never expelled at least temporarily during this period were the lands directly controlled by the pope. Furthermore, whatever pragmatic reasons may have existed for such relative tolerance, it was also reinforced by ideology, because the Holy See often maintained the authoritative traditional rationales for the continued presence of living Jews in Christendom—in particular, that Jews were to be converted in advance of the Second Coming, and that in their degraded current state they served as exempla of the fate of nonbelievers.[26] Thus Augustine's *City of God* "interprets the divine prophecy of Jewish survival as a mandate for the faithful: Slay them not, that is, ensure their survival and that of their Old Testament observance; and scatter them, guaranteeing that the conditions of their survival demonstrate the gravity of their error and the reality of their punishment."[27] In this version of the sacred history, there was indeed a thing called "the Jews"—and they were put on indefinite hold, in anticipation of the events surrounding the Second Coming.

In their writings about Jews, churchmen such as Bernard of Clairvaux, Peter the Venerable, and Abelard emphasized anti-Jewish themes that were new or revived from previous centuries without constituting a full-scale rejection of Augustine's doctrine.[28] From the eleventh century onward, there was greater antagonism toward Jews in the regions of Christendom we now know as northern and western Europe.[29] Miri Rubin, for example, cites the Dominican Giordano of Rivalto's emphasis on the Jews' "agency in Christ's death and their abiding desire to harm, to 'recrucify' him" as reflecting "the impact of the developments of the thirteenth century."[30] Again, what is striking here, yet perhaps still so much a given of our common culture that it is easily overlooked, is the notion that "the Jews" in Giordano's time were the same as those supposed to have brought about Christ's death, and hence characterized by the same motivations.

Of course the manifestations of this antagonism were not only scholarly or theological. Some were graphic.[31] Others were folkloric, such as the increasingly sharp anti-Jewish tone taken during the thirteenth century in Christian miracle stories such as the one about "a Jewish child thrown by his father into an incandescent oven as punishment for taking communion with his young Christian friends"[32]—perhaps an early example of the "repressive father" theme that was to become so prominent later in European modernity.

I spoke above of northern and western Europe. It is plausible to map a generalized deterioration of "the Jewish condition" thoughout western Europe from the twelfth through the fourteenth centuries, and then to view similar processes as taking place in Iberia a century or so later.[33] Indeed, it is tempting to see the expulsion of the Jews from Spain in 1492 as having come toward the end of two centuries of expulsions that exhibited, as one historian has recently summed it up, "remarkable unanimity among the rulers of Europe."[34] Yet such a schematic view is misleading—and with its implied endorsement of the old trope of Spanish backwardness, it risks leading us into an old, continuing, yet less than illuminating debate about Spain's place on some implicit or explicit timeline of European and world history. To paraphrase Walter Benjamin, the notion that such uncivil behavior was "still" possible in Iberia risks invoking the famous "Black Legend" of Spanish intolerance and cruelty in the New World, itself a legacy of contests between England and Spain at the beginning of what we call the early modern period.[35] Perhaps the worst consequence of suggesting that what happened in Spain had happened earlier elsewhere in Europe would be the reinforcement of the notion that Spain fully became part of Christendom, or of Europe, only when the *Reconquista* was completed. Nothing is further from my intention; yet it would be equally absurd to suppose that, for example, a polemic composed in Paris or a sermon from Clairvaux were part of some separate "French" history of Christianity and difference, and thus were not pertinent to what was said and done in Iberia.

Arguments about the epochal nature of 1492 do nevertheless tend to assume that in that year there was a Spain that was part of Europe and acted as the standard-bearer, as it were, for Europe's meeting with the world beyond its shores. The philosopher Enrique Dussel has made the claim, again plausible enough but also rather circular, that "modernity" is marked first and foremost by the incorporation of the entire world into the "modern world-system" and thus begins with the constitution of Spain with reference to its periphery—in short, that "modernity begins in 1492."[36] Others, famously, have identified the onset of modernity in the double consciousness of *conversos*—Jews and their descendants who remained in Iberia at the price of real, nominal, or generally ambiguous conversion to Catholicism.[37] Still others have suggested, with somewhat different implications, that Spain's bureaucracies and categorical approaches to the management of racialized populations placed it in the "vanguard" of modern nations.[38] To avoid charges of mystification, any such efforts should always acknowledge their relative arbitrariness and specify what it is they are trying to clarify about epochal or spatial designations such as modernity, Europe, or the world-system. By privileging Jewish difference in my analysis, I am trying both to highlight the dynamics of Christian identity formation that shaped European Christians' responses to those different from themselves, and to undermine any notion that 1492 represents an absolute new beginning. I do not seek—quite—to argue for an earlier commencement to modernity (such as the Fourth Lateran Council of 1215); but my argument does assume that the ever-unachieved (and only partially articulated) Europe is indeed already making itself, ideologically, bureaucratically and territorially, long before 1492, as a Christian unity.

To start the story in 1492, to maintain that momentous year as a reified marker of epochal differences, facilitates misreadings even by such a master as Walter Mignolo. When he writes that Christianity, as "cause and consequence" of colonialism, preceded "the civilizing mission,"[39] Mignolo occludes the long history of identification between Christianity, civilization, and indeed humanity that facilitated the description of Jews, Muslims, and others as bestial, and of non-monotheists as barbarous. Elsewhere he suggests that a denial of coevalness—the transformation of difference in space into difference in time—was particular or even unique to European colonial ideology in the late nineteenth century.[40] Such an assertion ignores the "pre-contact" construction of the Jews as, in the term that Jeremy Cohen has borrowed from medieval Christian scholars, "living letters of the law" rather than coevals. Indeed it ignores the entire legacy of Christian supersessionist history, which sees contemporaneous Jews as anachronisms, frozen in their stubborn nature at the very moment when they rejected the messiahship of Christ. Moreover, Mignolo's suggestion that what are "really" differences in space were recast as differences of time indirectly but powerfully reinforces the idea that the people back in the place called Europe were all basically the same. Against, for example, Barbara Fuchs' insistence that the politics of difference within the metropole are part and parcel of the politics of identity in the colonial encounter, Mignolo's silencing or casual summary of difference within Europe implies that spatial proximity can be safely assumed to imply relative lack of differentiation.[41]

Most pertinently, perhaps, Mignolo suggests that because Jews and Muslims were "people of the book" whereas Indians were seen as idolaters, the experience of contending with the former differences was largely irrelevant to New World encounters.[42] Many see it differently, as I will explore in this book.

To be sure, Christian Europe never became quite the unambiguous entity described in modern historiography.[43] One advantage of considering the place of Jews there, both as Europe became a problematic whole and then in the context of European encounters with peoples and places beyond, is the ability it affords to demonstrate clearly that what may be taken as particularly Spanish (the relations between conversion, expulsion, elaboration of differences, and construction of a collective self) neither began with Spain nor were unique to it—except insofar as Spain was blessed with more Jews than were other parts of Europe.[44]

SHRINKING THE PLACE OF JEWS IN AN EXPANDING EUROPE

Various explanations have been offered for the evident increase of intolerance in medieval Europe and the exclusion of Jews in the fourteenth and fifteenth centuries. They range from the economic (the need for capital accumulation by early nation-states) to the theological (the reformist movements growing out of the Fourth Lateran Council).[45] Of course, "Gentile tales" about Jewish perfidy—primarily ritual murder and host desecration—had often been available for centuries to facilitate acts of expulsion.[46]

The standard approach to European Jewish historiography assumes that economic and social crises tend to lead to intolerance, whereas situations of economic expansion are generally conducive to Jewish immigration and opportunity. Such, for instance, is the general explanation of the earliest shifts of European Jewish population centers from western to central and eastern Europe in the later Middle Ages. The assumption seems at first blush unobjectionable, but does it fit the general situation in western Europe over the three or four centuries of the later Middle Ages? One historian characterizes the period in broad terms thus: "From the eleventh century until the slump and crisis of the fourteenth and fifteenth centuries stretch the High Middle Ages, an epoch of economic growth, territorial expansion and dynamic cultural and social change."[47] Certainly, even though the first formal expulsions of Jews from western Europe did not take place until the end of the thirteenth century—roughly, that is, just before the "slump and crisis" period—they were a transformation and in some sense a culmination of some two centuries of increasing polemics, agitation, libels, legal restriction, and other constrictions of Jewish life.

In fact, these changes were not merely dynamic but in many respects disastrously disruptive. Jews were not merely scapegoated and hounded out when times got bad. They were first exploited and then, as the British phrase has it, "made redundant" with the development of a Christian urban trading and literate class and often with the increasing financial rationalization of the central state.

It is in these terms that R.I. Moore understands an agreement between the Capetian King Philip Augustus and the count of Champagne in 1198 regarding mutual promises vis-à-vis each other's Jews. The agreement, which facilitated the imposition of charges for protection, for the return of goods after seizure, or for permission to return to the kingdom after temporary expulsions, was enforced until the conclusive expulsion of 1394.[48] Moore understands this increased extraction of capital from Jews as part of the elaboration of a "persecuting society," something more than just the pursuit of short-term economic benefit by ambitious local monarchs. Rather, the much more broadly intertwined changes in class hierarchy, legitimation, and state building that constituted the consolidation of state power in these centuries underlay the imposition of ideological control and the persecution of groups such as lepers, heretics, and Jews.[49]

To be sure, it is all too easy to read Moore's evocative phrase, "the formation of a persecuting society," as suggesting that twelfth-century vilification and exclusion inevitably culminated in twentieth-century genocide.[50] Against this, we are well reminded that the late-medieval effort to create a synthesis of bureaucratic and ideological unity was riven both by the frailty of the newly centralizing powers and by the sheer entrenchment of diversity in various forms.[51] The Jews did not disappear permanently from Latin Christendom; indeed, reconsideration of their situation in northern and central Europe in the later Middle Ages suggests that while their integration there may not have led to such spectacular cultural collaboration as did the fabled Iberian *convivencia*, their lives were characterized by a fundamentally continuous though sometimes interrupted *Zusammenleben*.[52] It is tempting here to endorse as my own Moore's claim, made in a subsequent book, that "[t]he cultural onslaught to which Jews and Judaism were subjected with mounting ferocity from the 1090s was essential to the construction of Latin Christendom."[53] But I do not know how central was the material role of Jews—nor, of course, whether or how the effort to unify Latin Christendom could have proceeded without the onslaught against them. In short, I do not know what was "essential."[54]

Beyond the question of persecution, this book is about what I might call the origins of an incorporating society. These centuries fascinate me as a scholar of Jewish difference and its relation to the politics of difference more generally, not because of any supposed teleology of genocide inside Europe, but because of the rationalization and regulation of identity and difference that took shape there at that time. In retrospect, these processes appear to have been central to the management of the effort to become Europe beyond its own boundaries, especially overseas. I do share, however, Moore's conviction that Jewish difference troubled and facilitated the drive toward rationalization and unity in profound and unique ways.

The mendicant orders (most pertinently here the Dominicans and Franciscans) likewise facilitated the broader economic and social transformations in the midst of which they first flourished. These links were explored some years ago in an essay connecting the rise of these orders to the "spread of the cash nexus," which, it is claimed, entailed a reactionary expression of revulsion at money and those who earned their living with it.[55] The mendicants filled several roles in response to this legitimation crisis. Unlike the older monastic orders, which largely sustained themselves by their own productions (mostly agricultural and textual), the mendicants provided a model for renouncing profit and capital accumulation while remaining involved in town life. Both their backgrounds and their missionary styles of argument were familiar to the new bourgeoisie; on the other hand, by offering the Gospel as their wares without monetary exchange, they reinforced the idea of a truer and nobler Christian commerce.[56] At the same time they also helped to regulate money exchanges and harmonize the changing economy with established Christian doctrine by separating, as it was believed, "the useful activities from the exploitative ones."[57] This helps explain some of their particular anti-Jewish vehemence.[58]

The later Middle Ages were a period not only of economic expansion and elaboration but also of the territorial expansion of Europe. The territories targeted for "conquest, colonization and cultural change" in the tenth through the fourteenth centuries were at the fringes of medieval Christianized realms— that is, in formerly Celtic lands, in Iberia, and in what we now think of as eastern Europe. For example, Robert Bartlett notes the scholarly consensus that a hardening of anti-Jewish feeling occurred in the later Middle Ages and then notes a similar xenophobic trend on the peripheries of Latin Europe at that time. He takes as a prime instance the increasing hostility toward non-Germans in Baltic German trading towns.[59] Explaining that "such harshness was not a monopoly of immigrant or colonial groups," he goes on to quote a fourteenth-century Bohemian tract, written in Latin, that describes the Germans as a "crafty and deceitful race" insinuating itself everywhere. The tract elaborates on the best way to take care of the problem:

> Oh God! The foreigner is preferred, the native crushed underfoot. It would be profitable, just and customary if the bear stayed in the wood, the fox in his den, the fish in water and the German in Germany. The world was healthy when the Germans were placed as a target for the arrow—in one place eyes were torn out, in another they were hung up by the foot, in one place they were thrown outside the walls, in another they gave their nose as a toll payment, in one place they were killed peremptorily in the sight of the princes, in another they were forced to eat their own ears, in one place they were punished one way and in another in a different way.

As Bartlett convincingly claims, "this passage is an appeal for a pogrom."[60] Yet its pertinence here, it seems to me, is not that it suggests medieval precedents for modern anti-Semitism or even genocide. On the contrary, its lesson is that the same terrifyingly murderous rhetoric may be applied to any number of abjected identities.

More broadly, at least two lessons about the formation of a persecuting society in the Middle Ages can be drawn from observing that the process of gradually delegitimizing and then physically displacing Jews was simultaneous with the overall expansion of the contiguous bounds of Europe. First, we need to remain sensitive toward traces of covertly providentialist or even subtly anti-Jewish notions of Jewish exceptionalism. Resisting these tendencies lets us fully appreciate the extent to which Jews and Judaism per se played a distinctive role in shaping the tensions of European history while we remain open to understanding how the situation of Jews was much like that of certain other groups, as is brought to light in the anti-German screed just quoted. To the extent that Jewish difference is treated as unique in this book—and without, of course, suggesting that culture or religion, as opposed to something else that might be called "material forces," is the motor of history—it is so treated primarily in respect to the problematic of the origins of Christian universalism in the early history of Christianity, rather than to any irreplaceable structural role of Jews in the medieval European economy.

Second, we are clearly reminded that structures of administration (land grants, missionary establishments) developed in the expansion of Europe at its contiguous boundaries were later applied overseas and that the tensions of group identity were part of the process of expansion. At the far and newest end of Christian Europe—in Estonia, for example—social structure was marked for centuries by a class and ethnic distinction between elite German speakers and Estonian-speaking peasants, while trust in pre- or non-Christian gods was maintained alongside the acknowledgment of the supreme God of Christianity and sacred spaces were both Christian and non-Christian.[61] Moreover, much as earlier missionaries in contiguous parts of the Eurasian land mass had worked to transform the sacred landscape of the places where they preached so that local inhabitants could see it both as Christian and as their own, so too New World missionaries transformed the sacred landscape, in New Spain as elsewhere, so that its numinous power could be directed toward Christ and the Christian sacred history.[62] For those whom we now call Spaniards, as we will see below, conquest of contiguous Muslim-ruled land was sometimes cast as Crusade while New World conquests were sometimes cast as continuations of the Iberian *Reconquista*.

The point, of course, is not to determine whether contiguous colonization, or rather the rhetorical obsession with the separation of Christians and Christianity from Jews and Jewishness, or rather again the ideological and military struggle against Islam and against *dar el-Islam*, was more fundamental than the other phenomena in shaping the consciousness, strategy, and experience of European Christian colonizers. The point is to train ourselves to keep it all in mind at once as we reflect on this massive history and its continuing effects on us. We will never have a settled, synthetic picture; the past won't sit still for it.

PLAN OF THE BOOK

Jewish difference, then, was refracted and articulated in a multitude of ways, as were many other differences. Moreover, the overseas colonizations we might still regard, somewhat simplistically, as having commenced in 1492 were—even if the lands targeted had been completely unknown—part and parcel of the efforts to expand, rationalize, and unify Christian Europe that had been going on for centuries. This book proceeds by studying the implications of these lessons in accordance with several broad themes. Historicizing the problem of "identity"—the content, extent, and limitations of selfhood, whether individual or collective—is the first theme. In the aftermath of both confident European modernity and the European colonial system, understanding what identity is (or was) has become a crucial project in the attempt to articulate new understandings of territory, history, polity, and personhood. In the first chapter, then, I specify the period from the twelfth through the sixteenth centuries as a time of powerful development and transformations in Christian European understandings of selfhood and identity, both personal and collective.

The next chapter engages the confrontation between the ideological edifice of Christian community on one hand and imaginary Muslims as well as Muslim power on the other. In a study concerned with rhetoricized figures of difference vis-à-vis Christian Europe from the twelfth through the sixteenth centuries, it is impossible to ignore Muslims (variously referred to in Christian medieval sources as Saracens, Turks, or Moors). Indeed, the figures of Muslims under these various names—whether as objects of polemic or as characters in festive ritual dramas—were intertwined in complex ways with the figures and realities of Jews and Indians. Moreover, since Islam represented a presence "inside" Christendom and a material power at its edges, the question of Muslim difference complicates significantly what might otherwise appear to be an overly schematized dichotomy between Jewish difference (internal, prior) and Indian difference (external, subsequent).

If Jews represent a paradigmatic (not quite an "essential") form of difference within the formation of Europe, and Indians a comparably significant difference without, it suggests that the boundaries of Christendom—a term existing in a complex lexical and chronological relation with Europe—exist within two registers. In one, Christendom is a spiritual kingdom, the set of all believers. In the other, it is the territorial extent of the lands ruled by Christian monarchs. The third chapter accordingly explores how Jews and Indians served as symbolic building blocks in constructing these dual bounds of Christendom.

Beyond but also fully implicit within the question of Christendom—especially with regard to the actual and potential set of all its members, as well as its actual and desired boundaries—is the question of the boundaries of humanity, the topic of the fourth chapter. This question was a substantial and explicit concern within medieval Christian European thought. The temptation to designate non-Christians as nonhuman was sometimes indulged, but not always—not least because doing so placed at risk the project of bringing all souls within the church. Certainly the nature, human or otherwise, of Jews and Indians were matters that engaged the cultural work of polemic, speculation, and representation, though neither the stakes nor the terms of the disputed humanity of Jews and Indians were quite the same.

Textuality in the broadest sense was a key locus of authority, control, and contestation in the Middle Ages and the early modern period, including the early period of colonialism. It operated across these linked fields of Christendom, Islamic difference, competitive scripture, and humanity, and is the subject of this book's fifth chapter. Jews, Christians, and indigenous Americans all had texts in various forms, each of which was vital as a central cultural reference. The appropriation, transmission, interpretation, and mystification of these texts differed significantly, as did the understanding of the relations between them. As discussed above, contemporary studies suggest that the displacement of Jews starting in the eleventh and twelfth centuries had much to do with a new spread of literacy among western European Christians, yet issues posed by the Jewish textual tradition continued despite the expulsion of communities and the burning of their sacred texts. The simultaneous translation and suppression of Mayan textual forms and their transformation by indigenous scholars are likewise important in a history of active resistance that continues today.

One of the lessons of postcolonial theory is that rhetorics of dimensionality are themselves contingent, linked to domination and hierarchic order. The field covered by this theory is both historical—a reconsideration of colonialism—and contemporary, and the two moments always interact with each other. To some extent, the logic of this book is dictated by the insight that the same imbrication of the colonizing and the colonized, of the historical and the contemporary, is effective "backward" to the Middle Ages as well as "forward" into postmodernity.[63] Hence my concluding reflections focus on the axes of anteriority and priority and of exteriority and posteriority—that is, of inside and before, outside and after. Far from suggesting that Jews are an other in time and the Indians an other in space, however, I am primarily interested throughout this book in how these specifications cross, disrupt, obscure, and potentially illuminate each other.

Moreover, the chapter divisions here are not about separate subjects (or even about separate media, as it might appear from having a separate chapter about textuality—or about different groups, as it might appear from having a separate chapter on Muslims). They are intended to articulate different facets of a single problem: how the creation of social meaning takes place amid constantly shifting relations of power and difference. To take perhaps the most obvious example, the question of group identity is inseparable from the question of humanity's boundaries. Anna Abulafia suggests that in complaining in writing that it was " 'to the injury of Christ that a man of Jewish race has seized for himself the see of St. Peter,' " Bernard of Clairvaux was not articulating what we would today think of as racial determinism. Rather, in a gesture that presumably would have been readily recognized by his audience, he was criticizing as Jewish the usury practiced by the Pierleoni family, to which the new pope belonged.[64] Textuality and humanity are equally tightly linked, as when Peter the Venerable diagnosed the Talmud as the source of the supposed extinction of reason in Jews, which led them to act like animals.[65] And the Jews' possession of a text upon whose authority Christianity likewise depended is not only part and parcel of the problem of anteriority and succession, but was also, for the church father John Chrysostom, a kind of pernicious idolatry worse than that of the Greeks: "an altar of deception in their midst which is invisible and on which they sacrifice not sheep and calves but the souls of men."[66] In short, having a false scripture can be worse than having none at all.

THE SHOCK OF JUXTAPOSITION

Muslim difference, Christendom, humanity, and textuality serve here as so many prisms through which we can begin to view the figures and realities of Jewish and Indian difference in the making and remaking of Christian identity. In the largest sense, this book is intended to expand further the field of juxtapositions we are able to consider as part of an immense legacy of rhetoricized identities and differences in contexts of differential power.[67] What we are accustomed to calling the coincidence of the expulsion of Jews from Spain, the fall of Muslim Granada, and Columbus's departure in 1492 is at once compelling and misleading, suggesting the need for sustained analysis of the kind that has only recently begun.[68] Such analysis is too often still used almost carelessly as a rhetorical foil for the supposed epochal boundary it is taken to represent, as in Tzvetan Todorov's observation:

> Columbus himself constantly links the two events. "In this present year 1492, after Your Highnesses have brought to an end the war against the Moors . . . [and] after having driven all the Jews out of your realms and dominions, Your Highnesses in this same month of January commanded me to set out with a sufficient armada to the said countries of India," he writes at the head of the journal of the first voyage.[69]

Unfortunately Todorov never returns to this coincidence in his book on *The Conquest of America*, which is largely concerned with an explanation of Cortés's victory through reference to the semiological superiority of the Europeans, whose "literacy" is contrasted with the Mexicans' supposedly omenhaunted, cyclical understanding of time.[70]

Another revealing aspect of Todorov's account—surely linked to his desire to set Columbus up as the emblematic modern hero—is his denial of any particular significance to the fact that Columbus's faith was a *Christian* faith:

"When we say that Columbus is a believer, the object is less important than the action: his faith is Christian, but we have the impression that, were it Muslim or Jewish, he would not have acted differently; what matters is the force of the belief itself."[71] To say as much is not only to reinforce the ancient and hoary rubric category of the "Abrahamic" religions or the "peoples of the book," but even more to reify something called faith as an autonomous agent in history. Surely this is no more the path to historical understanding than is the reduction of missionary passion to a bare rationalization for conquest and exploitation.

Another scholar, David Stannard, displays a similar confusion about the specificity of the links between Christianity and the colonizing ethos. He refers to "the Western Judeo-Christian culture that undertook the New World enterprise" and immediately goes on to identify as central to that culture "the typological mode [of interpretation, which] is essentially a New Testament, Christian instrument by which the past is made significant and justified."[72] Questions of the politics of hermeneutics, of supersessionist doctrines, and of their deployment in the colonial encounter cannot be raised from such a perspective, which exemplifies, in the very iteration of the hyphenated "Judeo-Christian," the mode of interpretation it seeks to specify and criticize. Ancient Hebrews, if anything, become proto-Christians while the Jews living before or contemporaneous with the New World enterprise are invisible or irrelevant. In short, Jewish difference is canceled out, further obscuring what is specifically Christian (and *not*, or surely not in any simple way, Judeo-Christian) about the work of global colonization from a European base.

By contrast, once "we" articulate the conviction—unarguable given the history of the twentieth century—that Jewishness remains a distinction that makes a difference in the cultural politics of Europe and its West, we no longer need share either Todorov's impression that the important thing is some vague religious force or Stannard's idea that the New World enterprise was undertaken by a monoculture. "Our vision is often more obstructed by what we think we know than by our lack of knowledge," writes Krister Stendahl.[73] The value of this book stems, I hope, from my not thinking I knew more than I did; perhaps it will likewise reveal to others new shores unknown until now.

CHAPTER ONE

Until the Conversion of the Self

Speaking from the side of Christianity, the other in this event (namely, Judaism) is not just the indifferent alien; it is one's own other, the difference of one's belonging, that which one's self-identity can neither exclude nor contain, the conflict of interpretation in which one lives and which one cannot transcend.
Gerald Bruns, "What is Tradition?"

Celsus remarked that "If all men wanted to be Christians, the Christians would no longer want them," and, although Origen vehemently denies the charge, we may wonder at what provoked the insight.
Judith M. Lieu, *Christian Identity in the Jewish and Graeco-Roman World*

The focus on the colonizer's rhetoric of the gift . . . allows us to raise an issue that . . . could well be identified as the reluctance of the giver, an instance that points to the limits or resistances of such rhetoric. I am not referring here to the claims on the impossibility of giving as a founding paradox in Christian theology but rather to what seems to be at stake in the self-figuration of the colonial enterprise as an act of giving—cultural and religious: the preservation of the original meaning of the gift during and after its transmission and, ultimately, the identity of the giver.
Osvaldo F. Pardo, The Origins of Mexican Catholicism

A "conversion identity"—an identity paradoxically dependent upon a radical change in identity—is historically constitutive of both the Christian community and the Christian individual. Steven F. Kruger, *The Spectral Jew*

Any project that attempts simultaneously to focus on the reciprocal effects of a dominant identity such as Christian Europe on others and on the formation of that identity is doomed to a vexing instability—using, and thereby reinforcing the seeming givenness of, what are actually contingent collective names.[1] Historians and theorists of colonialism have examined the capacity of the subaltern to speak, and have attempted to recuperate the vision of the vanquished.[2] As a result, perhaps by now we are better equipped to understand how domination is formed and constrained both by expert discourse on the dominated[3] and by shifting mixes of absorption and abjection of various constitutive outsides, whether geographic or symbolic. Christian Europe is a creative response to shared problems of human existence, yet the moral aesthetic, central to Christian Europe, of the autonomous and self-responsible believer entailed dramatic tensions, and often catastrophic swings, between impulses toward exclusion and inclusion as intrinsic elements of the formation of that response.

FRONTIERS OF IDENTITY

It may be that, along with the well-noted privilege in much Christian doctrine of the principle of autonomy,[4] there is something equally intrinsic to the universalizing logic of Christianity that constantly undermines this ideal of autonomous selfhood—that is, of identity. Being born to Christian parents does not guarantee one's own Christianity (certainly not, for example, in quite the same way that being born to Jewish parents has for centuries been said to guarantee one's Jewishness or even seal it as inevitable), and one of the richest moral motifs of this doctrine is that becoming Christian is a constant process. Christian identity is thus always under interrogation, never safe, fascinated by the dangers of what it is not. It is hardly surprising, then, that some missionaries sought martyrdom as a sanctifying imitation of the death of Christ.[5] Even in the absence of a named, external infidel, medieval Christians understood "the formation of the Christian's will" as a constant effort, a struggle against impulses within the self that are never conquered and banished once and for all, so that the Christian self is never fully formed, is never separated from that which is non-self, and is never quite safe.[6]

But the problem was not a new one in the dynamics of Christian self-making, nor was it seen as a flaw in the system. As Peter Brown notes, already Pope Gregory the Great (d. 604) followed the model of the classical philosophers in viewing the remaking of the self not only as possible but as a goal worth sacrificing the cultural comforts of home for.[7] Moreover, "Jerome's incisive sentence—'Christians are made, not born'—meant that all Christians were converts"—divided from themselves, never finished.[8]

What is remarkable is that the problem did not disappear after the first Christian centuries—after, that is, the possibility of being a Christian *and* a Jew was eliminated by generations of vigilant policing from both sides of the boundary.[9] It seems the separation was never complete, the divorce never finalized. Traces of that abjected, divided self, often explicitly identified as the figure of the Jew or of Jewishness, continued to haunt Christendom. Up to the modern period, for example, as Claudine Fabre-Vassas puts it in the course of documenting the central place of pigs and porciculture in defining European Catholic identity, "[e]very pig contains a Jewish trace, as does every Christian child."[10] Making a Christian thus entailed separating the neophyte from animality and from Jewishness. The abjected little Jew remained rhetorically present and articulate in the polemical *Dialogi Petri et Moysi Iudaei*, by the convert to Christianity known as Petrus Alfonsí: "To defend the arguments of the Christians, I have used the name which I now have as a Christian; to present the arguments of the adversary, the name which I had before baptism."[11] It is doubtless accurate that Christians in the later Middle Ages, sensitive to questions of the sincerity of conversion in an age that had already grown more introspective, were concerned about whether it was possible for someone born Jewish ever to fully shed that identity and become wholly Christian— but such concerns were hardly limited to those who had experienced the conversion from Judaism in their own lifetime.[12]

Reaching out to convert, especially to the extent it was accompanied by coercion, must have added a further element of self-doubt. The theologian Ramon Llull (d. 1315) urged compulsory attendance at Christian sermons by Jews and Muslims, yet also wrote that "no man can constrain another man to desire or to love by force."[13] Although conversion of those born Jews to Christianity throughout the Middle Ages was generally an incidental phenomenon, it took on mass proportions in Catholic Iberia in 1391 and after, inducing a culture of systemic doubt concerning both Christian and Jewish identities, and contributing accordingly to a growing obsession with genealogy.[14] Moreover, the conversations risked in the context of at least some conversionary efforts compounded this risk and doubt. Colonial and church authorities were made uneasy by friars who took the trouble to learn native languages.[15]

It might be argued that the formation of an image of the other is in no way particular to the dynamics of Christian self-making. Homi Bhabha cautions: "The 'other' is never outside or beyond us; it emerges forcefully, within cultural discourse, when we *think* we speak most intimately and indigenously 'between ourselves.'"[16] Bhabha's formulation might seem to leave no place for the autonomous existence of cultural formations that are not dominant in any given encounter. However, the broader interdisciplinary move by scholars to examine the particular contexts of domination and differentiation in various times and places has directly illuminated the problematic nature of dominant identity from the point of view of the dominated and in terms of subaltern agency.[17] The lived experience of Jews and Indians thus was not a separate, irrelevant, or extraneous matter from their image as the "other." Their voices and perspectives are relevant because their own particular characteristics and resistances constrained the imaginary field in which Christian European identity could be articulated.

Since the philosophical ideas of difference and otherness have been given sociohistorical context mostly in postcolonial cultural studies, it is easy to suppose that the cultural dynamics to which they refer arose first or predominantly with modern European imperialism. Yet the Europe that engaged in that project resulted from an already long history of rhetorical, ritual, legal, and other efforts to create and maintain structures of collective identity and difference.[18] In Iberia, the later Middle Ages were a time of conflict and creative interaction, and also of active separation between Christian, Jew, and Muslim, rather than a time of mere slippage into intolerance. Modern scholarship, anachronistically taking as a transhistorical norm the monocultural ideal of the European-derived nation-state system, persists in speaking of the coterritoriality of Catholic, Muslim, and Jewish cultures in Iberia as though they were three separate species that happened to survive reasonably well together and benefit from something like symbiosis.[19] More recent critical reconsiderations, often drawing explicitly on strategies for analyzing power and culture in the colonial and postcolonial nexus, have begun to reshape this received view of medieval Iberia and the rest of what we call the European continent.[20] What was, in the standard historiography, that freakish medieval situation ended on the brink of the Renaissance, precisely the period during which national vernaculars began to be promoted and standardized in western Europe and in which monumental national histories and epics began to be conceived. At the same time, that process of active separation of various groups was fostered by and helped to shape the intrusive Castilian state—a development that stimulated the expansion and rationalization of a textual bureaucracy which, in turn, was to foster the administration of Castilian empire overseas.[21]

We are used to thinking of Iberia—at least since the time of the mass conversion of Jews in 1391, through the eventual expulsion of the Moriscos in the early seventeenth century and beyond—as a chronotope in which an "extra-ordinary concern" prevailed about "boundaries, definitions, self-definitions, and classifications."[22] Yet when Caroline Walker Bynum wrote those words, she was actually thinking about western Europe in the twelfth century. As she notes, polemics in the twelfth and thirteenth centuries had more to do with the evocation of an other, to be excluded in rhetoric as a means of self-definition, than with any attempt at dialogue or even conversion.[23] Thus, when Saint Anselm (d. 1109) wrote his *Cur deus homo*, his purpose was to edify Christians, not to convince anyone else of the truth of Christianity.[24] And if we are accustomed to seeing the conversionary effort in missionary and adventurist guise, it is worth remembering that such a figure as Bernard of Clairvaux exemplified and legitimated the transition from a warrior ethos to a monastic ethos.[25]

Specific cultural technologies for the legitimation, maintenance, and regulated crossing of intercultural boundaries were part of these processes of active separation and self-definition. They were to continue to serve as important resources in subsequent colonial encounters. The relationship between Catholic European policies toward Jews in Europe and toward native peoples in Central and South America is not merely a matter of analogy. These two sets of relationships represent two moments in a broader attempt to achieve and maintain coherence within a collective that was both expanding and riven by doubts about the coherence and legitimacy of an identity it represented to itself as both Christian and European, freighting the terms with much baggage. Drawing out some of the patterns of this contingency can help to dispel the numbing effect of rhetoric that characterizes past centuries as enjoying "an instinctive belief in the natural superiority of Christians over mere 'barbarians.'"[26] Such language takes as a given the long process by which such belief could come to be questioned so rarely that in retrospect a leading historian could plausibly call it instinctive, and it occludes many fissures in that belief.

WHEN IS EUROPE?

Partly as a legacy of these peculiarly Christian problematics of selfhood and difference and partly as a heritage of ancient Greek analysis, Europe even today remains intensely concerned with the problem of its own identity. To a certain extent, this constant worry about articulating and analyzing identity is what constitutes the identity of Europe.[27] As we develop the problematic of dominant identity and various subordinate differences in medieval and early modern Europe, this recognition of the European anxiety about identity helps to guard against at least three potential pitfalls: caricature, pathos, and normatization. It is worthwhile identifying these pitfalls because my interrogation of Christian Europe is meant to humanize, not to exoticize.

Caricature

Early in Stephen Greenblatt's *Marvelous Possessions*, he summarizes the Christian dogma adhered to by "the Spanish" as seen from an alien perspective. The summary bears lengthy quotation.

> The Europeans who ventured to the New World in the first decades after Columbus's discovery shared a complex, well-developed, and, above all, mobile technology of power: writing, navigational instruments, ships, war-horses, attack dogs, effective armor, and highly lethal weapons, including gunpowder. Their culture was characterized by immense confidence in its own centrality, by a political organization based on practices of command and submission, by a willingness to use coercive violence on both strangers and fellow countrymen, and by a religious ideology centered on the endlessly proliferated representation of a tortured and murdered god of love. The cult of this male god—a deity whose earthly form was born from the womb of a virgin and sacrificed by his heavenly father to atone for human disobedience—in turn centered on a ritual (highly contested, of course, by the second decade of the sixteenth century and variously interpreted) in which the god's flesh and blood were symbolically eaten. Such was the confidence of this culture that it expected perfect strangers—the Arawaks of the Caribbean, for example—to abandon their own beliefs, preferably immediately, and embrace those of Europe as luminously and self-evidently true. A failure to do so provoked impatience, contempt, and even murderous rage.[28]

If the failure of "perfect strangers" to conform immediately to the doctrine produced "murderous rage," then just how confident was this "culture" really?[29] The problem underlying this apparent inconsistency in Greenblatt's description is characteristic of New Historicist analysis at its most culturalist, least historical, and most susceptible to a descent from characterization into caricature: Greenblatt collapses all of the Spanish into representatives of one "culture."[30] His statement in isolation (though not his entire book) elides vitally important distinctions among Spaniards who were present in the New

World or otherwise engaged in the colonial encounter, such as distinctions between *encomenderos* (landed colonizers) interested in cheap native labor and missionaries passionately defending the humanity and hence susceptibility to conversion of those same natives.[31] At the same time, Greenblatt's caricature also stands as a thumbnail characterization of the aspirations toward a common Christian European identity whose articulation—over the course of several centuries, and never fully realized—is studied in this book.

Pathos

If one pitfall is the reduction of a diverse and divided culture anxious about its own identity to the culture of "Europe" to which Europeans at most merely aspired, its obverse presents a similar "plot device" to be avoided—that of unified resistance by the colonized to efforts at domination by the colonizers. The temptation here is to evoke a hitherto unrevealed similarity between Jews and Indians as partners in resistance or shared complaint as fellow victims (such as is suggested by a title like Stannard's *American Holocaust*). Although recalling the undercurrent of resistance does help to avoid the impression that Jews and Indians served as passive, inert *foils* for Christian identity, over the course of centuries explicit Jewish and Indian identities were elaborated in ways that substantially overlapped with the modalities of Christian identity. Meanwhile, the resistant rhetorics and practices of Jews and Indians constrained the field of Christian autonomy, and thus profoundly contributed to the particular forms that Christian Europe took in the postmedieval era.

Normatization

Both of these pitfalls tend toward a third: the normatization of the objects of study. By the normatization of European Christianity I mean rhetorical complicity in its own presentation as the given, the "we" who know who we are and who are recognized as valid interlocutors of each other and of each Other. Such normatization is at work in passages like the following, from the press release accompanying the magnificent 1994 edition of Fray Diego Durán's *History of the Indies of New Spain* published by the University of Oklahoma Press:

> Although Durán abhorred practices such as human sacrifice, he expressed admiration for many aspects of Aztec culture. He attempted to destroy the remnants of the old beliefs, but he also wrote "so that the

memory of these people will live forever." Despite the fundamental differences between Aztec culture and our own, the basic human experiences and responses that we share with them are responsible in part for the fascination with the Aztecs that continues to the present day.

The reference to the difference between "Aztec culture and our own" places the potential audience for this book, along with the publishers, on the side of Diego Durán, who has presented Aztec culture for *us*, who are not the Aztecs. One might as well have identified Durán, who was born around 1537 and raised largely in Mexico,[32] with the Aztecs rather than with Anglophone readers of his book more than four centuries later. The choice to identify him instead with "us" is reinforced by the odd parallelism between the last two sentences of the paragraph quoted. The first states that despite Durán's attempt to destroy the old beliefs, he wanted their *memory* to live. The second distances Aztec culture "from us," but then asserts a sympathetic identification with the Aztecs. The chronotopic imperialism of ethnography is here in a nutshell: destroy their beliefs, retain their memory; distance ourselves from them, and indulge a fascinated identification with them once they are neutralized.[33] Exoticism and empathy combine powerfully to make it clear that there is no need for an Aztec voice, or even for compunction about "our" complicity in the silencing of that voice. Yet once a reader pauses to question the inclusive "our," the rhetoric loses its unquestioned and naturalized seductiveness. This disruptive intervention, this dissension from inside the dominant "we," remains necessary as a reminder of our place inside the net of domination. Juxtaposing Jews and Indians helps us to speak inside the "we" while retaining the barb of our own difference.

In the passage praising Durán, the logical analogy to Christian doctrines of supersession and the incorporation of Judaism should be clear enough: Jews, *in this sense* like Aztecs from the perspective of a progressive and expansive Christianity, represent something different, something which is properly but not quite dead, but whose record is worth preserving. Aztecs, like Jews, acquire a spectral presence prior to the advent of Christian Europeans and (unlike Jews) outside the history of salvation—displaced but not at rest, exercising, as the press release asserts, a continuing (magical?) fascination on us, living (at least in memory) forever.[34] The analogy between Jews and Aztecs here would be almost too obvious to mention, were it not for the fact that this supersessionist doctrine is often still concealed or confused in contemporary scholarship.[35]

THE COLONIZING SELF IN THE MIDDLE AGES

Within the terms of the supercessionist Christian chronology, Homi Bhabha places the shaping of the "modern Western disciplinary society"—and with it the identity vested in the "dehistoricized figure of Man"—in the mold of nineteenth-century high-European colonialism.[36] Yet it is clear that new juridical regimes and disciplines of self-control were central to reform of the church and to the new monastic disciplines as early as the twelfth century.[37] These new elements of self-making in the late medieval period were, in turn, to play a role in the self-fashioning of colonizing missionaries during the Renaissance itself—that is, during the formation of great European nations and the early period of colonialism and exploration.

Three of Greenblatt's criteria for Renaissance self-fashioning seem especially relevant to consideration of the role of the Jewish and Indian other in the development of a European Christian identity:

3. Self-fashioning is achieved in relation to something perceived as alien, strange, or hostile. This threatening Other—heretic, savage, witch, seductress, traitor, Antichrist—must be discovered or invented in order to be attacked and destroyed.

4. The alien is perceived by the authority either as that which is unformed or chaotic (the absence of order) or that which is false or negative (the demonic parody of order). [Moreover] the chaotic constantly slides into the demonic, and consequently the alien is always constructed as a distorted image of the authority. . . .

10. The power generated to attack the alien in the name of the authority is produced in excess and threatens the authority it sets out to defend. Hence self-fashioning always involves some experience of threat, some effacement or undermining, some loss of self.[38]

Criterion 10 suggests far less certainty on the part of European Christian colonizers than the sketch from Greenblatt's *Marvelous Possessions* quoted earlier, and it supports the claim that efforts at conversion tend to place the identity of the missionary in question. Criterion 4 sounds as though it was written with two privileged "aliens" in mind: the Indian (often seen as the wild man, unformed and chaotic, positioned at "the boundaries of humanity") and the Jew (false and negative, hiding the true nature of Scripture).[39] Indeed, the one representation repeatedly slides into the other. However, it is criterion 3, the foundational need for an alien foil and the concomitant threat posed to Christian identity by that foil, that is most relevant here. In twelfth-century Latin Christian thought, the problem of personal guilt came to prominence and the theoretical question of individuation was a shared concern of both the scholastics and Bernard of Clairvaux.[40] Inwardness and hence "identity" thus were already becoming explicit topics of concern—and schemata of reward and punishment, commendable and intolerable behavior, were increasingly being elaborated and rationalized in a more comprehensive societal framework.

If, nevertheless, Renaissance self-fashioning was new in the way that Greenblatt has claimed, shall we say that something happened in European cultural history between the twelfth and sixteenth centuries that made self-fashioning the aggressive and individualistic process that Greenblatt depicts? Bynum suggests one specific moment of closure for the twelfth-century mode of self-formation: the same Fourth Lateran Council that in 1215 not only required Jews to wear special clothing and applied other measures to segregate them, but also renewed the Crusades, forbade the establishment of new monastic orders,[41] required annual sacramental confession,[42] reformed criminal procedures,[43] and officially announced the dogma of transubstantiation.[44] However, as was indicated in my introduction, these segregationary measures were not always honored. Moreover, such regulations—issued as they were from on high—present the classic dilemma of whether they should be read as leading indicators of new repression or as indicia of the mixing that was taking place on the ground and was not necessarily stopped by this legislation.

It is tempting to see a clear and systematic difference between the monastic discipline in twelfth-century Benedictine or Cistercian monasteries, where the material on which the self worked was the self, and that of sixteenth-century New World colonization and conversion, where that which had to be converted was embodied, initially at least, in another entirely non-Christian person, and where work on converting the self could be supplemented or even supplanted by work at converting the other. The renewed energy at bringing non-Christian peoples into the fold long before 1492 was encouraged by the new mendicant orders founded in the thirteenth century yet also helped explain their creation. It is no accident that the end of this earlier period with the Fourth Lateran Council also coincides with two other major events in church history: the founding of the Franciscans in 1210 and of the Dominicans in 1215. These new orders, along with the Jesuits, were to bear most of the burden of missionizing toward the native peoples of the Americas, at least in the first century or so of the Spanish encounter in America. The assumptions that drove their debates about how to address these native peoples, and the techniques they employed in evangelizing the natives while preserving their own Christian orthodoxy, were largely the product of their work in expanding and policing the spiritual and territorial boundaries of Christendom. Thus, understanding how they were both products and agents of significant changes taking place in Europe even before the momentous coincidences at the end of the fifteenth century is critical to understanding how those same changes helped structure European actions and assumptions in the New World encounter.

Yet even if Christian self-making in the twelfth century was still largely focused inward, resources for the outward turn were already being accumulated. Europe came into the twelfth century with the church considerably strengthened. The existing monastic orders had been substantially reformed with the political and material backing of the nobility, while church property had grown significantly in the previous two centuries.[45] During the pontificate of Pope Gregory VII at the end of the eleventh century, a new vigor had already come to characterize the relations between church and world. As Gerd Tellenbach suggests, it was as early as Gregory's papacy that movement outward, to convert the world outside, came to take priority over a contemplative and cloistered effort to convert the self inside; "the world was drawn into the Church."[46] Though Tellenbach is speaking here primarily of the increased confidence and ambition of the papacy as an institution, the image may also help to express the radicalism of the change that was about to take place in Catholic monasticism. Even today, the images called forth by the words "monastic" and "monastery" have to do with enclosure and settlement.

This establishment of the new mendicant orders was even more significant given that one of the Fourth Lateran Council's decisions forbade the establishment of new orders, largely to reduce the diffusion of "heretical" views, even though Church reform and the repression of heresy had been the Dominicans' founding goals.[47] As missionaries, however, the mendicants walked a doctrinal and psychological tightrope at the edge of the established church at a time of enormous transformations in European society. For centuries after their inception, Dominicans and Franciscans worked at the exacting task of combining vigilance over doctrinal purity with exhortation among Christians and conversionary missions to non-Christians, both within and beyond Europe. As Christian Europe extended its contiguous borders to the north and east and then overseas they, like their Jesuit fellow missionaries, faced complex and consequential dilemmas about the proper mix of Catholicism and existing traditions and identities. What blend of suppression, synthesis, and renaming would assure that the Catholic sacraments were inculcated while those at whom the mission was aimed could still recognize themselves?[48]

The anthropologist Mary Douglas has argued that widely differing human groups share anxiety about issues of "purity and danger," a fascination heightened when intercultural contacts intensify or take new forms.[49] In Europe, of course, such anxieties preceded the age of colonization. For example, R.I. Moore links the new persecution of lepers, heretics, and Jews in the twelfth century to the increasing hierarchization of western European society. Citing Douglas, he refers to what he calls "pollution fear"—"the fear that the privileged feel of those at whose expense their privilege is enjoyed."[50]

While in the stratified society of the twelfth century this pollution fear may have been connected to anxieties about the legitimacy of hierarchy, the new discourses and strategies for management of difference were part of a more general expansion.[51] In the interest of consistency and not just purity, doctrinal changes were associated with the elaboration of "a legal system which aimed at securing a consistency of behaviour, as well as of belief, throughout the whole of western Christendom"—and, by the mid-thirteenth century, with "a full-blown missionizing campaign, involving the allocation of significant Church resources, the development of regularized channels for confronting Jews with Christian argumentation, and the adumbration of innovative argumentation intended to break down Jewish defenses."[52] The new mendicant orders found themselves in the forefront of this campaign aimed at Jews, as they were at the forefront of efforts to suppress heresy and to evangelize non-Christian peoples at the boundaries of Christendom.

It is tempting to describe the difference between the self-fashioning of the new mendicants and that of earlier orders as a new restless selflessness, contrasted to the presumptive complacency of the Benedictines. Indeed, Dominicans and Franciscans explicitly renounced the Benedictines' self-contained and often comfortably secure abbatial economy. For Saint Francis, at least, this renunciation was explicitly linked to asceticism. Thus the text of Matthew 16:24—which reads, "If any man will come after me, let him deny himself, and take up his cross, and follow me"[53]—was crucial to the Franciscan ethos.[54] Yet the contrast between the older, "cloistered" monastic disciplines and those of the missionaries who pushed to extend Christendom at Europe's borders and in the New World should not be drawn to include a simplistic analogy between an older discipline of self-directed self-making and a later discipline directed only at the Christianization of others. At least since Augustine's depiction of the constant struggle between the Christian and the devil, Christianity had explicitly required vigilant fortitude among its virtues. In the traditional orders that vigilance was understood as being channeled primarily into monastic patience; but since those who filled the monasteries were themselves often former warriors, we should not wonder overmuch that inside those walls a "bellicose liturgy" was nurtured.[55]

SELF-FASHIONING AND CONVERSION: THE CHURCH MILITANT

Throughout the period including the later Middle Ages and the initial period of conquest overseas, conversion in Latin Christendom was directed both outward toward the inclusion of non-Christians and inward toward the perfection of the Christian individual. It may be fair to say that the primary struggle for Christianization had been understood in the older monasteries as an internal struggle for self-discipline. As part of the missionary enterprise, which was no doubt terrifying and alienating enough, Franciscans were now taught that this self-perfection would come externally, in the process of the pained effort to admonish the faithful and to convert the rest. It was understood that these tasks were not easy or conventionally rewarding, but that "[t]hose who inflicted sufferings, tribulations, shameful things, injuries, griefs, torments, martyrdom, and death upon the friars were their friends, for by these things, the brothers would attain their reward, coming to hate their bodies' vices and sins."[56] In this understanding, the greater the missionary challenge and the more suffering withstood, the more rapid and complete would be the perfection of the friar's Christian self, and the more effectively would he help all mankind prepare for judgment.

Thus, in the missionary orders the balance between internal struggle and external struggle shifted; the notion of monastic patience gave way to the idea of battle for Christ. The tendency to refer to conversionary tracts as weapons and to missionaries as soldiers had been prepared during the early Crusades when soldiering was transformed into a potentially holy enterprise. Earlier, when arms were taken up between representatives of different Christian rulers, church leaders such as Burchard of Worms found it necessary to stipulate the appropriate penance to be observed by one who committed homicide in war at the command of the legitimate leader.[57] Burchard also dictated that "[t]he one who by forethought of hate or because of greed kills a Jew or a pagan, because he extinguished the image of God and the hope of future conversion, will make a penance of 40 days of eating bread and water."[58]

Non-Christian humans, for Burchard, enjoyed a certain measure of worth—a certain "right" to remain alive, as we would say today—both in having been created in the divine image and in their potential to become Christians.

Although the association between warmaking and sin evident in Burchard's writings could still be maintained in the eleventh century, by the beginning of the twelfth a new view, articulated for instance by Guibert of Nogent, simultaneously valorized and spiritualized war made for the sake of Christianity. As early as 1110, in his *Gesta Dei per Francos*, Guibert drew a contrast between the material motivations for war among the Old Testament Jews and the nobility of the Crusade. "Israelis carnalia pro ventrium plenitudine bella miremur"—that is, carnal Israel made war to fill its belly.[59] Furthermore, he described the Crusade as providing a new dispensation for knights: "God ordained holy wars in our time, so that the knightly order and the erring mob, who, like their ancient pagan models, were engaged in mutual slaughter, might find a new way of earning salvation."[60] The same transvaluation of battle was applied to those who fought to recover Spain from the Muslims in the earlier centuries of the *Reconquista*, and of whom the Cluniac friars said that they were destined for Paradise.[61]

From the beginning, the missionizing activities of the mendicant friars were likewise described in martial metaphors. Whether heretics or non-Christians were a mission's immediate target, the real enemy was always the devil, as Dominic stated in a speech to a new recruit: " 'I will give you arms, with which you are to fight the Devil all the days of your life.' "[62] In the battle between princes and the church during these centuries, the New Testament allegory of the "two swords" (Luke 22:38) also became a central topos.[63] Different views on the relation between the church in general and the papacy in particular, on the one hand, and among Christian monarchs on the other were variously expressed as beliefs that the church should keep its sword at the ready, keep it sheathed, or unsheath it only in concert with the use of temporal power. Yet all parties to the debate apparently thought it fitting that the church should be understood as *having* a sword, or perhaps as *being* one of the swords of Christ.

MISSION AND INQUISITION

We may begin to suspect that the new fashion of speaking about friars as soldiers, along with the legacy of crusades against the Muslims in Palestine and Iberia, eventually helped make possible the view of conquistadors as being engaged in righteous battle for Christ. Right at the beginning of the Dominicans' activities, Pope Honorius III had written a letter in which he likened them to "invincible athletes of Christ armed with the shield of the faith and the helmet of salvation and not fearing those who can slay the body."[64] Both the Franciscans and the Dominicans, then, were founded with the mission of mission—in the case of Dominicans a mission to all non-Christians, whether pagan, "people of the book," or heretic.[65] The eventually powerful institutions they did set up helped transform the notion of combat from internecine feudal bloodshed to that of the church militant, purifying within and expanding without.

These centuries also saw the development of new methodologies and standards for investigation and judgment. In Europe an increase in the use of torture (associated with what legal historians call "inquisitorial procedure") as opposed to ordeal (associated with "accusatorial procedure") began in the 1100s and led to a general use of torture by the end of the fourteenth century.[66] Hence, contrary to the impression one might retain from an isolated historiography of the agony of Spanish Jewry, inquisitorial torture was a quite widespread practice, rather than something for which Jews were singled out.

Talal Asad thus cautions against a simplistically condemnatory account of Christian dealings with others—especially conversion efforts—and of the pain inflicted, since the "transforming work" involved the indiscriminate application of techniques to further "the European wish to make the world in its own image."[67] He also points out that the suspicion by Spanish "old Christians" of Jewish *conversos* and Moslem converts (called *Moriscos*) and the inquisitorial gathering of knowledge about their practices raise important questions about the political and epistemological grounds of ethnography and comparative religion.[68] One such question concerns the way in which *conversos* interested in maintaining aspects of their Jewishness learned how to do so from the Edicts of Faith that had been designed precisely to ferret out and thus eradicate marks of continued Jewishness[69]—a strategy similar to the appropriation by Native Americans in more recent years of the ethnographic accounts of "their" cultures.

To my knowledge, this perception has not yet been linked to recent discussions of the "ethnographic" techniques and sensibilities of Spanish missionaries and other colonial functionaries in the early period of the colonial encounter. This is especially surprising because to some extent the exclusions were carried out on the same territory. The Inquisition was active in New Spain; in 1523 an edict was issued in Mexico opposing heretics and Jews. Although the apostolic inquisitor Juan de Zumárraga carried out nineteen anti-Judaizing trials between 1536 and 1543,[70] Richard E. Greenleaf asserts that he conducted them with restraint.[71] During the same period, Zumárraga tried nineteen putative Indian heretics, and his harshness in at least one of these cases led to the loss of his title as apostolic inquisitor.[72]

Meanwhile, of course, the Inquisition was especially active in "old" Spain, testing the Catholicism of, among others, *conversos*—Jewish converts to Catholicism and their descendants. Geoffrey Harpham makes the dramatic claim that the *conversos* represent an extraordinarily precise example of the dilemma of identity as both modern and traditional, chosen and given, an early form perhaps of the "double consciousness" identified by twentieth-century critics such as W.E.B. duBois and Paul Gilroy. Harpham neatly expresses the tensions that, from the perspective of the twenty-first century, seem likely to have informed the poetics of *converso* identity: not quite Jewish, not quite Christian.[73]

Harpham also discusses the Inquisition as the first rationalized bureaucracy—a form of "nascent modernity."[74] The suggestion of a linkage between this arguably first modern panoptic and bureaucratic *institution*—the Inquisition—and an early example of modern divided *consciousness*—the *conversos*—is tempting. But are the two necessarily linked? After all, this was not the first time that groups of Jews were forcibly converted. What about the First Crusade?[75] If we identify processes of double consciousness at work in the cultural politics of difference in late medieval Europe, we should be most cautious in identifying them too closely with the *Reconquista*, the Inquisition, and the liminal status of *conversos* remaining in Spain—not least because, after 1492, the situation of *Moriscos* was structurally analogous to that of the *conversos* themselves.

STASIS AND THE MANDATE FOR INCORPORATION

Because medieval Christian attitudes toward non-Christians, as toward those whose faith was suspect, were driven by the conflicting impulses to spread the Gospel and to protect an achieved, static doctrinal purity, the ideal of stasis was central to notions of redemption in early and medieval Christianity. In Augustine's writings on redemption, for example, he stressed freedom from change and the achievement of stasis. He expressed anxiety about the inevitable corruption that accompanies the life cycle in this world, and accordingly "saw salvation as the crystalline hardness not only of stasis but of the impossibility of non-stasis."[76] Perhaps Augustine had a vision of that blessed state in which one might, once and for all and without the need for further vigilance, truly be Christian.

This emphasis on purity, fear of corruption, and obsession with the resurrection of the individual believer's body is linked to the universalism and faith orientation of Christianity in a more than accidental way. The focus on the fate of the individual in this world and the next (as opposed, for instance, to concerns of family well-being or the relation of the *ethnos* to divine attentions) is related to the way Christianity spread through the Roman world, understood through Paul's famous proclamation of the irrelevance of marks of collective belonging such as class, gender, or ethnicity to identification "in Christ Jesus."[77] At the same time, Christianity relied implicitly on notions of belonging—including race, genealogy, and kinship—that were shared with Jews as with other human groups. These common rhetorics, as Denise Buell has suggested, underlie the more "faith-based" forms of identity rhetoric, including the contrasting pair orthodoxy/heresy. Despite Paul's explicit devaluation of group identities (as of gender and class identities), the new communities of worship were spoken and written of in genealogical terms.[78] Perhaps the explicit devaluation of genealogical concern and continuity, along with their implicit displacement onto the ideological plane of orthodoxy, contributed to doctrines that sought as an ideal the arrest of biological cycles and the sublimation of sensual desire,[79] along with a terror of bodily corruption and the threat it posed to the dream of the resurrected Christian body. If the body was subject to corruption and change, with what could it be identical?

If identity is such a central problem both for Christianity and for Europe, how could it not be so, given this aversion to change, paradoxically coexisting with the Christian mission outside the collective self? The Christian ideal suggests that all will be redeemed when they are "identical" in their faith in Christ, and the practice of Christianity has dictated that one way for a Christian to personally be worthy of redemption is through helping to realize the global ideal of universal Christian identity. As Jeremy Cohen writes, on the level of ideology "a growing preoccupation with the notion of the immanence of the end of days" was a stimulus for the drive to purify Christendom in the twelfth and thirteenth centuries.[80] For those motivated by some form of imminent millennial expectation, questions of personal and universal redemption are inextricable, and some of the more comfortable and secure means for attaining the former must sometimes be placed at risk in the attempt to achieve the latter. How could missionaries not be extremely curious and ambivalent about non-Christian difference, or arrogant and anxious in their efforts at conversion? How could one possibly avoid debate about the degree to which local customs should be adopted, tolerated, or decisively uprooted?[81]

What part did fear of change play in the anti-Jewish impulses of the four-teenth and fifteenth centuries? What happened, in the context of the colonial encounter, to the impulse toward stasis as a guarantor of purity—literally of incorruption—and as the promise of redemption? Our "habit" of considering friars collectively as members of their various orders has tended to occlude another question: How did the expectations of eternal life for the individual (that is, the individual friar) in a millennial situation intersect with the desire to convert all of humankind?[82] As J.H. Elliott puts it, "Arcadia and Eden could now be located on the far shores of the Atlantic."[83] At least at first, a new world may have seemed to offer a resolution of the tension between the Gospel imperative and the desire to avoid corruption.[84] By the early sixteenth century, notions of corruption may have been closer to the subversion of spiritual and social processes and further from the emphasis on physical corruption and redemption of the earlier period—but still the concerns were with corruption and redemption.

This tangled quest for static identity and for redemption suggests that studies of colonial discourse are misguided insofar as they assume Christian European ethnocentrism to be a property essentially shared with any expansive, imperial culture. The cultural expansiveness of the Gospel imperative and the competing desire for stasis and incorruption contributed to an extraordinarily reflective (and wordy) discourse on cultural contact, prominently including analyses of similarities and differences between Christians and non-Christians, the possible origins of those differences, and the various reasons for the divergence. Not every ethnocentrism implies such a generalized epistemology and drive toward unification, nor does every empire; the multiconfessional Ottoman Empire comes to mind as an instructive counterexample.[85] It was an epistemology made necessary not only by the problematics of identity in an expanding medieval Europe, or by the evangelical imperative that drove and justified the expansion of Christendom, but by the varieties of cultural contact and forms of difference with which it had to deal. Not only Jews, after all, but Muslims prominently resided inside, beyond, and sometimes precisely on the confessional and geographical boundaries of Christendom—and, for the most part unlike Jews, the Muslims had their own swords.

CHAPTER TWO

Muslims

Let us rid Spain therefore of the names of the Jews and the Moors, for today their name alone does more evil than their erstwhile presence did.

Brother Géronimo de la Cruz, 1637

[T]he Merovingian chronicle that goes under the name of Fredegar ... [an] account of the Saracen conquests, written about 658 ... opens with the statement that Aeraglius emperatur—*this is how the so-called Fredegar spells* Heraclius imperator—*discovered, through the practice of astrology, that his empire was to be laid waste by circumcised races. He requested, therefore, that the Frankish king Dagobert baptize all the Jews of his realm, and passed like orders throughout his own empire, which was nevertheless soon invaded by another circumcised people, the Saracens.*

Benjamin Z. Kedar, *Crusade and Mission: European Approaches Toward the Muslims*

How Holy Mary revealed a great treasure of gold and silver to a king who wrote songs for Her....

She told him: "Your prayer [for money to finance the war against the Moors] is already granted by my Son. Therefore, have no concern for your lack of funds, but be of good heart, for I shall give you a very great treasure which lies hidden under the earth which people much worse than Moors put there...."

So God willed that on that occasion the king should find nothing. However, after a whole year passed, he led an attack on Granada, and on his way to join his army he passed by that way again, and the Virgin showed him in another

place great treasures of silver, gold, rich and precious stones, much cloth of silk,
beautifully worked tapestries, and other very noble objects of gilded silver which
belonged to the Jews, Her enemies, whom She hates worse than the Moors.

Songs of Holy Mary of Alfonso X, the Wise

Europe's emergence into history took place—and could not have taken place oth-
erwise—through the mediation of Islam: in the beginning by means of a defen-
sive recoil, afterward by an offensive explosion.

Hichem Djait, *Europe and Islam*

As Western Christianity renewed in expansionist vigor, first at the cultural and
territorial margins of Europe and then overseas, it worried about the integrity
of the Christian body, which was at once spiritualized and subject to all manner of corruption, especially as the injunction to incorporate all of humanity
left the boundaries of self perpetually at risk. However, what we might call "the
Muslim question" inescapably disrupted what otherwise would have been a
neat dichotomy between my two defining boundaries of the self in Christian
Europe—Jews, both "anterior" to Christendom and internal to it, and Indians,
encountered both outside Christendom and, as it were, after it.

ISLAM AND OTHER DIFFERENCES

Focusing on Muslim difference raises the specter of the longer list of non-
Christian identities in the face of which Western Christendom continued to
redefine itself—a list suggested, for example, by Ramon Llull's proposal long
before Columbus's voyage, in his 1305 *Liber de fine*, that the pope establish
"four monasteries specialized in the education of missionaries: one monastery for missionaries to the Saracens, one for missionaries to the Jews, one for
those to the 'schismatics,' one for those to the Tartars and other pagans."[1] A
review of various lists of the Church's enemies by one Ademar of Chabannes
(ca. 989–1034) suggests that in his time and place, Jews rather than Saracens
tended to be listed first.[2]

Even when polemics against the enemies of Christendom were primarily
directed toward Christians themselves, these enemies were not always rhetorically interchangeable with each other, nor did they always occupy distinct or
fixed positions on the grid of otherness within and without. To be sure, it is
easy enough to comb the record to find representations of Muslims, especially
in military guise, as representing an external threat, and Jews by contrast as
representing a threat of subversion of Christendom within. Thus one of the

few illustrations in the manuscript of Alonso de Espina's fifteenth-century *For-tress of Faith* shows the fortress being defended by a heavenly and Christian host against Muslim warriors and other threats including "Jews in chains who try to persuade [the Christians] by words." Yet in the same text Muslims could, because of their adherence to aspects of "Jewish" ritual such as circumcision, be allied implicitly with the Old Law, transcended in the new dispensation, and incorporated within the Christian saving history.[3] And Muslims, like Jews, could be portrayed as mocking key aspects of Christian ritual and sacred history, sometimes compounding their threat as military enemies.[4] In Spain's process of becoming, moreover, an identification and fascination with Moorish style and heritage,[5] combined with the obsession of ridding the peninsula of Islam, produced an ambivalence perhaps comparable in revealing ways to Christianity's desire to rid itself of the Jewish trace while simultaneously embracing the mantle of true Israel. But that suggestion remains to be explored.

Jews—along with pagans and heretics—were at any rate one of the categories among or alongside which Christian writers tried to fit Muslims.[6] Many of the same tropes and accusations leveled against Jews were also leveled against Muslims. One was the charge of Muslim "carnality"—not only in polemics against Muslim marriage practices and the idea of continued sexuality in heaven, but as a critique of their rationality, as in Thomas Aquinas's *Reasons for the Faith against the Muslims*: "Since [the Muslims] are carnal, they can think only of what is flesh and blood."[7] This was related to the view, increasingly prevalent by the thirteenth century and beyond, of Muslims as "irrational." Similar to accusations that Jews indulged in contemptuous sacrilege, Muslims were portrayed in chronicles of the First Crusade as mocking the Passion of Christ. Back in England, Jews were portrayed in medieval mystery plays as followers of "Mahound," while the late thirteenth-century Hereford Map depicted them as worshipping an idol labeled *Mahum*, another variant of Muhammad's name in medieval Christendom. And in sixteenth-century Spain, laws of pure blood originally designed to exclude New Christians of Jewish ancestry were also applied against Moriscos, New Christians of Muslim ancestry.[8]

Indeed, the poetics of projected Indian, Muslim, and Jewish identities were remarkably susceptible to mutual substitution. Depending on the alliances and divisions that one is led to promote prospectively or perceive retrospectively, various substitutions and elisions can be made, and over the centuries, most of them have been made: "Iudio" for "Indio" and vice versa, or "Moor" for "Jew."[9] Any temptation to read one of these three terms as the "fundamental" figure of difference against which the others take their ultimate historical meaning—Jews because of the persistent Christian habit of identifying both with and against Israel, Indians and other colonized peoples because the encounter with them defines "modernity," Muslims because their comprehensive ideological and temporal competition forces Christian Europe into a consciousness of itself—must founder on this welter of multidirectional associations.[10] As in the *Cantiga de Santa María* quoted as an epigraph to this chapter, Jews could be designated as an enemy hated by the Virgin "worse than the Moors." Yet earlier, Bernard of Clairvaux (as reported by a contemporary Jewish chronicler) reminded Crusaders that while "[i]t is good that you go against the Ishmaelites . . . whosoever touches a Jew to take his life, is like one who harms Jesus himself."[11] A chronicler of the Fourth Crusade similarly reported several leading clerics' opinion that the Saracens were worse than Jews.[12] Pope Alexander II praised bishops in Spain who were protecting Jews from those who advanced against the Saracens, drawing a clear distinction between the justified continued existence of the former and the need to fight the latter.[13] Much later, the bishop of Segorbe complained that the rebellious and recalcitrant Moriscos should be expelled as the less guilty Jews had been.[14] The legal theorist Victoria, meanwhile, argued against the possibility of making just war against the Indians based on their ignorance of the Gospel. As we might expect in a discussion of actual military conflict rather than mere "daggers of the faith," Victoria bolstered his argument by drawing a contrast between the Indians and the Moors who—rather than the Jews this time—were said to have rejected the Gospel message.[15]

The association between the Indians and the Moors was readily available, and not only because there were Spanish soldiers in Mexico who had fought the latter before fighting overseas.[16] Indians could, and apparently readily did, come to portray and actively occupy the role of Muslims in the kind of *moros y cristianos* pageants that had been mounted in Catholic Iberia for centuries. The friar Motolinía's *History of the Indians of New Spain* contains a detailed account of what must have been an impressive and lengthy historical pageant of the Conquest of Jerusalem in 1539. All the parts were played by Indians, though it is a bit difficult to keep that in mind as we try to follow the almost dizzying list of identities they portrayed and the costumes they wore. Some played Spanish soldiers; others were identified as having come from other parts of the Holy Roman Empire, while also wearing Spanish uniforms. There was also an army of New Spain, wearing much more colorful native costumes. There were even armies of Moors and Jews inside the besieged city, and the leader of the Moorish army was identified as none other than Hernando Cortés. The army of New Spain included "two Caribbean companies" that fell at the hands of the Moors, as the real Caribs so readily had at the hands of the Spanish. The climax of the play came when the sultan "Cortés" ushered in a number of as-yet unbaptized Indians who had been playing Turks, and who were then baptized on the spot. A play about Saint Francis followed, and then a *Sacrifice of Abraham*, which was curtailed due to the late hour. Wouldn't we like to know as much about transcripts of that performance, both overt and hidden, as we now do about the earlier one?[17]

Another "Moorish" mock battle, this time without Indians, took place in Granada in 1561. It was ordered by Luis Hurtado de Mendoza, the new mayor of the Alhambra. Hurtado's family, known as defenders of the Moriscos, were opposed by the twenty-six-member chancery that governed the rest of Granada and sought the elimination of distinctive Morisco identity and culture. In this mock battle, Luis himself was dressed in Moorish garb and rode among the camp of the "Moors," which in Max Harris's reading was otherwise made up of "real" Moriscos. The opposing army is not described; it may have included Old Christians. Harris suggests that Luis's gesture of dressing as a Moor was an overt expression of identity with and support for his Morisco subjects. Just a few years later, with increasing repression both followed and spurred by the revolt in the Alpujarras that began on Christmas Eve 1568, this kind of gesture became unthinkable.[18]

About a century after the coincidence of the conquest of the Kingdom of Granada and Columbus's first voyage, the relation of type and antitype in Spanish Catholic encounters with the Other came full circle. Reports of successful mass conversions in the New World reinforced the impression that Muslims who had refused the Gospel in Spain must be motivated by Satan, while one Spanish bishop cited Bartolomé de las Casas's prescription for the evangelizations of the Indians as being applicable to the effort to convert the Moriscos of Valencia.[19] Thus the New World could serve as a counter-model for debates about the proper way to approach the evangelization and integration of the Moriscos. Indeed much of the discourse on the Moriscos, and the Church's attitude toward them, points to the inclusive moment in Christian identity. Around the turn of the seventeenth century, the Church was not as clear about justifying expulsion as was the state[20]—much as many Church officials, in the fifteenth and sixteenth centuries, had resisted the imposition of *limpieza de sangre* regulations against *conversos*.

The campaigns to integrate and then to expel the Moriscos were a continuation of the internal making of Europe at the same time as Christian European powers were creating their overseas empires.[21] Yet the contest with Islam was not only military, but—like that with Judaism—also textual. Long before the conquest of Granada, Peter the Venerable had explained that the Saracens were "converted" to Muhammad's fables, the Jews to those of the Talmud.[22] As in polemics against Judaism, the depiction of the opponent was commonly so distorted and negative that the effort was clearly meant to reinforce Christian certainty rather than to persuade non-Christians of the Gospel truth. Anti-Muslim polemics were not embedded in as long a history of contact and intimacy as polemics against Jews, although some Christian portraits of Muslims expressed a nervous concern about the possible deleterious effects of interactions between live Muslims and live Christians. Peter the Venerable, for his part, had more hope that he might actually convince Muslims than the obviously obtuse and obdurate Jews. Yet even Peter's work was more effective at maintaining the doctrinal purity of Christians.[23] Later on, in fifteenth-century Spain, most writings about Islam were again more concerned with their Christian audiences than with any possibility of converting Muslims to Christianity.[24]

Still, especially considering the broad sweep of "Christian-Muslim relations" during this period, it is clear that holding too strongly to a view of Christian anti-Muslim polemics as being turned inward only reinforces the notion that Christian Europe made itself by itself—a notion that should be quaint by now but continues to reappear.[25] The several translations of the Qur'an into Latin during the later Middle Ages well illustrate the contacts that existed between Christian and Muslim scholars. Even in this highly polemical age it was possible for translators, at least provisionally, to place philology before disputation.[26]

Under pressure from missionaries, Muslims, like Jews, were forced to attend live disputations in the late Middle Ages.[27] Yet the Qur'an was not only a competing sacred text; in the case of the Mozarabs—Christians who lived under Muslim rule and shared Arabic culture—it found its way into the Christian sacred texts and helped shape them. Thus, for example, the *basmalah*, the Arabic invocation of the name of Allah, introduces each of the Gospels "in the Arabic translation made from the Old Latin version by the Andalusi Christian Ishaq ibn Balashk," and is found as well in numerous other Mozarabic documents.[28] Quite evidently, those who made such texts did not see Allah as an especially "Muslim" name for the one divinity any more than contemporary Americans see God as a Germanic Christian term, yet at the same time we have to assume that they were conscious of the invocation's Qur'anic context. Thus a phenomenon such as this is best thought of not as an example of Arab Muslim influence on Christian culture, but as demonstrating the need to question the rhetoric of comparison between stable and separate Jewish, Muslim

(Arab), and Christian collective identities.[29] Once that observation has been made, it should no longer seem anomalous that Arabic religious script found its way into Mudéjar architecture built for Christians,[30] much as we should no longer be surprised to read Cynthia Robinson's recent meticulous account of how the energetic Christian evangelist Ramon Llull deployed arboreal imagery, drawn from a multi-confessional store, in the articulation of his conversionary tracts.[31] Even the famous proclamation of Christian truth to newly encountered non-Christian peoples known as the *Requerimiento* had an Islamic legal model, for the jurist Averroes had declared that, prior to conquest, "an enemy must have heard the announcement of the new religion (Islam) following the injunction of Q. 17:15, 'We have not been accustomed to punish until We have sent a messenger.'"[32] And a key aspect of the Morisco identity that so vexed Christian rulers and clerics that they eventually took the drastic step of expelling these at least nominally Christian subjects was the literature known as *aljamía*, which was not simply the Romance vernacular in Arabic characters or an index of assimilation, but an expression of a desire to maintain their own Morisco idiom and community.[33]

The ways in which Christian European identity shaped itself vis-à-vis Muslims and Jews, however, were molded by structures of relation that were simultaneously shared, analogous, and in contrast with one another. To a considerable extent, Christian Europe came into being simultaneously with the rise of the new and aggressively expansive Islam and as an overt response to that expansion.[34] Augustine's rationale for tolerance of Jews within Christendom— as debased witness to the truth of the Gospel and as those destined to be converted at the end of days—hardly carried over into a tolerance of Muslims. On the contrary, Muslims became the pagans par excellence and Muhammad a synonym for idolatry.[35] Inverting the way the problem of the authority of Jewish scripture was managed through the doctrine of Christian supersession, Islam's link to shared sacred texts and figures was explained by narratives depicting Muhammad as a former Christian who had lapsed into a novel heresy.[36]

Moreover, it would be too easy to see Muslim difference as located solely outside of Christendom in space. If anything, it was a cultural difference that was then metaphorically spatialized. The Latin terms which have come down to us as "frontier," as used in Spain, originally referred exclusively to the boundaries between Christians and Muslims.[37] Indeed, since we cannot avoid employing the very terms, such as "Spain," whose contentious histories we mean to interrogate, we can stop at least to note that what actually *became Spain* is part and parcel of what *became the Reconquista*: the whole of non-Portuguese Iberia defined, at least retroactively, as properly Christian and hence Spain, much as I contend here that the becoming of Europe was inseparable, in imagination and not only in fact, from its becoming more or less fully Christian.[38] To that extent it still seems accurate to say that the longed-for and then accomplished "reconquest," capped with the Muslim loss of Granada in 1492, provided a powerful inertial force for the Christianizing conquest of the fortuitously encountered Spanish Americas.

Meanwhile, earlier and looking eastward rather than westward, *frontera* and Crusade came together when, sometime between 1145 and 1147, Pope Eugenius listed various regions as being open to Crusaders' efforts. Again, these regions represented the borders of Christian Europe at the time: Iberia and the Levant, but also (most surprisingly to us, but only because we have become so thoroughly accustomed to identifying Muslims as the exclusive targets of crusade) the frontier between German and Slavic lands.[39]

Yet of course the idea of an unambiguous frontier between Christendom and *dar el-Islam* belies the fact of Christian populations living under Muslim rule and vice-versa. Indeed, Christians living in lands where there were few if any Muslims had their views of Islam shaped by Christians who lived under Muslim rule.[40] The reality of Muslim power and the concomitant danger of retaliation figured into at least some of the decisions made by Christian authorities that bore on respect for and transgression of group boundaries. Thus, one contemporary chronicler explained that whereas the children of Jews were compelled to stay behind when the Jews of Portugal were expelled, the children of Muslims were allowed to leave with their parents because of the fear that Muslim exiles separated from their children might seek to exact revenge on Christians living in Muslim lands.[41] As early as 1499, Muslims in Andalusia faced the same choice as Jews had over the preceding century: conversion or exile. And long after the fall of Granada, monuments left as physical traces of Muslim rule served both Old Christians and Morisco converts as reminders of past dominance and continuing beauty.[42]

Moreover, whether in the Holy Land or in southern Europe (and unlike in the New World, except in the minds of certain apologists), Muslims occupied lands once—and, in the eyes of Christians, properly—ruled by Christian monarchs. As King Sancho I Ramírez of Aragón and Navarre declared in the late eleventh century,

> Let it be known to all the faithful that for the amplification of the Church of Christ, formerly driven from the Hispanic regions, I, Sancho . . . took care to settle inhabitants in that place [Montemayor] . . . for the recovery and extension of the Church of Christ, for the destruction of the pagans,

the enemies of Christ, and the building up and benefit of the Christians, so that the kingdom, invaded and captured by the Ishmaelites, might be liberated to the honor and service of Christ; and that once all the people of that unbelieving rite were expelled and the filthiness of their wicked error was eliminated therefrom, the venerable Church of Jesus Christ our Lord may be fostered there forever.[43]

Here, purification and reconquest went firmly hand in hand; Christendom was to be extended and rectified. But do we not perhaps also hear, under the identification of Muslims as "Ishmaelites," an echo of the old identification of the Church with Israel?

At the same time—most famously but not exclusively in Iberia—Christian monarchs and clerics had a long history of managing Muslim difference, along with Jewish difference, within their realms. The thirteenth century, in particular, saw the elaboration of rationales for exclusion that structured Christian attitudes toward Islam for a long time after.[44] Increasing surveillance of Muslim-Christian contacts accompanied increased segregation of Jews. Thus, for example, regulations issued at Valladolid in 1258 forbade Christian families from employing Muslim or Jewish women to care for their children, and likewise forbade Christian women from caring for Muslim or Jewish children. A century and a half later in the same city, an Ordinance on the Enclosure of the Jews and Moors was passed with the aim of limiting interactions between members of these two groups and Christians.[45]

CRUSADE AND MISSION

In hindsight it is hard not to see the struggle against Islam as having provided a crucial template for Christian missionary warfare, in New Spain and beyond, long before Columbus dreamed of sailing through the Indian Ocean to retake Jerusalem from the east.[46] Yet, as we will see in greater depth in the next chapter, the militant recovery of Spanish territory from the Muslims became understood only in retrospect as a unified process known as the *Reconquista*, while the militant conquest of the New World was neither simple nor unvexed by conflicting ideas and actions. For one thing, crusade and mission were seen as complementary, rather than as mutually exclusive, among the mendicant Dominicans and Franciscans. Moreover, the notion that wars of Christian conquest were entirely justifiable given the evangelical imperative was contrary to the desire of some Christian writers to portray the spread of Christianity as a peaceful process, unlike the martial advance of Islam.[47] On the other hand, the resort to military "persuasion" by those whose Messiah had preached the turning of the other cheek was hardly lost on Muslim polemicists, who complained that forcible conversion and conquest were against the teachings of Jesus.

The closely linked justification of crusade and mission proved crucial for the later rationalization of Spanish Catholic conquest in the New World, which was to rely on Pope Innocent IV's articulation in 1245 of the view that the pope, as vicar of God on earth, had jurisdiction over all humanity, not merely over Christendom. Accordingly, the pope had the authority to "punish not only a Christian for contravening the law of the Gospel but also a pagan for transgressing the law of nature and a Jew for deviating from the law of Moses or inventing heresies against it." More consequentially, perhaps, Innocent asserted the pope's power to authorize war against infidels in order to create space for the preaching of the Gospel.[48]

Significantly, those involved with evangelization in the New World did not always accept both of these rationales for Christian interference in non-Christian realms. The historian Xavier Rubert de Ventós, holding up Father Vitoria as an exemplary defender of the Indians, notes that Vitoria was willing to justify violent evangelization only where the preachers were under physical threat or where the target audience refused to listen—not merely because it refused to accept the Word. Meanwhile another commentator, Suárez, flatly denied the notion that the pope had jurisdiction over transgression of natural law within "the republic of infidels."[49] Despite such dissenting views, Innocent IV's articulation of the extension of the papal vicariate to every human being was a key moment in the ideological prehistory of early modern European imperialism.

The claim of universal papal authority and responsibility was intensified during the fourteenth century by Pope Clement VI, who offered an account according to which there was no part of the world that had not been Christian in the past. Clement cited Romans to prove that Christ's followers had made the Gospel heard literally throughout the world. Thus every land had been sanctified, and non-Christians had no right of dominion anywhere.[50] In a sense, this argument—that everyone everywhere had in fact heard the Gospel and those who did not adhere to it were being unfaithful—both complements and anticipates later arguments in the aftermath of the colonial encounter that since the truth of monotheism is available to natural reason, those who refuse it must be under the sway of the devil.

Thus Christian theorists separated the two processes of conquest and conversion, insisting on the volitional nature of conversion while justifying conquest as necessary to afford the unbaptized the chance to hear the Gospel.[51]

The imperative to spread the Gospel was so powerful at times that Catholic preachers were willing to die for the principle. Christian preachers ventured to Muslim lands, risking and sometimes seeking martyrdom for their temerity, confident that they would thereby "ensure eternal punishment for their unrepentant listeners," as Benjamin Z. Kedar puts it.[52] The Muslim world was a fertile ground for Christian practices and rhetorics of chosen martyrdom, although this practice was controversial and unpopular. Indeed, the Muslim authorities' ability to block Christian preaching led one thirteenth-century Christian writer to suggest preaching to the Jews instead of seeking the palm of martyrdom. Nevertheless, in the early thirteenth century Saint Francis of Assisi is said, upon hearing of the martyrdom of five Franciscans in Marrakesh in 1220, to have responded: " 'Now I can truly say that I have five brothers!' "[53]

MUSLIMS AS JEWS

Although Muslims and Islam presented quite different challenges of difference than did Jews and Judaism, it is also clear that Muslims and Jews were commonly conflated in the Christian imaginary.[54] As described below, the titles of several late medieval Christian polemics attest to the conventional association of these two forms of threatening difference. This led to the thesis that centuries of dealing with the problems of Judaism and Islam *jointly* served as the model for Spanish policy in the Americas, as is concisely stated by Sabine MacCormack, who asserts that "the long familiar religions of Islam and especially Judaism," as well-known objects of scorn, provided the occasion for elaboration of a vocabulary of difference which could be readily applied in the New World.[55]

In a broad sense Jews and Muslims were indeed often viewed with the same kind of suspicion, and with doubt as to their potential for incorporation into the universally human body of Christ. It has been famously claimed that in its strident universalism, Catholic Christianity ultimately found no place other than the not quite human for those who refused to accept Christian doctrines deemed self-evident to the well-intentioned, rational man.[56] We might expect this emphasis on the deviation from Christian humanity, and thus on the bodily difference and inferiority of non-Christian groups, to be heightened during periods of agonistic contact combined with efforts at exclusion. Yet there is, to say the least, no consensus that Spanish representations of Moors in the sixteenth century stressed their bodily differences rather than differences of bearing or dress.[57] Perhaps we may provisionally attribute this to the greater contact with real, and not only imagined, Jews and Muslims in Iberia. From at least the thirteenth century, the unusual situation of the Spanish church as part of a society constantly facing the rival Muslim power much more than most of Christian Europe did—and, in the course of what became in retrospect the *Reconquista*, increasingly confronted with large Muslim and Jewish populations inside its own domain—had placed that branch of the church at the forefront of actual conversionary efforts.[58] To be sure, the situation of Muslims under Christian rule differed throughout the peninsula, and in the Ebro region in the earlier period at least, missionary efforts were aimed at Jews and foreign Muslim potentates, not at local Muslims. But even here the situation began to change by the early fourteenth century, after the Council of Vienne focused on the anomaly of Muslims freely practicing Islam in territories ruled by Christians.[59]

A brief review of titles of some of the major Spanish Christian works of apologetics and polemics of the time, and of their authors' backgrounds, confirms the point that Moors and Jews were frequently caught in the same rhetorical lens. Thus Raimundo Martini, author of *Dagger of the Faith against Moors and Jews* (1278), claimed that "no enemy of the Christian faith is closer and more unavoidable to us than the Jew."[60] Martini had studied Arabic and spent time working in Tunis, risking martyrdom there.[61] Nevertheless, as this quote suggests, Martini's *Dagger* was aimed primarily at Jews. On the other hand, Petrus Alfonsí's *Dialogi contra Iudaeos* is an important source on Islam—and indeed, since he was from Andalusia himself, it would have been a striking omission had he failed to polemicize against Islam.[62] As an even neater mirror image to the disjuncture in Martini between the primacy of Muslims in his title and their secondary importance in his text, there is a chapter in the *Extravagantes* of Pope John XXII titled "De Iudaeis et Sarracensis" that actually fails to discuss Jews.[63]

The common conflation of Jews and Muslims as non-Christians did not, however, hinder Christian writers from casting their own heroes in the Biblical model, as when a Spanish chronicler compared the early thirteenth-century Fernando III to Joshua and the people of León and Castile to his victorious followers, the children of Israel.[64] Later in the New World, the terror of Muslims served as a convenient and convincing benchmark for the cruelties of the colonial encounter. The chronicler Oviedo, describing the experiences of Cabeza de Vaca's hapless shipwrecked party, declared that their native captors had subjected them to "greater cruelties than even a Moorish slave master could impose."[65] The comparison could also be turned against the conquistadors themselves, whom Bartolomé de las Casas described as committing barbarities "worthy of 'the Turk.'"[66] On the other hand, when "el Inca" Garcilaso de la Vega joined the Spanish Christian effort to put down the Morisco rebellion in the Alpujarras during the late 1560s, he rejected any attempt to link the inhabitants of the New World to the perfidious Jews and Moors.[67]

MUSLIMS, JEWS, AND THE WORK OF CONVERSION

Those professionally concerned with the conversion of nonbelievers might contemplate the differences between various forms of obduracy and the different strategies accordingly considered appropriate in missionary efforts. Continental conversion models aimed at Jews and Muslims were hardly models of unambiguous success any more than the attempt to extend to the New World the Christian project of perfecting and uniting humanity.[68] Father Gerónimo de Mendieta (1526–1604), a leader of the Franciscans in Mexico, turned to a parable in Luke (14:16–24) of a man who invited many guests to a great supper, all of whom refused. At that, the host ordered his servants to bring in all the unfortunates from the streets and lanes of the city. Informed that there was room still, the host instructed his servants to go out and compel still others to enter. Mendieta saw the three forms of invitation as prototypes for the different forms of mission to the Jews, Moslems, and Gentiles. Mere announcement of the Gospel was enough for the Jews, "who sin out of pure malice"; "[s]ome degree of compulsion was necessary for the followers of the 'false prophet'"; while the Gentiles, who had not been exposed to Scripture at all, required the greatest degree of forceful persuasion.[69] Force is directly proportional to charity in this interpretation: those who have the least excuse for failure to adhere to the Gospel message are left most to their own devices, while it is precisely the innocent who deserve the greatest compulsion. In this instance at least, it seems there is a neat gradation of moral blame from Jews, as the most familiar and intimate non-Christian group, through Muslims, who might have been misled by a false but in any case later message, to the innocent Indians. Mendieta perhaps did not remember or even know that hopes of converting Islam, similar to his own hopes of converting the Indians, had peaked in the thirteenth century but gradually been dashed in the wake of repeated Crusader defeats.[70] Even more strikingly, the rise and fall of missionary hopes for the full and sincere conversion of the Indians roughly paralleled the rise and fall of hopes for full and sincere conversion of the Moriscos back in the metropole.[71]

The implications of Mendieta's exegesis for the salvation of the Jews are unclear, since the parable from Luke ends with the host's declaration that "none of those who were first invited shall taste of my supper." However, to the extent it suggested that Christians should or did in fact deal patiently with

Jews, it was rooted in earlier rhetoric. Earlier on, Muslims in power had been rebuked for failure to deal patiently and tolerantly with Christian adversaries, as it was claimed Christians had done with obdurate Jews. Peter the Venerable reminded his imaginary Muslim interlocutors that upon "[h]earing the Jews blaspheme, the Christians do not go into a fury, but listen patiently and make scholarly, wise reply."[72] Peter was imagining his Christians, too.

For Spanish Catholics, the work of suppressing the remaining traces of Islam in the peninsula went on simultaneously with the mission to and administration of native peoples in the New World. The vexing challenge of maintaining purity while incorporating difference persisted.[73] As late as 1567, after all of Iberia had been under Christian rule for three-quarters of a century, the threat of Arabic culture remained sufficiently strong that it compelled repression by royal decree.[74]

Still, resolute determination in the earlier efforts to expel Jews—not only from Spain, but from other Christian realms as well—could serve as a model for those who urged similar steadfastness in the effort to rid Spain of the Moriscos. Thus the Dominican Jaime Bleda, late in the sixteenth century, cited in a letter to the king a cautionary tale about a French noble. When the nobleman suffered shame in an encounter with Jews while on pilgrimage to Santiago de Compostela, he realized it was because he had defended Jews at the time of their expulsion from France. To Bleda, this story served as a warning to those whose Christian vigilance might waver in the face of the threat to piety and unity the Moriscos presented.[75]

At the same time, the experience gained in governance of Muslim difference clearly was useful in the New World. Administrative models worked out earlier vis-à-vis Muslim minorities in Catholic Spain were applied to those in the Americas who chose to surrender rather than be enslaved.[76] But solutions were not always available to other dilemmas posed by Indians that were analogous to those the Spanish Catholics had faced in dealing with Muslims and Jews. Forced mass conversions of all three groups—in the first instance aimed at Jews after the anti-Jewish violence in Spain in 1391—raised the problem of doubtful sincerity.[77] The predicament of the Moriscos, especially perhaps in the desperate decades between the revolt in the Alpujarras of 1568 and the expulsions of 1609–14, can easily be described in terms of double consciousness, bad faith, and constant dissimulation similar to that of *conversos* from the end of the fourteenth century on—almost leading one to wonder whether these Moriscos might stake a rival claim to being the first moderns.[78] The languages, beliefs, and practices of the Americans presented similar conundrums about where cultural difference impeded the process of Catholicization and thus became intolerable, leading to an eventual decision against the ordination of natives in sixteenth-century Mexico. In the view of Mendieta this would have been unwise; because one could not yet be sure that the conversion of the Indians had irrevocably taken hold, backsliding was still a risk.[79] Inga Clendinnen's *Ambivalent Conquests* confirms the psychic power of the fear of such backsliding in its graphic description of the hysterical violence committed by Franciscans against a huge number of Yucatecan natives following the discovery of "idols" there in 1562.[80]

The conversion of the Mudéjars (Muslims under Christian rule) of Valencia was an Old World object lesson in the difficulty of determining the validity of forced conversions, while the perseverance of customs such as "'playing music at night, dancing the *zambra* and eating couscous'" was considered adequate grounds for arrest by the Inquisition in Toledo in 1538.[81] A bath taken by a Morisca, considered a covert continuation of Muslim practices of ritual purity, was also suspect.[82] As in the Americas, continued cultural difference fueled Christian anxieties not only about the efficacy of formal conversion in making its target the same as the Christian, but also about the effect of conversion on Christians themselves. If sharing the Gospel was considered a gift, the missionary effort cast into doubt what that gift really was, as well as the identity of the giver.[83]

INCORPORATIONS TERMINABLE AND INTERMINABLE

Although it is possible that the increased pressure to erase the marks of external cultural difference was a function of the racialization—that is, the internalization—of that difference,[84] it seems clear that in the sixteenth century there still was a general belief that what we would call the "assimilation" of the converted Muslim population was possible. This forced assimilation involved the breaking of spatial, kinship, and customary boundaries.[85] Indeed, an edict of the Inquisition in Seville from 1548 required the spatial segregation of Morisco families from each other in order to lessen their pernicious mutual influence, and one Spanish writer actually proposed banning endogamous marriages among Moriscos in favor of marriage exclusively between Moriscos and Old Christians—which would, at least by implication, have barred marriage between Moriscos and anyone of either Muslim *or* Jewish ancestry.[86] In Segovia, Muslims now formally converted to Catholicism were moved out of the *moreria* (the old Muslim quarter) so that their neighbors would be "reliable Old Christians." To be sure, this social engineering caused ambivalence and tension all around: Christians demanded the acculturation of these former

Muslims but resisted their integration. Indeed, only a generation earlier these people had been forced to sell their property and move into the *moreria*. As further evidence of ambivalent dominance, while edicts of expulsion would appear to have been the strongest evidence that group difference was irreducible and could be dealt with safely only through permanent removal, in at least some cases the expulsion of Muslims from Spain was actually intended as a further inducement to sincere conversion.[87] When the expulsion orders came, a number of local clerics vigorously argued that "their" Moriscos should be exempted from the order on the stipulated grounds that they were "good and faithful Christians," devoted, humble, and diligent.[88]

Whether they were to be assimilated or expelled, it made sense for Muslims, like Jews, to be considered marginal humans, "demarcat[ing] the limits of the Christian possible," for their insufficient humanity could help explain their hostility to the Gospel while leaving them still potentially susceptible of incorporation.[89] Nor is it surprising that even in depictions of those occasions when Muslims and Jews, like Indians, did convert, their image continued to trouble Christian doctrine and identity. Thus a late thirteenth-century French manuscript depicted a converted Saracen kneeling before an image of the Virgin. As Muslims were commonly seen as idolaters, and especially as worshippers of images of Muhammad, one scholar suggests that the image projected onto the depicted Muslim what were actually Christian anxieties about the danger that adoration of images might slide into the sin of idolatry.[90]

Perhaps more obviously than Jewish or Indian difference, Muslim difference transgressed the Cartesian schemes of clearly bounded space and linear progressive time. The ambiguity of a manuscript image of a Muslim converted to the worship not of an idol but of an icon (or so, of course, the believing Christian would have it) likewise adds a note of caution to any account that might otherwise purport to sketch the dimensions of late medieval and early modern difference. Any such rhetoric of closure, Kathleen Biddick has suggested, relies on implicit notions of periodization and supersession that are part and parcel of the Christian understanding of humanity, identity, and saving history. Reexamining the images of Muslim difference remains an indispensable part of the effort to reveal the contours and dynamics not so much of an unchanging core of religion called Christianity, but the larger, largely occluded, and most certainly dynamic formation we may begin to call " 'Christian-ness.' "[91]

To be sure, neither these images of Muslims nor the larger set of representations that contained and shaped "Christian-ness" were uniform throughout western and southern Europe or throughout the twelfth through sixteenth centuries. In terms of the dimensions of interiority and exteriority that this book is trying to both illuminate and question, Muslims were at some times and places more of a practical administrative, military, and missionary problem to be dealt with internally or in contact zones. Despite the language of *Reconquista* that would retrospectively make the Iberian peninsula appear to be a field of dichotomous contrast on which Muslims had been pushed beyond a moving frontier outside Europe, the Muslim presence there is of especial interest partly because it shows how much work it took to invent a Christian Europe bounded by a neatly Islamic exterior. At other times and places Muslims served more as a rhetorical foil for texts aimed at reinforcing the integrity and consistency of Christian identity. In these contexts, the free play of stereotype and denigration was checked, if at all, by continuing fantasies of conversion in a potentially ever-expanding Christian world.

Even the most sophisticated and recent work on medieval Muslim-Christian relations can reiterate the identification of Europeans with Christians precisely by eliding the term "Christian," as evidenced by the subtitles of John Tolan's brilliant books from 2002—*Islam in the Medieval European Imagination*—and 2008—*Muslims Through European Eyes in the Middle Ages*. (Tolan has little if anything to say about how European Jews may have viewed Muslims in the Middle Ages.) More rarely, but even more strikingly, writers will still make explicit the identification of Europe with Christianity as if it were unproblematic. Thus Pope Benedict XVI refers to a rupture of an already existing European consciousness when it "broke out of the borders of the European, Christian world with the discovery of America," then mentions "the Islamic cultural sphere" and eventually reaches "[t]he third large cultural sphere, Indian culture or, more accurately, the cultural spheres of Hinduism and Buddhism." In such formulations Jewish is not European; Muslim is neither European nor Indian; and in the current papal vision the poor peoples of America have no culture to speak of at all.[92] In pursuit of better ways to comprehend and express how various formations of difference challenged and furnished resources for the always incomplete project of making that "European, Christian world," in the next chapter I examine further the spatial and imaginative containers of Christian-ness in that realm known as Christendom.

CHAPTER THREE

Christendom

Institutionally, the Christendom (Christianitas) *defined by eleventh-and twelfth-century clerics was a unitary whole with a center, Rome, and boundaries that were to be both defended against external enemies—the pagans and infidels—and extended until they encompassed the entire world* (Universitas). *The Church was like a mountain destined to fill all the space on earth, gradually eating up territory until it and the world were one. In this sense, Christendom was an institutional entity that steadily affirmed its differences against the outside—the Orthodox, Judaism and Islam—and a universalist utopia that accompanied, justified, and spurred on the expansion of the Latin west in the eleventh and twelfth centuries.*

Dominique Iogna-Prat, *Order and Exclusion:*
Cluny and Christendom Face Heresy, Judaism, and Islam (1000–1150)

As Robin Lane Fox has warned us, in the opening pages of his vivid book, Pagans and Christians, *the brilliant reign of Constantine "was only a landmark in the history of Christianisation, that state which is always receding, like full employment or a garden without weeds."*

Peter Brown, *Authority and the Sacred:*
Aspects of the Christianization of the Roman World

Late medieval Christendom was understood not merely as the extent of territory ruled by Catholic monarchs, but also as the space wherein Catholic faith held sway. In that sense, just as being Christian was never a stable identity but inherently always a work in progress, Catholic-ruled territories still had to be regularly, if not continuously, made and remade into part of Christendom. This permanent unsettlement, combined with the mandate to spread the Gospel to all of humanity, made Christendom not so much a contained space as a project. The more the ambition to Christianize the world came to the fore, the more embarrassing became the anomalous persistence of Jewish communities "within" Christendom. Jewishness was therefore one of the irritating differences that provoked the rhetorical and disciplinary energies eventually deployed in the catechization of New World peoples, the attempt to expand Christendom to the limits of a world suddenly writ much larger.

The expulsion of irritating difference in the name of creating a unified Christendom thus was not merely reflective of the flawed humanity of the dominant. It followed a certain logic specific to Christianity. "Shameful is the part that is not congruous to the whole," Augustine declared in the *Confessions*.[1] Augustine's rationale for the continued existence of Jews—as evidence both of the truth of Christian history and of the sad consequences of rejecting Jesus as savior—made sense only when there was a clearly perceived outside to Christendom for whom Jews could serve as such an object lesson. Thus, for example, once Christianity had been brought to England, Gregory the Great wondered which pagans might still remain for whom Jews could stand as witnesses to the Gospel.[2] Gregory's suggestion that Jews were no longer useful or necessary could—with some plausibility, if without affording much new insight—be said to be a harbinger of the two-century sequence of expulsions (intermittent and frequently inconclusive) of Jews from most of western Europe beginning in England in 1290. In this perspective, the expulsion of the remaining unconverted Jews from Spain in 1492 may be seen not as an isolated event, but rather as the last and most dramatic example.

The coincidence of that expulsion with Columbus's departure on his first transatlantic voyage in 1492 is so momentous as almost to blind us to the need to examine further the common context of those two events. The numeric designation of that year has served—almost always, and even in critical scholarship—not as a link but as a divider between Europe's long struggle to recover from the "Dark Ages" and its reinvigorated encounter with an "outside" and an Other. By now it should be apparent that such a separation obscures as much as it explains, if not more. The elimination of separate space for Jews and the extension of European Christian dominion were part of a single process. Becoming Catholic Spain was part and parcel of becoming Christian Europe.[3]

In fact, it is in the case of Spain that the attempt to articulate "Europe" as both contingent and dependent on particular cultural exclusions can be most readily historicized, largely because of the significant contacts Spanish bureaucrats and intellectuals of various sorts had with Jews, with Muslims, and with New World peoples in the centuries considered here.[4] The cultural history of Iberia in the centuries before and after 1492 illustrates, more richly than that of any other part of what came to be called Europe, the claim that the formation of Christian identity in engagement with Jewish difference was also a formative element in the colonial encounter.

Thus, the Spanish coincidence of 1492 needs to be constantly reinterrogated. In doing so, we must not be seduced into a totalizing narrative that obscures the multiple and sometimes conflicting dynamics of the relations between the *Reconquista* in Spain and the conquest of the New World. The graphically dynamic image of southwestern Europe and the middle of the Western Hemisphere, an image in which the Iberian peninsula seems to be straining to be fit back into the Caribbean, is indeed seductive. Spain, the first great European colonial power, is also the headland or prow of an adventuring Europe.[5] Thus we have been tempted by a compelling spatialized summary of centuries of experience seeming to link the overseas missions launched outward from the Iberian headland to the peninsular project we call the *Reconquista* as part of one seamless process, rather than as the more complicated set of relationships between Spanish Catholics, Jews, Muslims, and Native Americans that I have been exploring in this book. Along with the history of the expulsions of Jews, this notion tends to combine into a narrative that relies on the notion of a "core" northern European Christianity coming down from the heart of Europe to sweep out impurities in Iberia and then, with the impetus of this experience behind it, to invade and begin to transform the New World in its own image.

The seeds for this retrospective view may be seen in the work of the thirteenth-century archbishop of Toledo, Rodrigo Jiménez de Rada. But despite Rodrigo's enthusiasm and vision, "[o]n a broader scale, we are hard put to see any wider ideology of either crusade or reconquest seizing the Christians," as Lucy Pick notes. Moreover, Rodrigo also resisted an absolutizing insistence on a monolithic Christendom and instead rationalized the continued presence of Jewish and Muslim difference in a necessarily unperfected world.[6]

Accordingly, it seems more promising to focus, as more and more scholars do today, on the contingent strategic and rhetorical cross-identifications made at the time between those several collective identities, than to bring their fates together in a seamless narrative of Christian consolidation and conquest. The notion of such a grand and unified process promulgated by the archbishop and of its spillover into the New World nevertheless reigns within a certain literate sphere as the overall conception of Spanish history, as in this excerpt from a trade book on the colonial encounter:

> Spain, in particular, was scarcely touched by the Renaissance; 700 years of war against the Moors had produced a warrior culture filled with loathing and contempt for other ways of life, not a new spirit of inquiry. The *reconquista* of Iberia, which ended in 1492, would be the model for the *conquista* of America.[7]

This brief quote contains in a nutshell both the famous "Black Legend" of Spanish exceptionalism and the retrospective packaging of the *Reconquista* into a single seven-hundred-year war. Yet the portrayal of adventures in the New World as the next phase in the defeat of the Moors is not a recent invention of late twentieth-century anticolonialism. Miguel Angel Ladero Quesada documents the origin of this tendency to link *Conquista* to *Reconquista* in one unbroken sequence by citing the chronicler of Cortés, López de Gómara, who wrote that "[u]pon finishing the conquest of the Moors, that lasted 800 years, the one of the Indies was begun so that the Spaniards could always wage war against the infidels."[8] This statement is unwavering in its teleology: the New World, as it were, not only had to be there, but it had to be "discovered" precisely when it was, or the "Spaniards" could not have continued in their mission. Moreover, it suggests that for eight hundred years the definition of a "Spaniard" has been articulated and now will continue to be defined in opposition to those infidels against whom Spaniards customarily and properly make war.

The capture of portions of Iberia by Christian monarchs occurred sporadically through the ninth through thirteenth centuries and then was renewed in the late fifteenth century conquest of Granada. To overemphasize its continuity is almost inevitably to minimize the competing model of *convivencia* among Christians, Muslims, and Jews in medieval Spain. Thus, as María Rosa Menocal suggests, "[t]he *Reconquista*, as the ideological construct that pits itself against al-Andalus, is not only not medieval, it is as anti-medieval as they come"[9]—if, that is, we accept a measure of uneasy coexistence and productive cultural interchange as characteristic of whatever we continue to call "medieval."

Without recourse to such totalizing narratives, what might it have meant to reclaim "Spain" as part of Christendom? The answer depends in part on what is meant by Christendom. Christendom has been simultaneously conceived of as a set of persons sharing ideas ("the state or condition of being Christian"), a conception that leads directly to the disciplining of the Other and his incorporation into Christendom via conversion, and also as a geographical demarcation on the surface of the earth (in titles such as *Rim of Christendom: A Biography of Eusebio Francisco Kino, Pacific Coast Pioneer*),[10] a conception that leads to organizational techniques of spatial discipline.[11] The phrase "rim of Christendom" suggests more broadly the extent of the known and populated world.[12] In such conceptions the boundaries of Christendom, civilization, and humanity come close to merging.

Thus, in a sense, any lands not inhabited by Christians were seen as being beyond the edge, awaiting physical incorporation into the Christian whole. This geographic organization of Christendom was created along the model of the Roman Empire. Its body was divided into cells called "sees," which were contiguous with each other but did not overlap.[13] Early in the uneven succession of Iberian conquests by Christian monarchs, the linkage of Alfonso VI's rule to a spatially rationalized church hierarchy was critical to his success. Alfonso was also the first of the small Christian monarchs in northern Iberia to style himself territorially—first as "king of León" and then as *totius hispaniae imperator*.[14]

However, conversion and administration were not simply different, and in some ways antithetical, techniques for the production and reproduction of Christendom. Spatial disciplines also could be used. In the twelfth-century Cistercian monasteries studied by Talal Asad, confinement within restricted areas and even the limitation of visits to those places fostered monastic discipline.[15] And in the New World, a major missionary strategy aimed at simultaneously civilizing and converting the Indians was to concentrate them in mission pueblos, or *reducciones*. The methods employed by the Jesuits in their *reducciones* (and by Las Casas in his abortive attempt at an egalitarian agricultural settlement for Spaniards and Indians) were motivated by a practical desire to manage the Indians' manners.[16] They also had much to do with new Utopian theories of equitable organization circulating in fifteenth- and sixteenth-century Europe.[17] Spatial disciplines thus could work by containment as well as expansion. Such efforts were deployed upon peoples ranging from the Tarahumara in northern Mexico to the Tupi-Guaraní of coastal Brazil.[18] These pueblos were commonly organized according to a "grid pattern derived from town plans that the Romans had developed centuries before for their colonies in Spain."[19] The conversion of conquered peoples became sufficiently routine that those still unconverted were assumed to be uncivilized.[20] In the twelfth century—centuries before Columbus's voyage—there was a close analogy between two distinctions: the one contrasting Christians and non-Christians, and the one separating civilized people from barbarians.[21]

That is, except when it came to the Jews. By contrast with efforts at both conversion and geographical administration in the service of Christianization, in the centuries immediately preceding the colonial encounter in the New World, Jews in western Europe were repeatedly segregated out and then expelled (albeit by no means uniformly, and often not permanently, since Jewish communities had protectors and were not necessarily powerless). Even in cases of mass and forced conversion, they were not maintained bureaucratically and geographically in concentrated communities of new Christians. Where the continued presence of unbaptized Jews was perceived as an overriding danger—especially to the Christianity of their newly converted brothers—the clearest solution was expulsion.[22] Separate Jewish neighborhoods, where they existed in western Europe through the Middle Ages, were based on a varying mixture of distaste toward Jews, perceived and actual need for the authorities to be able to protect the Jews as a collective, and the communal autonomy (tied to collective responsibility) underlying Jewish presence in a Christian polity.[23] Even though the popes tended to defend Jewish residence rights, papal rulings during the latter half of the sixteenth century limited that autonomous space, forcing Jews in the pope's domains into restricted spaces intended to foster canonical supervision.[24]

So whether it was acted on through expansion, restriction, or (in extremis) through exclusion, part of the rhetoric of empire in Christianity was the positing of an essential unity—Christendom. Here the term "essential" is not merely an intensifier. Cognitive unity itself, the creation of a true religious common sense,[25] was of the essence of Christianity.[26]

Essence and unity were linked to imperial loyalties at a very early stage in Christian history, as in this fourth-century Roman recruit's oath: "By God and Christ and the Holy Spirit and by the emperor's majesty, which, by God's will, ought to be beloved and venerated by the human race."[27] This unity of conscience was, of course, part and parcel of an imagined territorial and political unity, an imaginary unity that continues to shape conventional understandings of the origins of western European identity out of the ruins of the Roman Empire.[28] But this is not merely a retrospective characteristic of such contemporary "conventional narratives"; the link between imperial and Christian unity and ubiquity had already been expressed, for example, by the fifth-century geographer Paulus Orosius, who wrote with seeming confidence that all he surveyed—east, north, south, and toward "the great islands"—were of "my law and name" as a Roman and a Christian.[29] Nevertheless, given the very particular place that Jews and Jewishness had within the Christian sacred narrative, and the resistance to conversion of at least a sufficient number of Jews to reproduce their communities of difference, it is no surprise that they persistently troubled this ideal image of the territorial and spiritual unity of Christendom.

BECOMING CHRISTIAN, BECOMING EUROPE

As the historian L.P. Harvey puts it, "the Jews were a problem that Christendom never solved to its own satisfaction."[30] But formulations such as Harvey's set no beginning or end term to Christendom, and do not suggest in any way that the chronotope of Christendom had its own contingent history. They accordingly perpetuate an older identification of Europe and Christendom that served to justify expansionary projects at the time, and that is now invoked as an explanation of those same expansionary projects. Thus James Muldoon, in a major work documenting the critical role of medieval legal theory in helping to legitimate and regulate the dominion of Catholic monarchs in newly conquered infidel lands, begins with a sweeping statement about the generalized Christian European impulse toward expansion and the repeated production of sites of cultural tension. Starting with the First Crusade at the end of the eleventh century, he suggests, "Expansion would seem to be an essential characteristic of European culture. To a great extent, it is connected with European religious values: Christianity is a missionary religion seeking to bring into the fold all mankind."[31] Muldoon explicitly identifies Europe with Christianity. Adding expansionism as an "essential" third term, he reinforces his other claims that aggressive expansionism is part of what it means to be European and that Christianity is the exclusive European religion. He remains silent about whether and how a drive to bring non-Christian Europeans, such as Jews, into the fold might inflect the notion of Europe as naturally Christian and as naturally expansionist.[32]

Unfortunately, even today many studies of the colonial encounter remain conveniently stuck with the assumption that before 1492 Europe "was" Christian in some essentialist sense. This is the most obdurate of the sediments and accretions of rigid fantasies about Christendom that this book aims to shake loose. Thus, in the preface to a collection of essays called *Early Images of the Americas*, Jerry M. Williams and Robert E. Lewis describe how the New World encounter "made possible the sociopolitical reworking of traditional European valuations of peoples such as Africans, Moors, and Turks who were at odds with Christian sensibility." The boundaries of Europe are defined in this quote such that "Moors" (presumably including Muslims in Spain) and all non-Christians are effectively excluded. By contrast, the same editors later note that "[f]irsthand knowledge of, and contact with, the conventions of non-Christian peoples—Africans, Jews, Moors, Orientals, Moriscos, Turks—served many chroniclers as the basis for launching observations and conjectures about the Indians which were based on limited experience."[33] That Jews appear in the latter list and not in the former is not quite arbitrary: to include it in the former might well have disrupted the identification of Europe with Christianity.[34]

It is worth looking again at how this problematic and shifting notion of Christendom is related to the idea of Europe—or, more specifically, to the term Christian Europe as used by modern historians.[35] Scholars do not seem to be in agreement on whether the terms are to be used interchangeably, or whether there is a historical shift from one to the other. Judith Herrin argues that Europe acquired a distinctive identity as early as the second half of the first Christian millennium; during these centuries "Byzantium, the caliphate, and Europa 'found' their own cultures, creating traditions to meet their needs."[36] On the other hand, Herrin regards the period immediately before Columbus's voyage as a watershed: "By the fifteenth century, the classical harvest"—i.e., the recapture of classical humanities—"heralded the collapse of Christendom, as the concept had been understood in medieval times"[37]— that is, of Christendom as the unity of territory and belief. Jacques Le Goff likewise posits "a cultural space common to all western Christian Europe" as one of the characteristic features of the twelfth and thirteenth centuries, but refers to Christian Europe as "shattered" by the end of the fifteenth century.[38] Robert Berkhofer reinforces this suggestion by using Christendom and Europe as an explicitly contrasting pair, stating flatly that "the transition in thinking can perhaps be seen best in the increasing use of 'Europe' for self-reference during the fifteenth and sixteenth centuries in preference to the older 'Christendom.'"[39]

In his pioneering survey of the history of the term Europe, Denys Hay suggests that Europe both replaced and was also closely identified with "an earlier Christendom."[40] He sees the change as having begun around the thirteenth and fourteenth centuries (page 58), stimulated in large part by the Crusades, which brought in their wake a sharpened realization that the Middle East and north Africa were even further from being Christian realms than they had been at the end of the Roman Empire. By 1458, in writings of Pope Pius II, "Christendom is seen as radiating out from a European base" (84), and in his *Historia de Europa*, Pius writes of "the events which happened among the Europeans, or those who are called Christians" (cited by Hay, 87). By the sixteenth century, the notions of Europe and of Christendom were indistinguishable (109), and Hay agrees that the latter term eventually became eclipsed (116).

Remarkably for a scholar engaged in historicizing the notions of Christendom and of Europe, Hay betrays a seeming confusion about the internal uniformity of medieval Christendom when discussing the relations between conceptions of Christianity and personhood. He states that in the Latin West in the Middle Ages, "the very existence of a vernacular noun 'Christian,' meaning no more (and no less) than 'person' gives a vivid indication that religion rather than race or government or geography formed the common basis of all groups in western society. To be a Christian meant full humanity in opposition to the brute beasts" (page 57). Of course, the notion that non-Christians were simply opposed to "brute beasts" is rather too hasty. Jews, for instance, were debated and interrogated—surely something one does not do with animals—even while they were being drawn as bestial. Furthermore, when Hay refers to "the common basis of all groups," does he mean that all groups who shared Christianity had "religion" as their basis for commonality? Does this mean that Hay at least momentarily forgot the Jews?

Some more recent discussions of the relations among religion, selfhood, freedom, and politics in the European West suggest that what appears as Christian unity actually represents a profound division, yet they read the past as though Christendom were actually that ideal space that was uninterruptedly Christian. The division, it follows from this reading, exists within a society otherwise uniformly Christian. Thus, for example, Charles Taylor observes that "in principle, the inhabitants of Christendom were Christians. But these same people were organized in two societies—one temporal, one spiritual."[41] John Milbank, aiming to dispel the ahistorical notion of a separate "secular" sphere that existed in latent form in the premodern period, insists to the contrary that "there was the single community of Christendom, with its dual aspects of sacerdotium and regnum."[42] Hans Hillenbrand describes the principles of the *corpus christianum* as having been in effect for "over a thousand years of European history, during which each man, woman, and child had been, by the fact of citizenship, a Christian of the kind prescribed by the sovereign."[43] Whether a past Christendom is portrayed as unified or riven, in the relation between European history and Christianity, the only people remembered in Christendom are Christians.

This is not intended to resolve the question of the fate of the idea of Christian Europe from the late Middle Ages through the first century of overseas expansion, but more to widen the cracks already opened by recent postcolonial and medievalist scholarship in our retrospective naturalization of that identity, both as a geocultural unit and as Christian. The words Karl Leyser used to describe ninth-century uses of the term "Europe"—as "a topos of panegyric, a cultural emblem rather than a solid, firm geographical and ethnic concept"[44]—seem oddly reminiscent of the nineteenth and twentieth centuries as well. To be sure, the plausibility of such usages in these latter centuries has rested massively on the accomplishment of empire by several powers within Europe from the sixteenth century onwards—a Europe disunified politically as much as it was religiously.

In any case, the recognition in the quote from Hay of what was to become a powerful trope in modern colonialism—the identification of the Christian with the properly human—needs to be refined before we can learn something from it. This task will be taken up in the next chapter.

MAKING EUROPE IN 1215

Not only was the Fourth Lateran Council a moment of symbolic closure for the twelfth-century mode of self-formation, it also was a key moment in shaping this image of Europe as monolithically Christian. "Introducing its legislative program, the council simultaneously declared the universality and unity of the Church, linked that unity to the mystery of Christ's transubstantiated body, and stressed the primary role of the clergy in perfecting that unity."[45] This summary from the pen of Jeremy Cohen captures neatly the efforts to generalize the reach of the Church as a geographical and spiritual identity, and appropriately stresses the new mandate to an aggressive, outward-oriented clergy. Meanwhile, the later colonial ventures that revived the notion of actually expanding Christendom to cover the entire globe and include all the earth's peoples were at this time still centuries away. Catholic officials were extremely conscious of the limitations of Christendom at the margins of Europe—in Iberia; in the Middle East, where the Crusades were continuing; and in eastern Europe, where settlement and the conversion of pagans went hand in hand, where bishoprics were laid out along with peasants' allotments and town sites.[46] Churches outside geographical Europe—in north Africa and the Middle East—were either in decline or persisting as minority groups in Islamic realms. The area within which the popes aimed to establish full dominion was at this point concentrated in the Frankish regions, Italy, the Holy Roman Empire, and England. Much of the dispute about papal succession in the coming centuries would have to do with rivalries among these western European protostates.

The new prominence of the communion host after 1215 placed it at greater risk in the presence of Jews.[47] Where communion was explicitly under discussion, both as a ritual in its own terms and as a key defining moment linking several dimensions of the "organic" in Christianity, how much more of an irritant must the presence of Jews have seemed. Not only had "they" denied Christ at the time of his Passion, but they continued to deny him by refusing communion now. Again, the substantial understanding of Christendom as "the body of Christ" must be stressed here. Every time Catholics took communion and their Jewish neighbors did not, the Jews were once again actively placing themselves outside the *corpus Christi*. In a context where ingestion is a central moment in identification, the refusal to eat can be a dramatic instance of the general rule that incorporation always undermines the apparent solidity of distinctions between inside and outside.[48]

The body of Christ was itself understood to be dispersed, in the form of the host, throughout all Christian realms, its substance communicated to and informing the space of Christendom. Thus, an account of the anti-Jewish Rintfleisch massacres in Franconia in 1298 describes crowds incensed by reports of Jewish host desecrations as being "on a trail of vindication and recovery, in search of all the hosts, all those parts of Christ's body which had been allegedly disseminated by and among Jews."[49] The fantasies, doubts, and envies circulating in the context of this overall unifying drive toward literal incorporation and its cognate, physical expulsion, involved, first, written and oral discourses and, eventually, specific institutionalized practices ranging from the special distinguishing clothing for Jews to the Inquisition against heretics.[50]

Even in these late medieval centuries the impetus toward a new unity of Christian Europe, as well as a new identification of Christendom and Europe as corporate entities demanding the highest loyalty, came not from scientists, humanists, or protonationalists but rather from the church itself. In this movement to assert papal authority as temporal and united, what brought Europe together *was* the church, and the agents of that perpetual work of unification were the Catholic clergy. Perhaps for those two centuries or so, with Christendom being limited from without and with a major push for purification and unity being mobilized within, Europe and Catholic Christianity were more thoroughly one than at any time before and since. Even without the New World encounter, the situation probably could not have lasted forever, and the purification of Europe could never have been as effective as many clerics would have wished.

In the Old World during the later Middle Ages, the fantasy of an essentially unified Christendom was challenged as much by the limits of Christian

Europe—which were never sufficiently stable or clearly enough defined—as by the presence of Jews and Muslims. Similarly, not only in the Americas but throughout the development of modern colonialism and its history of enforced servitude, the tensions between the confessional and geographic notions of Christendom helped to dismantle the ideal of Christian unity. Henri Baudet points out, for example, that in Portugal at the end of the fifteenth century—that is, before 1492, when Europe is supposed to have encountered the Other—"although the bodies of Negroes might be held captive, this very fact made it possible for their souls to achieve true freedom through Christianity."[51] Here the spiritualization of Christian identity is expressed in a duality between body and soul that, even at the time it was enunciated, likely strained at the limits of any claim to speak in the slaves' best interest, body or soul.[52] Yet the fact that the argument had to be made at all suggests that in this time and place, the categorical difference of these "Negroes" could not be taken for granted and therefore their continued enslavement required justification. If their presence as non-Christians *and* as slaves troubled the ideal unity of Christendom as a territory and a set of faithful souls equal in Christ, their potential to be made into Christians made their anomalous presence another place where the project of Christendom could be pursued. Moreover, Baudet's observation underscores the idea that for places to exist on the earth from which people could still be captured and brought to Portugal as slaves, someplace still had to be outside of Christendom. In other words, even if we were to suspend our suspicion that the distinction between the captive bodies and free souls of Negroes in late fifteenth-century Portugal was cynically made—were we to assume that those who perpetuated this slave trade really did so to facilitate the Christianization of Negroes—still, Christendom had to have a beyond from which the bodies could be brought in and within which the souls could safely be freed.

As that beyond expanded, ambiguities of status similar to those concerning the Muslim slave in Spain or the Negro slave in Portugal sometimes obtained concerning indigenous peoples in the Americas. Thus, native people in the Tarahumara region of northern Mexico, faced with Jesuit missionizing and the colonial state in the course of the seventeenth and eighteenth centuries, sought out missionaries and engaged in the process of conversion. Sometimes this was to their own advantage, since as Christians they would enjoy a measure of legal protection against some of the most violently exploitive effects of the colonial system. At the same time, as with so many other merely legal protections, those who converted did not necessarily benefit, especially since conversion was linked to forced labor.[53] As elsewhere and at other times, entry into the body of Christ did not necessarily afford one the full privileges of membership.

THE LIMITS OF CHRISTENDOM

Meanwhile, the impediments to incorporating non-Christians into Christendom were becoming more salient, and the work of doing so was becoming more problematic, more susceptible to the extremes—positive and negative—of imagination and fantasy. Allegorization of the body helped to reinforce a tendency to denigrate the literal or physical body, as in the Portuguese example discussed by Henri Baudet and cited above. Both Jews and Indians, throughout the literature that falls within the scope of this study, are commonly cast as more material and less capable of spiritual conceptions. In the case of the Jews, this reaches back as far as Paul's argument that the true Jews are those who circumcise their hearts and not their foreskins.[54]

A wonderful parallel to this Pauline argument is found in the writings of the early colonial historian and polemicist Sepúlveda on human sacrifice in the New World. Sepúlveda supposed that the Americans had committed "a diabolic category mistake," substituting the literal sacrifice of the heart for what they should properly have sacrificed only metaphorically, " 'the pious and sane minds of men.' "[55] Furthermore, after the first flush of missionary zeal early in the sixteenth century a disillusionment with the supposedly limited capacities of the Indians set in, such that by the Third Mexican Provincial Council of 1585 bishops present referred to the Indians as *rudes*, suggesting that, like the simplest of European peasants, these were folks simply incapable of capturing the more subtle points of Christian theology.[56]

The kind of category mistake identified by Sepúlveda was grounded in the Thomist theory of cognition dominant in Catholic thinking by the sixteenth century, which in turn was derived from Aristotelian theories of perception and conceptualization. In this theory, imagination mediated between intellect and sense perception in the production of cognition and understanding.[57] This mediate step was an unstable place where essential properties of phenomena such as the Eucharist might sometimes be stripped of their "accidents." The result could produce such "positive" insights as visions of Jesus on a church altar. Conversely, demonic forces might intervene in the working of the imagination to produce confused illusions.

This theory was drawn upon by Spanish missionaries in the Americas in their attempts to explain why, if the observance of natural law was fundamental to human nature and included monotheism embodied in the Ten

Commandments leading ultimately to Christianity, Indians had failed to follow precisely that path. The Indians were understood to be incapable of distinguishing between the products of imagination based on actual sense perception and "the fictions of their own disordered and undisciplined imaginations."[58] This projection onto the natives of the New World represents what we could fairly call a prototypical theory of the "savage mind." Provisionally, at least, it appears that no such effort was made to explain the Jews' failure to embrace the Gospel on cognitive—as opposed to moral or providential—grounds. Certainly the root justifications for the move toward regulation, separation, and expulsion of Jews in western Europe in the later Middle Ages could not have depended on this kind of renewed Aristotelian theory of miscognition. The works of Aquinas, especially the *Summa Theologica*, from which the New World missionaries derived their fundamental cognitive categories, came only toward the end of the earlier efflorescence of the exclusion of the Jews and their regulation in the twelfth and thirteenth centuries. Aquinas died in 1274 after having written the *Summa* during the last five years of his life.[59]

In the attempt to understand the ways in which American beliefs and rituals diverged from Christianity, approached it, or represented demonic perversions of it, the relation between polity and doctrine is most salient. In the disciplined formation of Christian Spain, the presence of Jews as continuing rivals to universal church authority had to be contained without undermining the revealed status of the Bible. This was ultimately done by insisting that the Jews fall in line with the Gospels' supersession of the Hebrew Bible—that they convert or leave. In the colonial encounter, on the other hand, where otherness was much more pervasive as small groups of Spanish Christians felt their way—even if with bravado—among vastly larger numbers of indigenous inhabitants, a much more sustained effort to account for the various dimensions of difference was necessary.

At least two plausible, if ambitious, lines of potential inquiry suggest what more may be learned about the management of Jewish and Native American difference, those two markers of the limits of confessional and geographic Christendom. The first of these lines would start with Sepúlveda's explanation of American sacrifice as a literalization of a spiritual command, and explore further the analogy between the suggestion that Americans were living in illusion and the diagnosis of the Jews' refusal to accept Christ as being due to their literalism. This analogy appears to support the suggestion that, at least before nineteenth-century imperial British Protestant ethnology separated out the ancient Israelites from otherwise universalist theories of cultural evolution,[60] the hierarchies developed in the ideological work of excluding Jews from

Europe and explaining the difference of Native Americans shared a broader logic. Jews, by their stubborn indifference to the spiritual transformation wrought by the coming of Jesus, could not overcome that primitive literalism and carnality which had rendered their own ancestors mere precursors of the church, the new and true Israel. Indians were confused, so to speak, by a similarly "undertheorized" understanding of language and reality, though dedicated efforts might still bring them to a truer appreciation of the Gospel, and hence within the bounds of Christendom. In the chapter on texuality below, I suggest some ways in which this analogy appears to hold true, and other ways in which it might obscure contrasts rather than reveal similarities between the kinds of difference that Jews and Indians represented for Christian Europe.

A second line of inquiry would explore the influence of the colonialist management of the difference of Native Americans—and of all the other forms of difference outside Europe—on the later career of Jewishness inside Europe. If the pressure applied to Jews during the centuries before European colonialism was related to the rationales applied to the management of colonial difference, the colonial experience (and the profits of colonialism in turn) vastly stimulated the shaping of European states that began in the later Middle Ages.[61] Thus, another book yet to be written might reveal that in later centuries, when a liberal-statist European discourse about the civilization of Jews and the dissolution of Jewish communities arose, this earlier adaptation of Aristotelian/Aquinian categories of cognition to the New World encounter was adopted mutatis mutandis by liberals preaching tolerance and patience toward Jews. It would be hazardous to place a starting date to the discourse on the common spiritual humanity of the Jew within the Christian European era. Yet it seems fairly uncontroversial to suppose that the discourse flowered with the Enlightenment and the attendant struggles over Jewish emancipation. The ambivalence of this later discourse is clear in the language used by the Enlightener Delisle de Sales in 1777 to affirm the common humanity of the Jews while distinguishing their humanity from their Jewishness: "The Jews are monsters neither physically nor morally; they must be pleaded with, educated, and not exterminated. . . . A Jew is a man before being sectarian, before being a usurer, even before being a Jew."[62]

Whether or not Jews were indeed human was not an entirely settled question in Europe when de Sales wrote, nor had it been settled in the centuries prior to the inauguration of European conquest in the New World. We know all too well that it was also not settled in the century and a half after 1777. Yet the very possibility of the argument for common humanity as the primary quality that Jews shared with their European fellows, like the argument made by

Las Casas for the common humanity the Indians shared with the new Spanish arrivals, was inseparable from the Christianity against which the humanity of Jews and Indians was being judged and sometimes found deficient. Mass forced conversion of Jews and Muslims inside Iberia might have seemed at first to reinforce the spiritual and territorial integrity of Christendom, but it also placed massive pressure on the possibility of confidence in the spiritual unity of all Christians, even as it marked the ascendance of a part of Christendom about to become, on the foundation of New World empire, ever more insistently Spain.

CHAPTER FOUR

The Universe of the Human

The abbot [Peter the Venerable] represents a watershed period, the eleventh and twelfth centuries, in which western society began to define itself in terms of what it rejected as nonhuman. . . . For the moment, human life was impossible outside of society, and the only society possible was Christian.

—Dominique Iogna-Prat, *Order and Exclusion:*
Cluny and Christendom Face Heresy, Judaism, and Islam (1000–1150)

[In a late medieval English Sermo de corpore Christi*] a Christian and a Jew traveling together enter a church, and only the Jew is visited with a vision of the bleeding Christ in the hands of Christians. To the question why only he could see it the answer is given:*

> "And thy kin made him die,
> "Therefore all bloody thou him sees."

—Miri Rubin, *Corpus Christi: The Eucharist in Late Medieval Culture*
[orthography modernized]

One of the many unfortunate effects of the tendency to see 1492 as the year modernity began is to suppose that since racial discourses are characteristic of modernity, they will not be found inside Europe before that year—or, at least, that we can safely speak of "boundaries of humanity" known unproblematically to European Christians before Columbus's first voyage.[1] Where, how, and whether to locate within some problematic category of shared humanity such figures as the Jew, the Muslim, and the Indian—as well as those who personified them—has long been an aspect of European Christendom's negotiations with its others. The question of the Indians' humanity was hotly debated in sixteenth-century Spain, leading to eventual attempts by such men as Bartolomé de Las Casas to establish once and for all that they were part of the human community.[2] While the friars who argued strenuously for the Indians' humanity may have been swayed by the desire to have the demands on Indian labor reduced and the time for catechization consequently increased,[3] the language of the argument was not new. The terms of that debate had been set from late antiquity through the later Middle Ages in rhetorical distinctions between Greek (or Roman) and barbarian and in notions of "race" sometimes used to categorize the set of Christian believers.

The rhetorics that deployed the relations assumed to exist between Christianity and the categories of race (usually as *genos* or *ethnos*) and kinship in late antiquity drew their versatile power from the synthesis of fixity—by which they were vested with an aura of the inevitable, the fundamental, and the given—and fluidity—by which they were shown to be susceptible to the vagaries of human choice and invested with attributes of virtue and vice.[4] As such a synthesis, the late antique and medieval concepts of race and kinship have, in retrospect, proven difficult for us moderns to pin down.

UNIVERSAL KINSHIP

Already for the Church father Clement of Alexandria, the notion that the category of "Christian" could come to include everyone made the limited collective identities of Hellene and Jew necessarily inferior.[5] Yet rhetorics of kinship, far from being discarded in this quest for universalization, remained central to Clement, who noted the necessity of surrendering the primary love of one's parents, but only in order to be worthy "to be a son of God and a disciple of God as well as also friend and kin" to fellow Christians.[6] Accordingly, the elements we are today accustomed to separating out as religion on the one hand and ethnicity or race on the other were then components of a single identity. For Clement, Christians were indeed a people, a *genos*—but a superior people in both salvation and its accessibility through faith.[7] Perhaps the easiest way to approximate this early Christian rhetoric of simultaneously universal and "racial" identity is to recall how common, at least until quite recently, has been our usage of the term "human race" to indicate the entire species. In late antiquity, "[b]y collapsing Christianity with humanity, early Christians could argue that Christians constitute the ideal form of the human race, whereas all other peoples (and their forms of piety) fall short."[8] More than garden-variety ethnocentrism, this Christian argument depended in turn on the potential of Christianity to include all of humanity; but it also left plenty of space for rhetorics that treated non-Christians as not quite human.

Later, the Christian thinkers of the twelfth century were taken with the idea of reason as a defining characteristic of the human race: reason, a shared capacity of all humans, was the ticket by which everyone who wished to could enter the Church.[9] It was not a far step to conclude (or at least to suggest as a handy rhetorical strategy) that those who failed, as Jews failed, to exhibit their possession of reason by being true Christian believers were not quite human.[10] If this damning evaluation is open to debate,[11] perhaps that is not so much because Christian polemicists at this time were more tolerant or more patient than this picture would have us believe, but rather because the dividing line between the human and the non-human was not then seen as being so rigid and absolute as it now seems to us.

"Religion" and "ethnicity" are not the only categories that, from a post-Enlightenment perspective, ancient and pre-modern speakers and writers refused to keep straight, much to the confusion of historians viewing their world through the lens of social-scientific categories. Categories of race and gender were subject to similar imbrications and slippages between fixity and fluidity—and they were, moreover, powerfully tied to questions of meaning, especially when it came to readings of the body.[12] Thus, for example, race, gender, and religion come together in a discussion of the question of male Jewish flux as that question appeared, not for the first time, in seventeenth-century Spain:

> In the early months of 1632, Juan de Quiñones, an official in the court of Philip IV, addressed a memorandum to the king's confessor, Inquisitor General Fray Antonio de Sotomayor, citing what he presented as incontrovertible "means for knowing and persecuting the Jewish race" which included the following:
>
> "among other curses which they suffer, bodily and spiritually, inside and outside the body, for having persecuted the true Messiah, Christ our redeemer, to the point of placing him on a Cross, is that every month many of them suffer a flowing of blood from their posterior parts, as a perpetual sign of infamy and shame."[13]

An old canard—the notion that male Jews suffered some form of monthly flux, mysteriously akin to female menstruation—was here drawn on to reinforce the notion that their non-Christianity was genetically fixed and subject to objective diagnosis, and also to relate the fantastic symptomology of inherited Jewishness to the supposed historical infamy of the Jews from the time of Jesus and all of their unrepentant descendants. In sum, religion and rationality were closely tied to race and gender in the self-definition of Christians and Christianity throughout its long engagement with Jews.

This should cause contemporary writers to be wary of their own assumptions about other fixed and fluid group characteristics when examining the encounter between Christian Europe and non-Christians outside Europe. In some accounts of the colonial encounter in Latin America an assumption of greater Spanish "rationality" relative to the Indians, an assumption already grounded in a kind of Weberian cultural determinism, is facilitated by a failure to examine the link between the exclusion of Jews from late medieval Europe (eventually and most dramatically from Iberia) and the politics of Spanish-Indian relations.[14] The putative rationality of encountered others is linked to their putative humanity, and we are accustomed—not least by the historically recent prevalence of biological accounts of speciation—to contrasting the human with the animal. The categorical distinction between human and animal is not a cultural universal, but it is a distinction of particular significance in Christian doctrine—developed at length for example in the work of Aquinas, for whom the presence of a rational soul was the distinguishing characteristic of the set of all Christians, whether actual or potential. Following Aquinas, the Spanish arrived in the New World believing that their religion was discoverable by natural law and should thus be obvious to anyone possessed of a rational soul and exposed to the Gospel message.[15]

Others shared Columbus's conviction that the peoples he hoped to encounter on his voyage were rational souls ripe and even eager for the Gospel. Beatriz Pastor Bodmer cites a letter sent to Columbus before his first voyage by "a Florentine physicist named Paolo da Pozzi Toscanelli," who tells him he will find rulers who have "a great desire to be instructed in our Catholic religion and in all the sciences that we possess."[16] Striking here is the link between the two claims—that the inhabitants of the imagined lands want to be instructed in both Catholicism and science. Toscanelli's imaginative and prescriptive description was just one of the ways in which "America" was prefigured before Columbus set sail.[17]

This kind of analysis can be taken too far, the risk being an account in which the actual contingencies of cultural encounters in history are flattened and subsumed within an overarching, deterministic logic of reified colonialism.[18] Such an argument about prefiguration relies on a functionalist sociology of knowledge, attempting to explain what Columbus expected to find on the basis of identifying what it would have been most useful for him to find. The citation of Toscanelli's letters remains of value as a reminder to us that those colonizers who argued most strenuously for the Americans' humanity, civilization, and virtue were not motivated solely by ethnographic generosity.

What of the putative humanity of Muslims and Jews, who had been exposed to the Christian religion for quite some time, yet who for the most part still did not convert? Were there any attempts in Catholic theory to identify those Jews and Muslims who did convert as rational, and those who stubbornly refused to convert as being ipso facto irrational? David Stannard argues that both Muslims and Jews, unlike Indians, were consistently regarded as human beings with souls.[19] Yet medieval ecclesiastic polemics were by no means free of associations of Jews with animals, an extension of the common view of the Jews as "carnal Israel." As early as the seventh century, Isidore of Seville referred to *synagoga* as a bestial gathering and to *ecclesia* as a gathering of men.[20] Later on, Jews were represented as monstrous beasts in some medieval Spanish literature.[21] Thus, for example, one of the *Cantigas de Santa María* describes "how Holy Mary caused the son of the Jew to be born with his head on backward, as Merlin had asked of Her," as a consequence of the Jewish sage's swearing "by the name of the Creator that Our Lord did not choose to become incarnate in Her, nor could it be so."[22] As in the seventeenth-century Spanish discourse on male Jewish flux discussed above, a theological sin committed by a Jew has consequences that are both genealogical and carnal.

With regard to the Jews, the logical conclusion of the claim that human reason suffices for the realization of the truth of Christianity was drawn by Peter the Venerable, who concluded "that if any man is naturally endowed with the mental faculties to recognize the truth of Christianity and the Jews have not acknowledged that truth, then the Jews must not be human."[23] The context for this rhetoric was Peter's concern over the attention being paid in his time by Christian scholars to Jewish Bible exegesis. Peter thus derives the Jews' bestiality from their overly carnal interpretation of Scripture. The link between Jewish emphasis on ritual and cultural practice had been tied to the supposed literalism of Jewish Biblical exegesis since Paul, yet the insistence that their attachment to the flesh signals their animality represented a kind of animus absent in Paul. The alternative would have been to acknowledge a plurality of interpretations, a threat that Peter the Venerable would not accept.[24] Indeed, what Peter most directly derides as "the monstrous beast" is not so much the Jew himself but rather the Talmud, the book in which these "carnal" interpretations are contained and which induces in Jews a kind of bestial stupor.[25]

In considering the question of the Jews' humanity in the centuries prior to and concomitant with the start of massive European colonialism abroad, one must recall the particular sort of inhuman devilishness in which Jews were frequently understood to indulge—a kind of rebellious and misanthropic treachery, not just generalized evil, but specific and malicious anti-Christianity.[26] We can contrast this to the double image of the Indian as noble and devilish in later phases of the colonial encounter in Latin America.[27] It may be fair to generalize and suggest that Indian devilishness has been associated more with wildness, and Jewish devilishness more with a maliciously knowing cynicism. Yet it is also well to recall that in Spain, as elsewhere in medieval and Renaissance Europe, many of the oral and written polemics against Jews were conducted by New Christians.[28] Converts away from Judaism such as Petrus Alfonsí also were some of the most creative participants in the intercultural exchanges among Jews, Muslims, and Christians.[29] That individuals born into a community derided as bestial sometimes became both paragons of humanism and leading detractors of their birth community is not the height of irony but rather a dramatic illustration of the powerful and protean nature (both creative and destructive) of discourses of genealogy and race.

Nor was the assumption of Indian wildness ubiquitous. It appears that there were moments in the Spanish encounter in Latin America where Indian resistance to conversion, like that of Jews and Muslims, was treated as an evil that knows the truth it is resisting. One such moment when clerical viciousness against Indians seems related to the perception of this particular kind of deviltry appears to be Father Diego de Landa's brutal obsession with rooting out "backsliding" among converted Indians in the Yucatan.[30]

We need not choose between a reductive list of paired contrasts (such as wild Indian/overcivilized Jew), on the one hand and a mere collection of isolated cultural references to Jews and Indians on the other. Here as elsewhere, the richest lessons for our understanding of the formation of collective identities are to be gleaned from tacking back and forth between similarities and contrasts in the rhetorical treatment of Jews and Indians. To collapse the two into a generalized figure of difference would simultaneously vitiate the historical argument and obfuscate the autonomous aspects of the respective cultural formations. Yet it is also wrong to fail to see the link in the Christian imagination that underlies, for example, the anti-Jewish blood libel arising at the same time as the wave of Jewish expulsions in the Middle Ages, or the accusations of ritual crucifixion combined with human sacrifice by Mayans.[31] Probably the view of Indians as nonhuman was more common and less of a rhetorical flourish. Their very descent from Adam and Eve was a topic of debate; if it could not be demonstrated, then their true humanity was in doubt.[32] By contrast, the unquestioned Adamic lineage of Jews, whenever they were considered in genealogical terms, would likely have worked to reinforce the charge that they had been present throughout the saving history of the Gospel, and thus their obduracy in refusing the Gospel made them if anything more culpable. By the later Middle Ages, the most common explanation for this Jewish obduracy was association with the devil.[33]

No doubt the accusation of deviltry is one aspect of pre-modern European culture that most consistently puzzles and troubles us. One of the key ways to open a discussion of baffling or repulsive behavior in a culturally or chrono-logically different situation is to ask, "What were (or are) these people afraid of?" This is how I understand Caroline Walker Bynum's narrative in *The Resurrection of the Body in Western Christianity, 200–1336*, a work that among other things cautions us not to take historical Christian rhetorics of Jewish "carnality" (and its sometime extension into inhumanity) as evidence that medieval Christians were solely concerned with their souls. Bynum articulates the obsession in early Christian doctrine with the proper understanding of the relation between the mortal body and the resurrected body, and explains that obsession as follows:

> Christianity spread among peoples for whom bodily change was theoretically inexplicable and to whom corpses were horrifying. For Romans and Jews (although in different ways), the cadaver that lay rotting in the grave was in some sense the locus of person; its putrefaction was both terrifying and polluting . . . the more Christian apologists adopted the natural philosophy available in the ancient world, the less explicable such flux seemed.
>
> Change was the ontological scandal to ancient philosophers. Their basic effort was to fix identity in a world where (as Tertullian understood Aristotle to say) change meant ceasing to be one thing and becoming another.[34]

These pressures—obsession with identity, desire for stasis, fear of change—help us to understand the desire for a stable category of human to which Christians could safely cling. The pressures were and continue to be manifested not only in a pervading Occidental perplexity in the face of mortality, but also in a continuing ambivalence toward what in recent centuries has come to be called historical progress. Moving forward into the new risks change and corruption. New ideological threats appear when, for example, a new hemisphere is encountered. New mortal terrors appear, summoning the defensive impulse to separate out these different, unexpectedly encountered humans as animals, wholly different from the human and Christian self.

Yet there were powerful reasons for keeping in check the view of the Indians as animals. During the early decades of their encounter with the New World, the Spaniards experienced a persistent tension between the temptation to write off the Indians as brutes and the need to assert their capacity for conversion, an assertion that underlay the insistence of Paul III in his 1537 bull *Sublimis Deus* that "the Indians are true men."[35] Columbus, however, did not put too fine a point on the matter, consistently referring to the Indians as "pieces."[36] Furthermore, according to the testimony of Las Casas, Columbus at one point believed that although all the people he had actually seen on his first voyage had been "very handsome," not far away there were "men with but a single eye and others with dogs' heads who ate men"[37]—perhaps those Plinian races he had heard about as a schoolboy.

Las Casas himself consistently argued for the Indians' humanity. Nor was he alone in this. It has even been asserted recently that works such as those of Las Casas, Cabeza de Vaca's *Castaways* narrative, and Alonso de Ercilla's *La Araucana* (a narrative of Chilean native resistance that is unusually sympathetic to the natives) are part of a Spanish literary countertradition that provides intimate and detailed description of American peoples' lives and questions the legitimacy of Spanish imperialism.[38] And yet even the motive (let alone the questionable efficacy) of someone like Las Casas in advocating bringing the Indians conceptually and practically within the fold of the human is very much a question of scholarly debate. A partisan such as Gustavo Gutiérrez argues that, like Noah, Las Casas was a righteous man in an evil generation.[39] A sympathetic Foucauldian critic claims that the discursive framework within which the missionary ethnographers Sahagún and Las Casas operated rendered their claims, so to speak, unenforceable.[40] Another scholar informed by notions of the archaeology of knowledge is even less sympathetic in the case of Sahagún, whom he sees not so much as being interested in preserving and analyzing the rich Nahua culture on its own terms as aiming to make that very cultural richness manageable within "a known, previously cohesive Christian cosmology."[41]

Still another revisionist, Patricia Seed, claims that pragmatic issues of self-interest underlay the dramatically humanist rhetoric of Dominicans arguing for the humanity and rights of the Indians.[42] Seed analyzes conflicts among the mendicant orders—specifically between Dominicans and Franciscans—as a reflection of their competition for rights in the New World. She also stresses the stakes for the Spanish crown of a self-accounting that gave high marks to its own efforts to convert the Indians and that hence inclined it to respond sympathetically to the claims made for their humanity: if they were not human, they could not be converted, and if there was no one in New Spain to whom the Gospel needed to be preached, then the crown had no sacred sanction for its dominion there.

One way to frame the play of fixity and fluidity in the debate over the humanity of the original New World inhabitants is to see it as part of a Christian dilemma: how to determine the boundaries of an identity designed to stretch to encompass the world, yet that required vigorous policing in the meantime. Thus, in discussing the proposal to allow natives to become priests, a proposal that failed in the end, Osvaldo Pardo notes: "[Father] Motolinía's enthusiasm for promoting the Nahuas to the priesthood appeared justified by his particular vision of the early church, in which the priesthood was open to recent converts. [Father] Mendieta's position, however, directly attacks the appropriateness of such a model, given the unique situation in Mexico, where the danger of the Indians' regressing to their old customs had not yet been eliminated."[43] Whatever particulars of training, temperament, and situation may have guided Motolinía and Mendieta to these respective positions, they represent starkly the twin horns of the Christian dilemma: how to go all the way into the world, and indeed bring that world into the Church, without running too great a risk of losing the Church's very identity.

One strategy for reducing the risk of such regression while humanizing the Indians was to take their children away at a young age, a practice that had already been sanctioned with regard to the children of Jews by the fourth Council of Toledo in 633, presided over by the same Isidore of Seville who had elsewhere remarked on the bestiality of *synagoga*.[44] At the end of the sixteenth century, in fact, the Jesuit José de Acosta cited decisions reached at the Fourth Council of Toledo regarding Jews as justification for the legitimacy and enforcement of forced conversions of Indians.[45]

To what extent were such arguments prompted or propped up by overt identifications of Indians as Jews? In the unexpected colonial encounter, what models were the Spanish supposed to use for modulating between the question of common humanity and the maintenance of difference? In one sense, discourses about the identity of Jews and Indians had been popular since the beginning of the sixteenth century. I refer, of course, to the speculations that the indigenous peoples of the Americas were in fact Jews, or at least Israelites—usually descendants of the ten lost tribes. In this regard, the identity of Jews and Indians was simultaneously established: they were the same as each other. Among the early Spanish writers propounding this theory were Diego Durán, Las Casas, and Mendieta.[46]

The connection could be used to serve various polemical purposes, not all of them mutually exclusive. It served first of all to buttress the biblical account of human monogenesis and also to guarantee the claim that the Indians were in fact human.[47] Here, as at so many other points, Catholic orthodoxy was consistent with at least a more humane theory of how the Indians should be understood and treated. At the same time, the Indians-as-Jews theory could serve to denigrate the Indians because the ten "lost" tribes, in the biblical account, were precisely those that had turned away from proper service and faith in God. This view of Indians as bad Hebrews was in turn consistent with the charge, quite familiar by that time, that contemporary Jews were likewise corrupt vis-à-vis their biblical ancestors and that the Jews' postbiblical texts, such as the Talmud, were deliberate products of bad-faith attempts to refuse the Bible's witness to the coming of Jesus. At the same time, the association might also have been worrisome in ways that encouraged its suppression. Did it occur to no one at the time as odd that while a few Spanish missionaries were doing their very best to convert vast numbers of Indians over in Mexico, grave doubts were still maintained about the efficacy of the conversion of Iberian Jews and Muslims, and hence about the Christianity of their descendants, accordingly designated "New Christians" for generations to come?[48]

New Christians could also be treated as something not quite human. John Edwards reports a story from the records of the Spanish Inquisition that is instructive in this regard.

In the Aragonese city of Teruel, around 1480, a young man named Jaime Palomos, an Old Christian, testified before the inquisitor during the trial of his patroness, a *conversa* named Brianda Bestant, the wife of the merchant Luis de Santangel. He reported what had happened one day in the kitchen of his employer. A Jewish wet nurse was nursing Adolica, the daughter of Brianda. Seeing this, the young man said to his employer:

"Why are you letting that Jewish bitch nurse your daughter?"

She argued, "She's not a bitch."

Jaime, doubtless repeating what he had heard either at home or at church, responded: "Yes she is, because the Jews killed Our Lord."[49]

Edwards plausibly emphasizes that the vignette demonstrates the "perceived connection between the blood of a person and the milk of her mother," and to be sure, it reflects common enough medieval concerns that an infant could be harmed by foreign milk as a polluting substance. But if we read the epithet "bitch" here as something more than a generalized epithet, it is also another example of the association of Jews with animals—here as often elsewhere, especially dogs[50]—because of their refusal of Christianity.[51]

THE RIGHTS OF HUMANS

Perhaps we can say more: that Jaime was expressing some resentment that he, an Old Christian, had to be subservient to a *conversa*, to someone not quite fully human herself. Only those fully human are capable of understanding, exercising, and taking responsibility for dominion and property. This is an argument of the "humanists," who claimed in effect that when encountering people who had not developed to the point where they can sustain a properly settled, political, and therefore human state, the more advanced men had not only the right but the obligation to serve *in loco parentis*. This argument in the early colonial encounter matches the one sometimes made in earlier centuries by Catholic theoreticians vis-à-vis the rights and powers of Jews. Then, however, the question had been not whether Jews could rule their communities, but rather whether it was justified to remove Jewish children from their parents. It was not so much the rights of parents per se, but the parental status itself that was under dispute. Thus the fourteenth-century legal writer Jean de Jean, following a position taken by Duns Scotus grounded in the official status of medieval European Jews as serfs of the lords, argued that Jews, as slaves, had no dominion over their children, and that their temporal lords had the right to remove such children and have them baptized.[52]

The American Indians' right to self-rule was taken to depend on their level of social development, understood as a criterion of their full humanity. In the earlier argument about Jews' rights to control their own children, the claim was made that because they were not free (they did not own themselves), they could not be fully adult or be genuine parents.[53] In the case of the Indians, this view was commonly opposed by the old-fashioned, Thomist, natural-law Dominicans such as Las Casas. Even in the case of the Jews, in fact, the argument of Jean de Jean and Duns Scotus defending the forcible baptism of Jewish children was a minority viewpoint. Aquinas, for his part, argued against the practice on several grounds, the most germane for this discussion being that "natural justice forbids removing children from their parents."[54] Such disputes reveal some of the dilemmas that followed on the polemical assertion that humanity and Christianity (actual or potential) were one.

Some of the early Spanish colonial writers seem likewise perplexed by the question of the Indians' humanity. Thus, in the writings of Bernal Diaz, "a primordial brotherhood ('sons of one father and one mother') seems to be confirmed by deep homologies of worship (oratories, priests, sermons) and at the same time blocked by demonic practices, practices that make the Indians radically alien."[55] They are children of Adam and Eve; they do some things that seem very similar to what Christians do; they do other things that are reprehensible. One factor that certainly would have tended to reinforce the impression of Indians as wild is that, largely because of the expansion of the territory claimed for Spain and the paucity of Spaniards available to exercise force within it, the Indians were in many cases capable of resisting violently or wildly.[56] As J.H. Elliott puts it, in contrast to the peoples within the administrative cores of the American empires, those at the margins were less tractable: "Widely dispersed, semi-nomadic, and unused to externally imposed discipline, they revealed an exasperating capacity to elude or resist whenever the Spaniards attempted to introduce some form of domination."[57] Hence the placement of the Indians on the scale of humanity and animality had to do not only with their capacity or willingness to undergo Christianization or even civilization, but with their tractability and their various degrees of settlement and (pre-Columbian) imperial incorporation as well.

HUMANITY AND SETTLEMENT

This last consideration suggests that at least some of the Spanish commentators made distinctions among the Indians based on whether they had reached the level of dwelling in cities. For the Salamanca school of theological-political theorists in the sixteenth century (Francisco de Vitoria and his successors), the city, as a necessary precondition to the practice of virtue, was a key to the definition of full humanity. For these theorists, nomadic peoples lacked one of the key criteria and were actually beasts.[58] Aristotle, who had defined "man" as a *zoon politikon*, was here in effect read as saying that anything outside the *polis* would not be quite human.

Occasionally we obtain glimpses of more overt analogies, drawn by the Spanish newcomers themselves, between negotiations of the religious and racial boundaries of Christianity and Jewishness (including the liminal category of converts) and negotiations of the boundaries between Catholic Spaniards and Indians (again, including converts). In a provocative study of anti-Jewish rhetoric used in sermons addressed by Spanish clerics to Indians in the New World, Judith Laikin Elkin notes the process by which the category of "New

Christians" came to include those of Indian origin along with those of Jewish origin, and asks why—as in the case of the New Tribes Mission to the Panare, to be discussed below—the substitution of "Jews" for "Indians" was so frequently used when Jews were almost entirely absent from the New World.[59] The most innovative of the several reasons she offers is that since the Indians had been removed from the bishops' power of inquisitorial oversight after 1539 and were never placed under the power of the Holy Office itself, the best object lesson that could be shown to them was autos-da-fé of Jews—"the ultimate parable"[60]—made to suffer the real Inquisition.

Because the humanity of the Indians was in doubt, dramatic expressions of sympathy for them worked especially well as an object lesson in Christianity. Bishop Juan de Zumárraga once was urged to have "less to do with the evil-smelling and poorly clad Indians." He replied, "You are the ones who give out an evil smell according to my way of thinking. . . . These poor Indians have a heavenly smell to me; they comfort me and give me health, for they exemplify for me that harshness of life and penitence which I must espouse if I am to be saved."[61] It would be quite remarkable to find similar expressions with regard to Jews.

STORIES OF BLOOD

While in some scholars' eyes, explicitly racialist notions of Jewish difference were not prevalent in pre-Columbian centuries, others claim that new and virulent forms of racism can be discerned as early as the thirteenth century.[62] This latter view does not dispute the specific relationship between scientific racism and modernity, but (consistent with the notion of a fixed/fluid relationship between Christianity and race) it contends that the category of race remains useful in the analysis of pre-modern discourse if we define it simultaneously as "a phenomenon of multiple category overlap, rather than as a distinctly reifiable or measurable 'thing'" and as something "always written on and produced through the body."[63] Forms of social kinship akin to godparenthood perfectly illustrate this kind of discourse, which is simultaneously overtly symbolic and about the relation between bodies. Thus, for example, prevailing social conditions and intimations of a growing church movement for differentiation are both signaled in the records of the Council of Tarragona, held in 1329, which noted, among the various forms of dangerous social intercourse between Christians on the one hand and Jews and Muslims on the other, relations of compaternity entered into by Christians attending the circumcisions of their Jewish and Muslim friends' sons.[64] Vigilance was applied not only to Jews and

Moors who became Christian, but to Christians who became the fictive kin of Jewish and Muslim parents and children.

The Tarragona council was also displeased with the attendance by Christians of Jewish and Muslim weddings and funerals. It is no mere coincidence that all these non-Christian ceremonies where the burghers of Tarragona were horrified to see Christians in attendance were centrally bound with the life cycle and generational reproduction. Pressures for social and biological separation increased in tandem and coalesced into the racial doctrine of purity of blood, or *limpieza de sangre*. This constellation of notions about inherited and immutable identity began to take shape in the half-century before the Expulsion and was further elaborated in the centuries after 1492.[65] It is important to stress these pressures for separation since the anti-Judaizing activities of the Inquisition in the period after 1492 and the Expulsion bear such a pathetic affect in popular historiography. When we remember that both *limpieza de sangre* and Inquisitorial investigation of *conversos* suspected of Judaizing were practices that began before Columbus's voyage, we are better able to consider that not only the general exclusion of Jews throughout Europe but these more specific Iberian phenomena preceded the efflorescence of European colonialism overseas.

It is doubtless correct to say that statutes of *limpieza de sangre* were argued for and instituted partly to ensure that the Spanish elite remained intact despite the Christianization of those former Jews who remained in the country,[66] and also at least in part to facilitate the preservation or acquisition of social and material capital. Yet anxieties about the integrity of the Christian body in the face of massive and sudden incorporation of those so recently not Christian were also prompted by perceived threats to the notion of Christendom as a vast endogamous group, "a family of brothers and sisters tied to God through overlapping bonds of marriage and paternity."[67] This concern with endogamy was common to Christians, Jews, and Muslims in Iberia, and a renewed vigilant stress on pure genealogies was shared by these Iberians in the wake of the disruptions caused by the massacres and mass conversions during and after 1391.[68] The statutes of *limpieza de sangre* targeted not only individual *conversos* but, in some cases, New Christians as a compact and highly contestatory social group opposed to the Jewish community and to Old Christians. By 1449, things had come to such a pass that the city council of Toledo passed a statute barring *conversos* from holding office or giving testimony against Old Christians. In response, Pope Nicholas issued a bull titled *Humani Generis Enemicus* (enemy of the human race), denouncing the notion that non-Christian origins could be used to bar a Christian from holding office. Yet the town remained troubled.[69] In 1467 a group of *conversos* actually "invaded the city and took possession of its bridges and gates."[70] The situation was again decried, on lines similar to those of the Pope's earlier bull, by Archbishop Alonso Carillo, who condemned the situation under which some of the guilds of Toledo excluded *conversos* while others excluded Old Christians.[71]

It would be wrong to regard exclusionary rules based on descent as a mere attempt to gain or maintain raw social power. In the case of the mendicant orders, at any rate, the rules were a response to a genuine ideological dilemma, one that resonates in striking ways with the tension in colonialist cultural strategy between the impulse to "bring the colonized up" and the need to maintain barriers and standards.[72] This may be clearly seen in the different stances toward the issue taken by the Franciscans and the brothers of the Order of Saint Jerome at the beginning of the anti–New Christian religious agitation in 1461. While the Franciscans took the initiative, the Jeronimite General, Father Alonso de Oropesa, was more hesitant, troubled by the way Old Christians were taking the offensive against New Christians accused of corrupting Catholicism.[73] Like Motolinía and Mendieta in the next century, the Franciscans and the Jeronimites played out the dilemma of Christian identity and incorporation. This time the Jeronimite stance was backed up by a bull issued by Pope Nicholas V in 1449 "condemning the authors of statutes of *limpieza de sangre* as schismatics and excommunicating them."[74] Again, the Jeronimites tended to blame contact with Jews for the ideological slips of New Christians, while the Franciscan writer Alonso de Espina in a text written in 1459 defended these statutes by cataloguing "the legendary atrocities attributed to the Jews of Spain and of Europe,"[75] thus reinforcing the notion of Jewishness as a curse that baptism could not expunge. It was also Espina who suggested that Jews were descended from the union of Adam with animals or with Lilith, thus offering a handy genealogy to support the notion that their descendants, in turn, would forever be constitutionally unable to join the universe of Christian humanity.[76]

Ultimately, however, the tolerant (and doctrinally conservative) policy of the Jeronimites was tested and broken by scandals in which numerous monks were reported to have observed the fast of Yom Kippur and the Sabbath strictures. The most egregious case of Judaizing within the order was that of the prior of the monastery at La Sisla, who "organized an audacious conspiracy which made possible the observance of the Jewish festival of Tabernacles each year."[77] Eventually the Jeronimites were the first to pass a rule barring New Christians from their order. This move was initially opposed by the king and queen, who in the meantime instituted an inquisition against the New Christians in the order as a partial alternative.[78] Yet the *limpieza de sangre* statute in the order was ratified in 1495, when it received the approval of Pope Alexander VI. Albert A. Sicroff's summation reveals the intricate links among "forced" conversion, Inquisition, and "racial" legislation:

> In an irony of fate the Inquisition, which was to have freed the *conversos* from global rules of exclusion, revealed enough damning proof of their religious infidelity to convince the Pope (himself Spanish, and hence especially sensitive to the *converso* problem) that he was serving religion by ratifying the Jeronimite statute of *limpieza de sangre*. . . . In order to avoid the dishonor cast upon the Order, Alexander VI accepted that, even while the Inquisition pursued its task, no one until the fourth generation of descendants of neophytes would be admitted among the Jeronimites.[79]

While this case is especially illuminating, rules of genealogical exclusion (notably from colleges and trade guilds) and laws against intermarriage spread during the 1480s and continued to expand during the first decades of the sixteenth century. At first glance, at least, there is a striking difference between this genealogical obsession in Spain and the colonizers' readiness to have children with natives in the colonies—children who in the sixteenth century were generally assimilable into one or the other of the parents' communities, with castelike restrictions coming into effect only in the next century.[80] On the other hand, scholars have recently become attentive to the ways in which *limpieza de sangre*, originally designating an ancestry free from the taint of Jewish and Muslim heritage as well as from any legacy of condemnation at the hands of the Inquisition, came in the Spanish New World possessions to include freedom from native or African ancestry as well.[81] The Inquisition was prominently present in New Spain, not least because many who applied for official positions there had to prove their *limpieza* vis-à-vis the categories of the Peninsula (absence of Jewish, Islamic, or heretical taint).

Nevertheless the logic and suspicions of the inquisitorial methods for proof of blood purity were eventually applied, in at least some cases, to those whose family trees included Indians, as in 1576 when one unfortunate applicant was refused a post with the Holy Office on the grounds that his wife had one Indian grandmother, and that (among other problems) it was possible that the Indians were of Hebrew origin.[82] By contrast, in one early clerical defense of the Indians' purity, the friar Gregorio García argued that even if they were descended from the Hebrews, they should not bear the taint of deicide since their ancestors might have lived prior to the life and death of Christ.[83] That such an argument was deemed viable suggests not merely the more obvious point that Christ-killing along with continued rejection of the Gospel constituted the main crimes of Jewishness, but also that the very notion of tainted blood was inseparable from the idea that all Jews who had lived since year one of *anno Domini* were "the Jews" who had been and always would be rejectors and killers of Christ. Whether or not we choose to call this discourse racist, it certainly entails the genealogical fixing of the antagonists in the fundamental Christian narrative of suffering and redemption.

Famously, then, while categories of race and ancestry in the Spanish New World had at least as much to do with formulae of mixture as with purity, the very origins of these categories were inseparable from the initial effort, on the Continent, to assure ideological reliability through tests for untainted ancestry—both because the initial categories of suspected taint remained operative in New Spain, and because the habits of categorization, investigation, and proof that began in Iberia informed the discourses of difference, transformation, and hierarchy in colonial Mexico.

Consistent with the suggestion that discourses of race, religion, and gender are frequently found combined together, the identification of the Indians with ancient Israelites was at one point used both to buttress the legitimacy of Spanish rule and to elaborate on the different levels of manly worthiness among the Indians. In 1681, Diego Andres Rocha, in his *Tratado único y singular del origen de los indios del Perú, Méjico, Santa Fé y Chile*, retrospectively argued the case for Spanish rights in the New World by claiming that the New World actually had a double population, Israelite and Spanish. Since Ferdinand had also been "king of Jerusalem" at the time of Columbus's voyage, it made the Spanish crown the proper ruler of the descendants of the Israelites. This enabled Rocha to make finer distinctions concerning the character of the Indians than did Diego Durán: he explained that the descendants "of the Hebrews [were] the timid Americans, and of the Spanish the brave ones."[84] One almost expects to hear that the timid male Americans experienced a monthly flux, as male Jews were said to have done back in Europe.[85]

Just how the discourse of racial difference inside Europe affected the attitudes and behaviors of Spaniards and other Christian Europeans toward newly-colonized peoples is still little understood. Were the affects of some Spanish toward the Indians influenced by questions about their own lineage? Numerous scholars have observed the ironic probability that some of the leading missionaries in the New World had *converso* backgrounds. Thus, for example, Tzvetan Todorov, remarking that "most likely [Diego] Durán himself came from a family of converted Jews," suggests that Durán had already attempted to reconcile Judaism and Christianity, and sees this as the reason for Durán's emphasis on similarities between Aztec and Christian (as well as Jewish) practices.[86] Todorov's line of argument is curious here, however. Let us assume that Durán did indeed come from a family of converted Jews, and that the conversions were recent enough and the family still sufficiently attached to Judaism for Durán to grow up with a strong and well-informed Jewish identity—a necessary assumption for Todorov's argument, since *converso* background without identification would provide no impulse for reconciliation. Even if Todorov's speculation that Durán had tried to "reconcile" Judaism and Christianity were granted, such musings would most likely have been kept to himself. Otherwise Durán—not just from a *converso* background, but a cleric—would have opened himself to charges of heresy, for the reconciliation of Judaism and Christianity was hardly on the agenda of the Spanish church in the sixteenth century. If indeed Durán were inclined because of his own family history to draw analogies between Aztec and Jewish cultural forms, it would seem more likely for him to abject both of them, rather than further link either to Christianity. At best Todorov's assertion remains a speculation, and in drawing too narrow and direct a link between Jewish origin and empathy for Indians, it constricts our potential view of a more complex field of associations.

Similarly, it has been suggested that Las Casas may have come from a family of converted Jews.[87] Even if this were the case, it would not necessarily help to explain his extraordinary sympathy for the Indians. It is nevertheless true that his references to Josephus and others of "the Jews' historians" at the beginning of his *History of the Indies* suggest that he did not stigmatize the Jews in a way that had become common enough for other ecclesiastics by this time.[88] Against this we can discern an opposite "de-Judaizing" move in his own life history: the point at which he turned from defending the exploitation of the Indians to arguing against their mistreatment, a conversion that he likens to Paul's epiphany on the road to Damascus.[89]

To approach the question of associations between Jews and Indians in the minds of Spanish Catholics from a psychohistorical perspective, as Todorov does in the passage cited above, is therefore extremely problematic. The very process that produced *conversos* would tend to hide any evidence supporting such arguments; precisely to the extent that Jewish associations remained important to *conversos*, they had to be hidden from public view and from the public record. On the other hand, the question itself must remain potent in the background. Here as elsewhere we must not assume that even the most passionately partisan rhetoric necessarily reveals the innermost consciousness—the "true" identity—of its author. It remains plausible that some of the most prominent Spanish chroniclers and polemicists who demurred from the most dismissive and chauvinistic depictions of the Indians were motivated at least in part by personal memories of their own non-Catholic difference.

Associations of Indians with Jews in an attempt to place them genealogically do not always appear in situations such as historical accounts, Biblical analogies, or debates about proper missionary technique—all highly rationalized contexts in which the terms of analogy bear specific argumentative burdens. The associations seem all the more effective where they appear casually, as it were, in putative reports of everyday events. Nor are these evident only for the earliest period of Spanish settlement, when the memories of living Jews would be freshest and when trials of suspect *conversos* were still being held both in Europe and in America. As late as 1739, the files of the Inquisition in Mexico include a report on demonic ceremonies among the Indians attended by "many 'Jews and heretics'" who flew the Indians "through the air to their European 'synagogues' and initiat[ed] them in their 'abominable sects,' with the result that the Indians have practiced these errors and taught them to their children so efficiently that the practice had spread to 'all the corners of New Spain.'"[90] Whoever may have actually "frequented these ceremonies," it is easy enough to see the psychic comfort that would have come from attributing Indian recalcitrance to the corrupting presence of known categories of non-Christians, rather than to the inadequacy or inappropriateness of missionary conversions.

Fernando Cervantes attributes this report to a wave of renewed anti-Semitism in European thought, beginning late in the seventeenth century.[91] Yet inasmuch as the report's source was the Carmelite confessor of a local Spanish woman in Oaxaca supposed to have participated in such ceremonies, its bare bones invite further speculation. Were the report's references to heretics and Jews actually prompted by statements made in confession, or did they draw on his own preexisting imaginary? Was the description of the ceremonies idiosyncratic, or representative of a common set of associations in rural Mexico in the eighteenth century? Was this "Spanish" woman actually from Spain? Perhaps the actual source of the report, at least some of whose details we may regard as fanciful (Jews don't, in fact, know how to fly) had to do with the Spanish woman's consorting with Indians in a way unacceptable to proper Oaxacan Spanish society. The reference here to Jews would serve mostly to reinforce the demonizing innuendos that followed upon associations with Indians.[92]

THE NON-CHRISTIAN BODY

To stress, as I have been doing throughout this book, both that the history of managing Jewish difference helped shape the New World encounter and that much can be learned about Christian identity formations from the juxtaposition of Jewish and Indian difference, is certainly not to suggest that the management of Indian difference was subsumed under the figures of Jewishness or of Islam in every major respect, or even in most. That is indeed one reason to resist a mere catalogue of the many instances in which Indians were either taken to be or confused with Jews.[93]

To be sure, salient differences between Indians and Jews with respect to their relations with Christian Europe are as instructive as the similarities. Signally, Jews and Indians were approached quite variously with respect to the questions of their humanity, race, and kinship. After conversion Jews could officially no longer be Jews (though they might remain stigmatized as such), but Indians could remain Indians (and probably at least for the first generations had no choice but to do so)—although here, too, there was a range of possible identifications.[94] Certainly some efforts were made to open the ears of the Jews, such as papal orders that they, sometimes along with Muslims, attend compulsory sermons by Dominicans and Franciscans.[95] Yet education of Indians, inadequate as it may have seemed even at the time, was more clearly central to the process of their conversion.[96] Likewise, in Iberia during the *Reconquista* (unlike, for example, in the Russian Empire during the nineteenth century), the efforts to convert Jews did not constitute a civilizing mission, as they did in the case of Indians in Latin America.

The most important point here is that, if treatment of Jews served as a significant model for colonial treatment, control, and exploitation of Indians, it was not the classical attempts to rationalize the continued existence of Jewish communities within Christendom that had this result. What these would have produced might have been something like reservations, where civilized Christians could have received object lessons in the abject state suffered by those who had not accepted the Gospel and civilization. Although, as discussed in the chapter on Christendom, such reservations were actually attempted, the attempts were aimed not at preserving Indians in their degraded state, but at habilitating them. Rather, if Jews (and Muslims) served as a model, the new combination of bureaucratic surveillance and expulsion would have been the most salient method applied to that model by the Spanish as they negotiated the distressing question of the Indians' humanity and potential for absorption into the Christian *polis* and the body of Christ.

Discourse on various groups of non-Christians, including Jews and Indians, was not shaped by their placement within some metaphysical or general category of "otherness," and thus we should not expect to find that the rhetorical stance toward Jews and Indians was a single, stable structure in which only the names changed. Rather these discourses were shaped by specific yet overlapping histories, at once overdetermined and contingent, sometimes filled with rhetorical and allegorical resonances and also recording surprise at the unexpected. The rhetorics themselves seem at times neatly aligned with material interest, and at other times to testify almost directly to humane empathy. To note once again that the imperative of Christian missionizing and Christian witness was the inclusion of all humanity within the Christian body is of course not to suggest that in any static way different non-Christian groups were objects to be fully humanized through conversion, or to be proven irrevocably less than human through failed or suspect conversion, but more modestly to insist once again on the persistent link between the fraught boundaries of both Christendom and humanity.

CHAPTER FIVE

Text and Translation

All who are wise will remain mute before them
Will be silent out of fear of their power.
For what can the persecuted say to the persecutor?
How can the subjugated turn upon the subjugator?
                    Jacob ben Reuben, *Milhamot ha-Shem*

At an auto-da-fé in New Spain on 14 June, 1699, Domingo de Soussa addressed
an audience of Old Christian Spaniards, their mestizo *offspring, and the newly*
christianized Indians. Quoting John Chrysostom, he added that, in worship-
ping the golden calf, "the Hebrew people opposed themselves to their zealous in-
quisitor, Moses."
     Judith Laikin Elkin, "Imagining Idolatry: Missionaries, Indians, and Jews"

The Gospel and the technology of writing in which it was embodied served to
exemplify, more than anything else, the shared and inseparable gifts of Christianity and civilization. Access to privileged texts—especially Gospel and,
more problematically, Jewish or Islamic scripture—was one index of shared
humanity while, as we have seen, resistance to the Gospel and its message
could sometimes be ascribed to perverse or inadequate humanity. Not only
Jewish and Islamic scripture but the texts of New World peoples were to be
studied and derided, translated and destroyed. Moreover, possession of literacy and a privileged relation to texts—their dissemination, interpretation,
legitimation, and suppression—was a mark of spatial integration within the
European Christian *polis* and its microcosms in the New World: settlements

of Europeans, natives, and their descendants modeled on the European Christian city.

Probably the single most troublesome trait of Jews and Indians, as far as passionate Christians were concerned, was their recalcitrance when told about Christ. But Jews and Indians, at least as individuals, stood in very different relations to that message. Confronted with such initial recalcitrance on the part of Indians, missionaries could sometimes ascribe it to the novelty of the information, an accident to be overcome with patience. On the other hand, Indians could be seen, like Jews,[1] as being hopelessly caught up in their linked carnality and literalism, morally debased and intellectually deluded by their ties to this world—a handicap when it came to appreciating the higher meanings of spirit and allegory. In any case, rejection of Christ was integral to the Christian conception of Jews and Jewishness captured in Christianity's own most sacred texts. And doctrinally, all humans, in their fallen state of original sin, were assumed to stand recalcitrantly aloof from the salvation of Christ.

The potent yet mercurial image of the Jewish people as actors in the Christian Passion is well captured in a passage from a missionary text—admittedly from a time and place far removed from New Spain in the sixteenth century. The text is based on the Bible and aimed at the Panare Indians of the Amazon.[2] In the redacted Passion, the Panare are blamed for Christ's death:

> The Panare killed Jesus Christ
> because they were wicked
> Let's kill Jesus Christ
> said the Panare.
> The Panare seized Jesus Christ.
> The Panare killed in this way.
> They laid a cross on the ground.
> They fastened his hands and his feet
> against the wooden beams, with nails.
> They raised him straight up, nailed.
> The man died like that, nailed.
> Thus the Panare killed Jesus Christ.[3]

David Lawton uses this text to illustrate how portable and indeed transferable the role of the Jew as paradigmatic blasphemer has become ever since the Gospels were composed and wherever they have been spread.[4] Yet however compelling Lawton's interpretation of the New Tribes missionaries' rendering of the Passion may be for the purposes of this book, it is precisely this sort of reduction that we are trying to interrogate here in the interest of a more nuanced approach to these issues. Are the Panare, in this "translation," equivalent to Jews or to sinning Everyman? Because Christ is considered to have died for the sins of all humanity, there is a sense—often emphasized in fundamentalist Protestant rhetoric, but not restricted to it—in which Christ is crucified anew in every human sin.[5] The rhetorical association of the missionaries' target people with blaspheming Jews, and the more general lesson that all men are sinners against Christ and can therefore be redeemed only in and through Christ, are both suggested in the missionary text.

Thus, although the Jew is the archetype of the blasphemer, the depiction of humanity as sinning is not always or only routed through the Jew. We who come long after might be tempted to view the reiterated invocation of the Jew as a figure of unredeemed humanity only in terms of a neurotic repetition compulsion. Yet the missionaries were bound to communicate their message by any means in their arsenal. Other creatures besides Jews could and did stand as object lessons in this effort: among missionaries to the Nahua, various friars exhibited ingenuity in conveying the torments of sinners in hell, some inflicting such torments on their own bodies, others on the bodies of small animals, while others had learned Nahua well enough to communicate suffering less graphically.[6] Missionaries sought solutions wherever they could in the symbolic arsenal available to them—including, of course, the Bible and the typological treatment of Jews within its stories.[7]

Articulating the linkages among textuality, power, and difference in the metropole and in the colonies is an immense project of historical criticism suggesting rich possibilities for scholarly collaboration. One point of departure for the colonial situation is Walter Mignolo's indispensable *The Darker Side of the Renaissance: Literacy, Territorialization, and Colonization*,[8] a tremendous effort to overcome the ethnocentrism of conventional notions of what constitutes a "text," and more broadly to link material textuality with territoriality and colonization. Yet a lingering suspicion of literal textuality in Mignolo's work apparently leads him to reiterate something like the old notion of "religions of the book." Accordingly, the question of the specificity of Christianity's relation to empire and the search for identitarian unity disappears in a proposed general "disequilibrium of power between religions possessing the book and those without it."[9] Mignolo, following Jack Goody, further asserts that religions of the book tend to be religions of conversion rather than religions of birth. Here, however, the analysis slips beyond an edifying materialization of books and book culture into a reification of the book, beyond a more dynamic history of media into a talismanic displacement of agency that closes the question of difference in the colonizers' home territory. It is not clear that the distinction between religions of conversion and religions of birth holds water (certainly the vast majority of Christians and Muslims have had Christian and Muslim parents respectively), but if it does, we certainly would be more inclined to identity Judaism as a "religion of birth." More consequentially, perhaps, Mignolo appears to reinforce the identification of "Western" hermeneutics with a Greco-Latin or Greco-Roman legacy—to be sure, in the interests of inducing a wider, deeper, more "plurotopic" reflexivity,[10] but once again occluding the importance of any legacy of difference "inside" a West whose reality is accepted and whose basic contours remain unexamined.

HOW TO DO THINGS TO OTHERS WITH WORDS

Given the long and complex tradition of biblical hermeneutics, how are we to imagine the rhetorical and political uses to which the missionaries put this privileged text in dealing with non-Christians, whether in the Old or New World? Clearly the Bible was appealed to as an ultimate authority, but wherever authority is explicitly grounded in sanctioned interpretations of a text commonly confessed to be divinely inspired and perfect, the contest for power underlying such appeals is closely related to the social framing of texts.

The particulars of that social framing involved the interplay of orality and literacy, communication and interpretation, prescribed formulae and performative utterances. Especially in a discursive field where canonicity, authority, and (competing) scriptures are so closely linked, it is salutary to recall the distinction between literacy, the ability to employ reading and writing as a technology of communication, and textuality, the entire set of connotations that accompany texts in society.[11] Neither literacy nor textuality is reducible to the other, and any or several aspects of what the two concepts cover may be present in actual situations. This is dramatically evident in the performance through which Christopher Columbus laid claim, on October 12, 1492, to the first solid ground he had stood on since leaving Spain. In addition to bringing the royal banner and flags ashore, Patricia Seed explains, the voyager had to manifest his intent to remain,

> which Columbus did, in his son's report, by "appropriate ceremony and words." Columbus's solemn declaration and due recording of the intent to claim the land were far from improvised. By the terms of his agreement with Ferdinand and Isabella, Columbus was required to make a grave declaration of the intent to remain and to record those words for

posterity by writing them down . . . . No specific device or words need be employed; what mattered was the solemnity of the utterance.[12]

Literacy—the skill of reading aloud marks on paper—and textuality—the authority conferred by the public recitation of the sounds represented by those marks—both appear here, and though one cannot be collapsed into the other, each is indispensable to the other. The case illustrates once again that the movement between the authority of the written and the oral is reciprocal. The exact wording of Columbus's statement does not derive from an existing text, and indeed, its authority depends on its oral enunciation. At the same time, it would have been ineffectual—the claim to possession would not have been a good one—unless it was recorded afterward.[13]

Later in the course of Spanish exploration and conquest in the Americas, the process of taking possession became more formulaic and came to include the famous *Requerimiento*, instituted as part of the Burgos laws in 1512. According to the reforms intended when the *Requerimiento* was adopted, it had to be oralized—read out loud—at initial encounters with natives. The *Requerimiento* served to mitigate the possible claim that resistance by the natives preceding colonial violence had been due to their ignorance of the law—the law in this case being that of the pope, who had chosen to donate the lands in question to the king and queen of Spain. Here again, textual authority is called on, as it is explained to the native audience that everything being said to them is " 'contained in certain [Latin] writings that . . . you may see if you wish.' "[14] In accordance with this law and this authority, the natives are "required" to accept the sovereignty of the Spanish monarchs and to permit the Gospel to be taught. The document warns of dire consequences—war, slavery, dispossession, harm, and evil—to its hearers who do not comply. Finally, the same stipulation is made as with Columbus's original solemnly made and duly recorded statement: the procedure is to be witnessed by a notary who is to deliver a notarized copy of the document for the records.[15]

Where did this relation between what Seed calls "taking possession and reading texts" come from? What, in particular, might be the link between the authority of Christianity grounded in the Christian Bible and the textual grounding of legalized conquest? Scripture provided a general model for the written text as a privileged site of access to truth and authority, but as shown in the case of Jews and Muslims with their own flawed scriptures—taken by Christian apologists as obsolete and corrupt respectively—written texts could serve the work of the Devil as well. Indeed, these flawed scriptures and the misguided, literalist hermeneutics supposedly applied to them were closely imbricated with doubts concerning the full humanity of even these literate non-Christians.[16] At the same time, the close connection between religious clericalism and literacy provided a further context helping to make plausible the moral validity and efficacy of the Spanish-language *Requerimiento*, or of Columbus's otherwise unspecified written testimonials,[17] as an ameliorative prerequisite to Spanish conquest.

One of the most compelling ways to bring the Gospel to those who had not heard it preached before, and to deploy its narratives to convey its message, was to recast those narratives so that the targets of missionary activity would see themselves as actors in the Gospel narrative and draw the appropriate lessons. Indeed, the anecdote about the mission to the Panare, albeit pertaining to much later Protestant missionaries, reflects a tendency common in the rhetorical record of Spanish conquest to draw both historical and allegorical connections between Jews and Indians. These assertions are fascinating, but as we already have suggested, they are by no means univalent—that is, they do not always simply situate the Indians rhetorically in the place of the Gospel's Jews.

On the contrary, in one valence Jews and Indians are placed not alongside each other as victims of dominant Christianity, but in an implicitly antagonistic relationship. In this view the Jews of the Bible are seen as the model for Christian ventures of discovery and conquest. At least one precedent for such modeling was available in Guibert of Nogent's *Deeds of God through the Franks*, which reports that Pope Urban's preaching of what became the First Crusade invoked the example of the Maccabees to inspire his audience of Christian soldiers.[18]

Martin Fernández de Enciso, who argued early and vigorously for Spanish rights of conquest in the Americas, drew just such an explicit analogy between the Spanish and the conquering Israelites on one hand, and the Indians and the inhabitants of Jericho on the other.[19] The analogy was far from isolated in European colonizing history, and some scholars have even taken it as the norm.[20] According to it,

God had given the Indies to Spain just as he had granted the Promised Land to the Jews. These had been awarded in order that idolatry might be suppressed in Palestine and in the Indies, respectively. Both the Jews and the Spaniards had the right to use military force to destroy idolatry. . . . [T]his memorial . . . was the ideological foundation of the *Requerimiento*. . . . Las Casas did not challenge Enciso's exegesis. Rather he suggested that the Christians had no need to follow the harsh law of Moses since Christ had taught them otherwise.[21]

Las Casas was hardly alone in taking the ancient Israelites as a model, much as he was hardly alone in separating a supposedly more humane Christian conquest from the obsolete harshness of that ancient model. In even more complex and profound ways, the Christian rhetoric of superseding "Old Testament" chauvinism while retaining the notion of a providential relation to a universal God served the missionaries well as they propagated a Gospel of peace in a context of vastly unequal power.

THE HERMENEUTICS OF CONQUEST

What *kinds* of interpretation are these—Guibert's, de Enciso's, and Las Casas'? What training, what hermeneutic tradition, allows the drawing of such analogies between ancient narratives and new situations? Specifically, is it the same kind of interpretation that linked type narratives in the Hebrew Bible to their realization in the Gospel? More troubling perhaps, what are the implications for the moral analogy underlying the scheme of this book—the shared pathos of Jews and Indians as problematic, sometimes resistant constitutive outsides for dominant Christianity—of the evidence that a plausible analogy could instead be made in certain situations between Spaniards and Israelites?

One way or another, comparisons between the Spanish, the Indians, and the Jews required strategic management of the interpretation of each of these groups' status vis-à-vis sacred textual authority. To begin with, the valence of analogies between the Spanish, the Indians, and the ancient Israelites had a great deal to do with how the older story was "edited"—which parts of the biblical narrative were emphasized and which were excised.[22] For Enciso, the justification of conquest was paramount. Other Spanish writers, especially later ones, selected different elements. Thus, Father Gerónimo de Mendieta drew a four-part analogy between ancient Jewish history and the first century of Spanish presence in the Americas. For the missionary Mendieta, the territory of America was not analogous to Palestine, and the Spanish as a collective were not the conquering Israelites. Rather, the Indians were the Israelites, Cortés their Moses, and the church their Promised Land: Before the arrival of Cortés in 1524 the Indians had been in bondage to idolatry, and Cortés led them to the church. The next four decades were "the Golden Age of the Indian Church," analogous to the period of Jewish independence in the Holy Land. Then, from

1564 until Mendieta's writing in 1596, a combination of Spanish government hostility toward the Franciscans, forced Hispanization, epidemics, and an exploitative and repressive labor system produced "the Babylonian captivity of the Indian Church."[23] In short, not all rhetorical references to Israelite history were triumphal.

To get at the hermeneutic traditions underlying these various analogies legitimating conquest, it will be worthwhile to return to the writings of Las Casas, and especially his treatment of the relation between Indian religions and true monotheism. Las Casas's creative response to this key question was fueled by a tension between two textual heritages: that of the classical philosophers and historians on one hand and that of the Bible and Christian writers on the other.[24] The Greek and Roman sources generally articulated a notion of the development of culture in which understandings of divinity were dim and crude at first and became more refined over time. This supported an argument for tolerant and gentle missionizing attitudes toward the Americans and for strategies that would build on their current practices and seek to purify rather than eradicate them. By contrast, the Biblical account was understood as presenting a sudden and adequate revelation, followed by repeated moments of human shortcoming in the face of that revelation's demands.[25]

Drawing on classical sources, Las Casas argued that the involvement of natural phenomena in American worship was evidence of the Americans' perception of divinity. At the same time, he wished to claim that there were many parts of the new lands where the inhabitants had once known about the true God.[26] Las Casas understood the falling away from this original knowledge in biblical terms, as having resulted from the dispersal of nations after the destruction of the Tower of Babel: "Human beings in the course of traveling from their origins in time and space set in motion a twofold theological error" consisting of a plurality of divinities and a confusion of natural features and powerful persons with divinity.[27] Approaching the question from a classically grounded perspective, Las Casas was thus able to describe the human sacrifice of the Incas as following a certain rationality: Insofar as sacrifice to the gods indicated a clear understanding of their position and power, the sacrifice of the people's own children evidenced the highest form of that recognition. Yet Las Casas also saw a moment of regress in the trajectory of the Americans' consciousness of divinity, and here he saw a characteristic of humanity's sinful state: mental illusion, the product of the workings of the devil. For Las Casas, who was in any case quite certain of the humanity of the Indians and thus of their common Adamic descent with the rest of humanity, the question of whether the Indians were directly descended from ancient Israelites was less important than how their own relation to both revelation and the progressive understanding of the single creator could be correlated with that of European Christians.

Other approaches to the interpretation of the relation between Jews and Indians tended, however, to stress not the rationality contributed to the hermeneutic repertoire by the classical tradition but the limits of interpretation itself as seen from within Christian doctrine and biblical authority—limits that revealed meaning "through a glass darkly" and that legitimated seemingly contradictory claims. In this vein, the Dominican Father Diego Durán's *History of the Indies of New Spain*, originally completed in 1581, is one of the most dramatic examples of the association between biblical Jews and Indians, to whom are ascribed Hebrew/Jewish origins.[28] Yet to a modern reader, his claim for this origin is extremely ambivalent, moving in about sixty words from an insistence that it is altogether "doubtful and obscure" to a nearly "positive affirmation" "that they are Jews and Hebrews," citing in between the evidence of their "strange ways, conduct, and lowly actions." Durán goes on to list a number of supposed analogies in the Indians' practice and in their own legend of their origins, all of which appear to him as proofs of their Jewish ancestry, before retreating at the end of the first chapter to an assertion that "the only knowledge which I have of the origins of these people . . . tells of the Seven Caves where their ancestors dwelt for such a long time"—in other words, it comes from the Indians' own account—and proceeding in the following chapter, as he says, "to give the true account of these nations and their migration from the place of the caverns."[29] As it reads now, there seems to be a jarring mixture of concern for empirical validation or doctrinal caution (though the Indians' account of the "Seven Caves" is the "true" one) on the one hand, and a rhetorical insistence on a Biblical genealogy on the other.

The apparent discordance might be resolved somewhat by referring not forward to our notions of empirical versus legendary histories, but backward to the interpretative method of Augustine, who wrote in *The City of God*:

> We investigate these hidden meanings of divine Scripture as best we can, some finding symbols with more, others with less success. However, what is certain to all men of faith is, first, that these things were not done and recorded without some prefiguring of what was to come, and, second, that they are to be referred only to Christ and His Church, which is the City of God, concerning which, from the beginning of the human race, there has been no lack of prophecy which we now see completely fulfilled.[30]

Hence Durán's rapid shift from cautious uncertainty to a hortatory confidence concerning the biblical genealogy of the Indians, eventually leading to a retelling of their "true" story about the Seven Caves, does not reflect a category confusion. On the contrary, the aspect of the account that is a "foreshadowing of future events"—doubtless the "return" of these lost tribes through their conversion to the Gospel—may well have been of more moment and solidity for Durán and for his early readers than the mundane "truth."[31] It was a turn from classical models of interpretation to the typological hermeneutics of Augustine and the Middle Ages.

Deploying the interpretive resources of the tradition of typological hermeneutics also could underwrite an attempt to liquidate the stubborn difference of the non-Christian through claims made on the basis of the non-Christian's own texts. Typology could be used to put Jews in their place. It might be thought that when confronted with Christian missionaries armed with Bibles, medieval Jews had a distinct hermeneutic advantage over sixteenth-century Indians, since they knew the Bible (and the Talmud, whenever that text was dragged in) at least as well as their antagonists did. Yet it is also true that the narremes of the Jewish texts had been used against the Jews at least since Augustine, who interpreted Esau and Ishmael as the synagogue, Isaac and Jacob as the church, the exile of Hagar and Ishmael as prefiguration of the Jews' disgrace after the advent of Christ, and the forty years in the desert as yet another foretaste of the Jews' sad exile.[32]

Much as the Hebrew Bible itself records the descendants of Esau, the rejected son, this derogatory Christian allegory preserved and defined a place for the Jews. The tenuousness of that place and its intimate link to questions of interpretation and textual authority are dramatized not only by the periodic compulsory attendance of Jews at Christian sermons,[33] but also by a series of famous disputations throughout the later Middle Ages in which Jewish scholars were called to debate the meaning of both Biblical and Rabbinic texts with Christian clerics and in which Christian victory was a foregone conclusion, since the Christian participants set the terms of the debate, as well as its public stage.[34] Here also, even though the Jews, unlike the Indians, were granted the hypothetical possibility of some form of textual truth, the lines of power were quite starkly drawn in this unequal dialogue. Robert Chazan summarizes the ground rules for a famous disputation in Barcelona in 1263. The encounter

> was to serve as a test for the new missionizing argumentation developed by Friar Paul, which utilized rabbinic texts as the basis for proving to the Jews that their own talmudic tradition in effect recognized fundamental

truths of Christianity. Confronted with such proof from their own tradition, Jews were supposed to recognize the error of their ways and to follow the path of the friar into the Christian fold. In the course of the public debate at Barcelona, Friar Paul was to advance a series of such Jewish texts in an effort to prove rabbinic recognition of Christian truth. The rabbi's role in the encounter was to be rigorously limited to disproving the friar's contentions. Disproving the friar's reading of rabbinic texts and their implications did not mean casting aspersions on the truth of Christianity. In the course of his defense, the rabbi was forbidden to say anything that might be construed as offensive to the Christian faith or to the sensitivities of his Christian auditors.[35]

This disputation was clearly pre-scripted and stacked against the rabbis and their texts, but the very fact that it was staged acknowledged the existence of a competing, non-Christian textual and hermeneutic tradition. By contrast, Indians were not granted even the possibility of an independent textual truth. Although they did have what we might gloss as books, these did not constitute alphabetic texts, which further contributed to the image of the Indians as uncivilized.[36] Rather, the Mayan codices were ultimately seen as demonic, and thus we have, for example, the case of the Yucatecan friar Diego de Landa, who collected Mayan books only to burn them after transliterating them into the Latin alphabet.[37] Both Landa and the early missionary Motolinía actually did specify as trustworthy the Mayan texts dealing with scientific issues such as the calculation of the calendar because they dealt with "the truth."[38] Indeed, the Indians had no lack of texts.[39] But with regard to virtually everything besides these scientific issues, the authority routinely granted to alphabetic texts in the European tradition was denied. Instead, the work of translation was seen primarily as part of the struggle to replace heathenism with the dominion of God.[40] It is no surprise, then, that the tentative efforts at integrating Indians into the holy orders foundered "on problems of reading and interpretation," and that provincial councils in New Spain in 1555 and 1565 "decided that Indians should be excluded from the sacred orders and recommended that they be forbidden to read printed texts or manuscripts."[41] Their conversion to European-style textuality was effectively blocked.

Scholarship on the literary efforts of the missionary friars nevertheless affords an increasingly nuanced account both of the friars' motivations and understandings and of the different interests at work on the Spanish side of the effort at intercultural comprehension and documentation. Thus we know that the Franciscans desired the spread of the use of Nahua among the natives, and generally sought to learn as much as they could about native cultures.[42] The friars acted out of a mix of motives, including a Christian sense of the worth of all human souls and a generalized Renaissance curiosity, along with a clear understanding that the pagan enemy had to be known if paganism was to be replaced with Christendom.[43] Thus the missionary Bernardino de Sahagún's encyclopedic effort at summarizing Nahua culture was not aimed at depicting "a culture that was valid on its own terms" so much as at understanding native worldviews in order to inculcate Christianity more reliably. Nevertheless, when Sahagún's manuscript was seized by the crown, it was not to destroy it, but because "the government of Philip II wished to incorporate it into its new project of centralizing the production and processing of information on the New World."[44] Missionary ethnography was thus absorbed into the colonial archive.

Still, early missionary ethnographers were sometimes capable of recognizing the Americans' power to retain textual memory. Diego Durán argued, against those whom he feared might claim that his ethnography would lead to the perpetuation of precontact Indian customs, "I swear that my intention is not to instruct the Indians regarding these [pagan] things, because they are already well informed. They are so careful in hiding their papers and ancient traditions, so secretive and so deceitful that they do not need an instructor!" His reassurances were inadequate; in 1577 Philip II issued a letter prohibiting "all writings referring to 'superstition and the way of life of the Indians.'"[45] Evidently, some of the Indians' humanity inevitably seeped through in the translation and recording of their texts and their ways.

Whatever the motive and whatever the method, denying the authority of culturally central texts was the central tactic of the hermeneutics of interpretively recasting Christian Europe's constitutive outsides. By the 1500s, when these Spanish scholars were at work on the central texts of the Americas, a legacy of Talmud burning provided ample precedent for the suppression of devilish books—and, as we have seen in the Christian-Jewish disputations, the interpretive authority of the Jews was rigidly circumscribed in the unequal contest with Christian audiences. Hermeneutic struggles at the heart of the earlier Christian-Jewish disputations likewise were based on more than a naively slavish belief in divine revelation of texts.[46] They arose amid a new order of doubt and debate about the status of scripture, and they signaled a deterioration of the modus vivendi through which Jews had been able to survive and flourish among Christian majorities in earlier centuries.

Tensions over literacy and legitimacy did not arise solely out of competition between Jews and monks in the eleventh century concerning the social roles associated with literacy. On a more subtle level, the very elaboration and spread of the habit of making records and regarding them as authoritative stimulated reflection on the process of writing and the authority of texts—a reflection that in turn created room for new questions about Christian faith.[47] By opening questions about the interpretation of texts and their authoritative nature, the conjunction of literacy and record-keeping complicated Christian doctrine, as when the eleventh-century grammarian Berengar of Tours questioned the Eucharistic doctrine of transubstantiation on the grounds that transformation of bread into Christ's body would make nonsense of the statement *hoc est corpus meum*—this is my body.[48] With competition for literacy and the social roles associated with it, along with the kinds of questions literacy brought in its train, it is no wonder that the genre of Jewish-Christian disputation (whether actually enacted or merely scripted) flowered in the twelfth century, or for that matter that polemical responses from the Jewish end multiplied in the following century.[49]

A period of increasing literacy, beginning in the eleventh and twelfth centuries, was also therefore a time of increasing ideological risk—especially in the parts of Iberia already under Catholic rule, where the presence of such large and powerful numbers of non-Christians stimulated the highly structured and energetic effort to purify Spain as a Catholic realm.[50] Because the imagination was believed to produce both divinely and demonically stimulated visions, it was often difficult to determine which of these two was at work in a given case of potential wonder or corruption. Spanish priests therefore emphasized the institutional authority vested in the church to administer efficacious sacraments invoking the goodwill of God. At the same time, several of them devoted energy toward identifying and denouncing doctrines falsely cloaked in the authority of revelation.

Jewish texts obviously had this potential, since at least some were acknowledged as having been divinely revealed. That is why Fray Lope de Barrientos "contradicted the claim that the [Jewish] Book of Raziel had been given to a son of Adam by the angel who stood at the gate to the earthly paradise":[51] his active denial banished Raziel from good Christian consciousness and reinforced the notion of the Jews as perfidious and deceitful. Nor was this only part of the effort to erase autonomous Jewish culture or community, since books like those attacked by Barrientos circulated among non-Jewish readers as well. Even the fragmentary and covert persistence of Jewish beliefs and rituals as an alternative bearing a plausible validity or authority served to sustain doubts about Catholic theology.[52]

One possible response to this doubt about the authority of Christian textual interpretation and to the threat of rival Jewish interpretations was, as I have discussed in chapter 4, to revive the charge of Jewish literalism. The convert from Judaism, Petrus Alfonsí (1062–1110), contributed in no small measure to this effort, though his attacks on the *aggadah* (the narrative or more literary portions of rabbinic literature) as literalist absurdities required that he suppress what he must have learned in his own Jewish education—that the rabbinic tradition did not require these texts to be interpreted literally.[53] Nor was the charge of "Jewish" reading restricted to Jews. Thus, for example, the sixteenth-century poet and theologian Fray Luís de Leon was accused of reading the Song of Songs literally, like a Jew, failing to lift the text above the eroticism of its plain reading.[54]

TEXTUALITY, SOVEREIGNTY, AND AUTHORITY

Ultimately, however, even if Christian hermeneuts believed the allegorical or typological meanings of authoritative texts to be superior to their literal meanings, the contest for the meanings of texts is inseparable from their very stuff, their physical character. Here again, the distinction between literacy and textuality—between the technologies of communication and the connotations of those technologies—is helpful. The contest depended not only on knowing how to read, or on questioning the interpretation of texts and their authoritative status, but on questions about the nature of sovereign authority and how to represent and convey it.

Material and semiotic aspects of some texts produced by the new clerical class affected issues as central as the nexus between Christianity and land. This revealed deeper sources of instability in the situation of medieval Jewish communities and in the imposition of European authority on lands and peoples of the New World. This is because land transfers were a central context in which the elite Christian laity interacted with literacy.[55] Prominent among these transfers were deeds of land from noblemen to monasteries, which served as penitence for the bloodshed in internecine power struggles that were increasingly delegitimated and discouraged by the Cluniac clergy. Through the sacrifice of seigneurial lands, the land itself acquired a sacred and potentially saving character, and was dedicated to the kind of monastic practice that was the ideal penance for the Christian warrior.[56] A description of the charter deeds by Brigitte Miriam Bedos-Rezak bears extensive quotation.

The charters to lands to be disposed of by nobles are produced and kept by the abbeys to which the land was donated through these written transactions. According to the terms of a text written in Latin, the donor gives land to an abbey and to its patron saint for the salvation of his soul and those of his ancestors. These charters are complex objects. They have a visual nature, but owing to the scarcity of literacy, their text contains less words than image, and their legibility, which is not linked to a given semantic content, depends on the multiple semiotic values attached to the letter as sign, entirely free of linguistic function.[57]

It is immediately obvious that this description of the charters as material objects, whose significance is prior to their "linguistic function," is strikingly reminiscent of the way "primitive" peoples are conventionally said to respond when first shown books and having those books read to them. Yet rather than describing a category mistake, Bedos-Rezak here is simply describing the actual working of these charters in medieval society—a lesson that might, in turn, lead us to view supposedly primitive peoples as understanding something about textuality that modern European understanding tends to forget.

Because the charters were produced by the monks who were also the beneficiaries of the deeds of land, rather than by the noble donors, a basic ambiguity concerning the origin of sovereignty and authority over the land itself lies at their heart. Who is actually giving the land to whom, and by what authority? The solution that they embody is to defer the question to an *ultimate* authority. The noble donor is not the writer; the clerical scribe is not the donor; rather, the authorship of the text is separated from both the scribe and the donor and implicitly removed to God, making the charter, and legal documents like it, akin to Holy Scripture.[58]

The nexus linking property, penitence, and propriety elaborated through these land grants and the charters that confirmed them offers yet another nuance to the social construction of the idea of Christendom as simultaneously a geographical, social, and ideological unity. Land was not only a measure of the extent of Christendom, but also a convertible currency for the salvation of the Christian soul. Yet the nobility who did possess land were doubly dependent on the literate monks who were the beneficiaries of their largesse. Authority and sovereignty over the land thus were simultaneously established and complicated by an appeal to scripture—the interpretation of which, as we have already explored, was itself becoming an issue. In displacing the question onto the authority of Christian textuality, the monks exacerbated the instability in its reception.[59]

This rich account affords revealing comparisons with the function of colonial rhetorics and documents that were cloaked with deictic authority ("it is so because of *this*"), such as the statement in the early Spanish colonizers'

Requerimiento that its hearers could, if they wanted, check the Latin texts in which its authority was grounded.[60] But the most enduring such authoritative textual artifact was doubtless the Bible itself, as presented in Sahagún's later account of the Spanish-Aztec dialogues of 1524. There, the Bible's authority is evoked in a tradition dating back to the early days of the adoption of Christianity as the official religion of the Roman Empire.[61] Sahagún depicts the missionaries indicating the Book as the source in which their authority is bound to that of the pope and of the only Author:

> And he [the pope] gave us,
> we bore it hither, his sovereignty,
> as well as the divine book.
> There it lies, there it keeps itself,
> His venerable breath, His venerable word,
> of the One Sole True God,
> the Possessor of Heaven, the Possessor of Earth,
> He by Whom All Live.[62]

Far from being spiritualized, the materiality of the Bible is unambiguously stressed in this account:

> Because we guard it,
> the divine book, the divine word,
> there where it lies visible, it lies painted,
> it lies arranged
> all that which is His precious word.[63]

Now, the missionaries' rhetoric can be seen not merely as an inventive ad hoc response to the problem of communicating the Word to an utterly alien culture, but as being grounded in a tradition where the materiality of texts was an inseparable aspect of their power. How indeed were the Indians supposed to know that this book was anything other than extremely great magic?

THE TEXTS OF CHRISTIAN SPACE

The texts that continued to be written by clerics for aristocrats relied on the medieval tendency to hypostatize scripture as sign and entailed some of the same doubts, being posited as authoritative for a broad range of persons only a few of whom had any capability of interpreting them. This heritage helps us in turn to understand the later Spanish obsession with textual power—historiographic, legal, and theological—an obsession that was in large part the medium for Spanish Catholic encounters with and regulation of both Jews and Indians.

Control of text and control of property have thus been closely linked in Western Europe for nearly a millennium. That link is neatly summed up in the unity of literacy, urban planning, and power in the early Spanish colonies, summed up by Angel Rama's phrase *la ciudad letrada*.[64] Rama's notion, corresponding in part to the English "Republic of Letters," brings together the complex ways in which our expanded notion of textuality simultaneously emphasizes the materiality of texts and their relation to symbolic power. The *ciudad letrada* is linked to Brian Stock's idea of textual communities, yet it bears a much more specific hierarchical charge. Its establishment was closely tied to the development of print technologies, but as Rolena Adorno stresses, its existence did not automatically produce either a democratization or a totalization of discourse, since the control of printing was itself the subject of energetic struggle.[65]

As with other technological developments, print heightened and changed the stakes of communicative power, serving particularly the process by which national and territorial identities came to be elaborated and, at least to an extent, fixed.[66] However, these developments must not be seen as the material component of an inevitable civilizing process. This caution is particularly pertinent in a discussion of the *ciudad letrada*, for that phrase weds two of the most potent aspects inherent in the idea of civilization: literacy and fixed settlement. Indeed, in the humanist *ciudad letrada*, the notions of literacy, civilization, the city (*civitas*), the political (*polis*), and the human all came together. Vasco de Quiroga, active in Michoacan, Mexico, in the 1530s, argued that the Indians did not possess dominion in their lands since they were not politically organized: In the eyes of the colonizers, as Anthony Pagden puts it, "no Indian society had, prior to the arrival of the Spaniards, been adequately constituted as a full civil community, a 'civitas.'"[67] Ultimately, the men of the *ciudad letrada* took upon themselves the linked tasks of determining the criteria for civilized humanity, determining how and under what conditions natural peoples could be tutored until they met those criteria, and determining the best way to manage those who remained outside.

The increasing social power of various sorts of texts and the struggles over the authority to use them are thus inextricably tied to the broader questions of spatial control, the permeability and rigidity of cultural boundaries, and the various possibilities of cultural mixing versus exclusivity that are the broadest concern of this book. The notion of the *ciudad letrada* evokes a nexus of themes including the power of literacy in Spanish colonial America, the legacy of the twelfth-century western European struggle to displace the substantial Jewish hold on the commercial and administrative functions of literacy even as the Jewish displacement from Christian towns was traced in pious Christian texts,[68] and Christendom as a space inhabited not simply by Christians but by settled civilized folk, and outside of which was a place where no real men were to be found—a place outside the text, always to be diminished.

The Christian Dimension

Great is the charity of the Church, who does not grudge her delight even to her rival, the Synagogue. What could be kinder than to be willing to share with her enemy him whom her soul loves? But it is not surprising, because "salvation is from the Jews." The Saviour returned to the place from which he had come, so that the remnant of Israel might be saved. . . . Let the Church hold fast the salvation which the Jews lost; she holds it until the fullness of the Gentiles comes, and so all Israel may be saved.

Bernard of Clairvaux, Sermon on the Song of Songs 79:5

The designations Christendom and, by extension, Europe are neither solely spatial nor solely spiritual, complex as they already are in their synthesis of what Peter the Venerable called "dilatation (a struggle against enemies without)" with "purgation (a cleansing through struggle within)."[1] Both identities entail a tangled notion of temporal closure. The law embraced by Christians was, unlike the old "Jewish" law, to be valid for all time: something had been once and for all putatively achieved.[2]

Or not. The end of Christian history clearly had not yet arrived. By the sixteenth century, Jerusalem had been lost to the Muslims once again. At the same time many churchmen believed, with Bernardino de Sahagún, that Christian triumph was following its course from east to west.[3] Sahagún solved the problem of Nahua origins, which could not be permitted to remain somehow outside the realm of the Christian sacred history, by assimilating the Nahua to the ancient Greeks and Romans.[4] However, the discovery of these unconverted humans in the extreme west was easier to fit into the culmination of the salvific history of time and space than the presence of unconverted humans—Jews and Muslims—within Christian Europe itself.[5] Through the grand trajectory of the history of salvation, the incorporation of the Jews (who were still stubbornly rejecting Christ), the Muslims (who held to a corrupt scripture and to the sacred geography of the Gospel), and the Indians (for whom the Gospel was a new message) in a vision of the final battles and the Second Coming played a part in the fervor for conversion and/or riddance.[6]

However, the initial enthusiastic confidence of the New World missionaries gradually soured as their optimism gave way to skepticism and suspicion concerning the efficacy and sincerity of their mass conversions.[7] As the millennial horizon receded, its increasing distance was tied to the recalcitrance of converts, both potential and actual. Yet, inevitably frustrated as it was, this impulse toward universal redemption was central in the implicit effort to rationalize the spread of Christian European empire as good and necessary for all human beings.

The example of the lucid, energetic, brave, and long-lived Bartolomé de Las Casas is instructive in this regard, for he remains the most dramatically appealing of the early Spanish New World missionaries. The fact that different scholars in different periods have wavered between viewing Las Casas as a genuine hero and as a "good cop" in a good cop/bad cop situation has much to do with the sheer volume of his writings. But it also has to do with our own difficulty, a difficulty inherent in the project of retrospection, in simultaneously entertaining two equally vital considerations. One of these is the specificity of what actually happened—that is, the power relations and ethical considerations at work once the encounter with the inhabitants of the New World was set in motion, the range and forms of debate that might be effective in shaping state policy without risking the wrath of the Inquisition, and so forth. The other is our need to retain a critical distance from the putative inevitability—and hence the inevitable and providential justice—of the Spanish colonial venture.

Like Columbus, Las Casas had no doubts about the role of providence. As Edmundo O'Gorman writes, what mattered to Las Casas was not the completion of the map of the world, but the discovery of new souls freshly available for the Gospel.[8] For all his humane attitude and rhetoric concerning the Indians, he was and remained a missionary. Surely he saw no contradiction between the two, and if we who come later see a tension there, it is perhaps our understanding of humanism that most needs critical revision.

Indeed, for all that Las Casas and many of the other early Spanish missionaries and ethnographers defended the cultural practices of the Americans, ultimately they all aimed to bring the Americans into the universal community of the church.[9] Las Casas was utterly uncompromising in defending the humanity of the Indians, and therefore he passionately desired their genuine, humane, and uncoerced conversion.[10] The Spanish monarchy was the agent of that evangelizing effort, and the debate was over the methods to be used. Raimundo Martini in the *Pugio fidei* (nominally, at least, a dagger aimed first at Moors and only then at Jews) had also, albeit with a measure of venom lacking in Las Casas, regarded the Romans as God's agents when they forbade the Jews from carrying out ritual commandments regarding circumcision and the Sabbath.[11]

JEWS AND THE FOUNDATION OF CHRISTIAN EUROPE

At stake in the issues I have been exploring with regard to the construction of the idea of a universal community of the church have been the various roles played by those outside Christendom's spiritual and geographical boundaries. I have argued that to understand the treatment of non-Christians encountered in the New World, we must attend to the specific place of Jews and Jewishness—understood as precursors to Christianity somehow still troublingly present among Christians and in Christian realms—among the foundational differences of Christian Europe, while bearing in mind the press of Muslim power, Muslim communities, and spectral Islam as a complementary shaping difference. Centuries after polytheism was banned in Christendom, Jews and Judaism were ambivalently tolerated, and the boundaries of Christian concern for and jurisdiction over Jews remained a vexing question. Thus it is necessary to cast the question of the Christian dimension backward to the founding—and never concluded—moment of separation between Christian and Jewish identities.

Of course Christianity did not begin as an identity clearly separated from that of Jews and Judaism. On the contrary, Gentiles—actual and potential converts to Christianity—were to a profound extent the founding Other for Jewish Christians in ways that presented perplexing issues of doctrinal consistency and communal constitution for the earliest Christian apologists and organizers.[12] The doctrine of "justification by faith" was originally intended as a means to include Gentiles within the purview of the Jewish Messiah's saving grace. Yet as the reception of canonical Christian texts became gradually removed from that founding intercultural moment, "[j]ustification no longer 'justified' the status of Gentile Christians as honorary Jews, but became the timeless answer to the plights and pains of the introspective conscience of the West."[13] Jews, Muslims, and Indians were thus, albeit in different ways, shadows of the divided Christian self that I analyzed in chapter 1—a self that constantly had to be fashioned anew, not an autonomous identity. This was the founding self whose elision in later understandings of the church militant is inseparable from the often frantically anxious insistence that those who are not yet Christian must ultimately or immediately profess and truly adopt faith in Christ as Redeemer. Moreover, if it was necessary for the stability and security of Christian identity that Jews be cast as living and abjected relics,[14] it seems clear enough that this relegation, too, was never accomplished once and for all, but entailed ritualization and reiteration, vigilant and anxious, down through the generations of Christianity. As a repeated fact of Christian self-making, this abjection of the Jews was efficacious whether the "Jews" involved were (as for Peter the Venerable) rhetorically frozen in a lost Biblical past or (as for Raimundo Martini) living bodies available for live disputation, or even merely "spectral" Jews, read in the figure of the Indian.[15] Jews remained stubbornly present, in the Gospel if nowhere else, stubbornly challenging the effort to convert, that is, to free putative Christians once and for all from any trace of their Jewishness— much as Islam, banished from a Europe that seemed finally to have achieved Christian territorial integrity, nonetheless remained both a specter of heresy and a material competing claimant to empire in the name of faith.

In the intervening centuries are sometimes found expressions of an attitude conveying moral and cognitive superiority toward the Jews, as in the writing of Joachim of Fiore, *Adversus Iudeos*: "I, however, wish to oppose [the Jews'] controversy and perfidy . . . because I feel that the time for pitying them is at hand, the time of their consolation and conversion."[16] Unworthy as they might be because of their moral failings, the sacred narrative of universal redemption in Christ required a renewed effort to bring the Jews within the fold. Such patronizing rhetoric echoes Bernard of Clairvaux's reminder that salvation would culminate by returning to the Jews, just as it had originally come from them.[17]

This clearly seems different from the rhetoric of someone like the conquistador Cortés, who saw himself as a good father, and the natives as being in need of his good paternal offices.[18] However Jews were seen, they were never regarded by Christian polemicists as "innocent" or "primitive." Whether they were honored as those to whom prefigurative revelation had been entrusted or reviled as those who had refused to acknowledge the old law's transcendence and fulfillment in Christ, they could under no circumstances be characterized as living under natural law. Thus, in the thirteenth century Robert Grosseteste argued that the period of the Mosaic revelation was an intermediary stage between natural law and the fulfilled divine law, necessitated because the human heart had become so hardened that people in fact no longer followed natural law.[19] The tension in this line of thought is obvious, reflecting the constant pulls between Greco-Christian naturalism and Biblical teleology,[20] between an account of law as a falling away from inherent perfection and an account that sees the first revelation as a step toward perfection. It is unsurprising, but revealing nevertheless, that the fifteenth-century Spanish *converso* apologist Alonso de Cartagena, in his *Defensorium unitatis christianae*, relied squarely on the progressivist understanding of the relationship between the earlier and later revelations. Revelation is perfected as time moves on. True, the Old Testament was a text for those who, childlike, needed to be instructed by fear of chastisement while the more perfect new revelation bore a message of charity. Yet Alonso asserted—as if anticipating the argument that those who had never heard the Gospel deserved more charity than the perfidious Jews who had been refusing its message for well over a millennium—that the Jews were much better able to absorb the Gospel.[21] Indeed, he might have said that Jews who became Catholics were the *real "viejos Cristianos."*

Centuries after the Augustinian consensus defending the continued existence of Jews in Christendom (albeit in a degraded state) had begun to crumble among Christian writers, the *converso* Alonso presented a view that differed from Augustine's in two distinct ways that made for a combination both original and appropriate to the *converso* situation. He implicitly identified the Jews of his own time not as "bad" or "corrupted" Jews, but as people in the same spiritual situation as the first generation of Jews faced with the Gospel, enjoying as it were the first-chance opportunity to embrace it. Yet that privileged potential could be realized, he held, only if all the Jews of his own time converted to Christianity, as he had.

JEWS, CHRISTIANS, AND THE INHABITANTS OF THE NEW WORLD

We may compare this curious balance to a common missionary stance vis-à-vis natives, which consisted of privileging their existence in a state of nature while damning them if they did not rapidly embrace the Gospel. Still, even if Spanish Christians were generally disinclined to view the Indians as having once been privileged to witness Revelation, the same was not necessarily true for native apologists. Another possibility, as we have noted before, was to argue that the Gospel had in fact reached the Americas in apostolic times. Thus Guaman Poma insisted that the ancient Andeans were descended from Adam, that they once had followed the "ley de cristiano," and that it was the Inca who had forced them into idolatry.[22] Guaman Poma's rhetoric clearly indicated the acceptance of racial categories among colonized (if noble) apologists. More-over, the identification of corruption with a third party substantiated his argument for a unity of interests between the "original" Andeans and the Spanish.

On the other hand, statements by Indians that "their first age was an epoch of Christians" were not always intended to reinforce their legitimation through a connection with saving history. Rather, when Augustinian missionaries in the Andes were told this, the intent was to denigrate the Christian Spaniards, since Andean myths commonly assumed the inferiority of earlier ages. Perhaps, by suggesting that the Christian Spaniards were like their own distant ancestors, these Andeans were indulging in their own version of the dread denial of co-evalness.[23] Nevertheless, the Augustinians who recorded this account took it as proof that the Gospel had reached the Andes long before.

The notion that Indians had fallen away from an original dispensation might recall to us, for example, Pope Gregory IX's condemnation of Jews in the thirteenth century as heretical not to Christianity, but to their own sacred Bible.[24] This active effort to differentiate the Jews of Gregory's time from the biblical authority of Jewish existence was a key element in the dismantling of the Augustinian argument for the continuity of Jewish communities in the Christian era. The chronological separation of latter-day Jews from biblically sanctioned authorization of continued nonadherence to the Gospel was most fully actualized in the denial that the name "Jew" was appropriately applied to them. This denial was justified by the folk-etymological interpretation (which appears in Jewish sources as well) linking *yehuda*, "Judah," with *yode*, "knowing"—that is, one who recognizes and proclaims the divinity. What we might call this denial of Jewish identity appears, for example, in Jean de Gênes's *Catholicon* of 1520.[25] This arrogation of the right to attach or detach the name "Jew" from those who thought of themselves as Jews is also seen in the availability of "Jew" as an epithet for a Christian too attached to the letter of the law.[26]

This should suffice to caution us against assuming that the "Jews" in the minds of medieval European Christians were quite identical with Old Testament Israelites (as they were not always clearly distinct from their Muslim contemporaries), but it does not gainsay a reasonable assumption that some measure of both chronological sequence and of continuity—a narrative coherence in Jewish identity—was also granted at the same time as dramatic denials such as those of de Gênes were being propounded. What Christian writers from Augustine to Durán understood as "truth" and what they regarded as matters of faith coincided more fully concerning Jews than they did in the case of peoples whose ethnographic or historical particulars were incidental to the history of salvation.

In the history of Christian rhetoric, Jews are not always explicitly ab-jected, because Christian spirituality so prizes internality and often also lays claim to the true heritage of the Jews. To the extent that Christian theology, influenced by Platonism, denigrated the external, material, and corporal in favor of the internal, ideal, and spiritual, the associations were likely to work in reverse fashion. Thus, in the thirteenth century Pierre de Capua distin-guished the "external Jew" from the "internal Jew"—that is, the Christian.[27] I doubt that it would have occurred to Christian European writers at any point to make a distinction between "external" (superficial) Indians and "internal" ones (Christians).

Of course, the internal other was also—at least in the medium of folk-lore—the familiar other. Thus, the problematics of translation were very dif-ferent in Christian-Jewish discourse from what they were in Christian-Indian discourse. Even at first encounter, the relations between Indians and Span-ish were affected by the absence of a shared language.[28] The need to translate Christian doctrine into various Indian languages offered inexhaustible oppor-tunities for debate among clerics and for a range of judgments, from celebra-tion of supposed common beliefs to denunciations for backsliding syncretism. It also afforded the Indian recipients of the Gospel a dangerous and uncertain yet productive space in which to work out their own accommodation to the new "faith."[29]

Furthermore, while after centuries of coexistence Jews in Spain may have been differentiated primarily by religion, in such regions of early colonial en-counter as the Yucatan the attempt was made to make religion the *only* connec-tion. The friars working there were not especially eager to teach Spanish along with their preaching of the Gospel and instruction in the sacraments, since access to Spanish might undermine their own authority and grant the Indians access to other, harmful teachings as well.[30]

EUROPE UNDONE

The midpoint of the twentieth century saw a war fought on both hemi-spheres. That war produced the most shocking genocide in human history, carried out inside Europe, which had been the standard bearer of enlighten-ment and progress for centuries. Since the end of that war, our notion of the human future has shifted from the guarded hope of unification exemplified in the creation of the United Nations to a prospect of cultural and ecological dis-integration. Why was the belief in a unified global civilization, with Christian (or post-Christian) Europe as its standard-bearer, once so strong that much of the postcolonial world looked to Europe as a model for change? What is the relation between the aftermath of Europe's rage to annihilate its Jews and its changed role in the world as the third Christian millennium begins?[31] And what do these questions have to do with assumptions about diversity and likeness among the members of *Homo sapiens* who drove, justified, and acted as restraints upon Christian Europe as it strove to articulate coherence and unity in the later Middle Ages—and as its various "potentates" competed, as Chief Justice Marshall would write in the landmark United States Supreme Court case of *Johnson v. M'Intosh* (1823), to acquire the Americas (and much of the rest of the world as well) in the following centuries?

In this book, I have suggested that a renewed desire for purity within Christendom both fueled and was supplemented by a renewed desire to extend Christian dominion over the entire globe. At the same time, the renewed and in some ways original hostility toward Jews can be related to ideological cracks in the edifice of medieval Christendom itself—or, perhaps better, in a renewed concern for the structural coherence and integrity of that edifice. Moreover, scholarship is beginning to illuminate the ways in which various figures of difference at the boundaries of Christian Europe—Jew, Indian, Muslim, and more—served to reinforce rhetorics of Christian identity.

Precisely how the heritage of Christian management of Jewish difference, mixed as it is with confidence, conviction, fear, and self-doubt, is related to the fatal and creative encounter between Spaniards and Indians remains to be specified further. The question of how we are to structure our own retrospective discourse on these matters, especially given the inevitable need to consider Muslim difference as well, should occupy us for quite some time to come, if the world we have made continues to support our universities and the rest of the machinery of scholarship. As Bernardino Verástique notes in his study of Vasco de Quiroga's millennialist evangelization of Michoacán, the "dual prophecy of terror and salvation" found in the Book of the Apocalypse "continues to function to this day as a fundamental layer of modern Western civilization."[32] He likewise notes the presence of a similar vision among a Mexican people know as the Purhépecha. Though I have profited from studies such as Verástique's, which accord due attention to the specific characters of different New World peoples, "Indian" doubtless remains a term that is too homogeneous and anonymous in this book. This is only one of the lacunae here that I invite others to address.

This book has aimed, by juxtaposing Jewish difference to native American difference without occluding the shaping force of Islam, to help us see and understand dominant Western identity as a never-ending project that neither began nor ended at Europe's borders. Instead, the notion of Europe (and the notion of Christendom with which it substantially overlapped) was invented, deployed, and insistently reiterated in the effort to naturalize rhetorical links between a doctrine known as Christianity and the exercise of legitimate power. Likewise, the dominant identity was never securely established in the temporal dimension, and hence was always busy anxiously revisiting and reworking the story of its Jewish origins. Jerusalem, contested for against Muslim rulers during much of the period examined in this book, was part of that origin story as well; the struggle to regain Jerusalem along with the *terra sancta* that surrounded it provided the context for much of the legal and religious rationale later applied to conquests overseas.[33] When "new" non-Christian populations were encountered, they had to be integrated into the developing saving narrative of the world's becoming one and becoming Christian. That integration centrally involved placing these populations in the time of Christian history. Those to whom this task fell commonly (but not always, and not always in the same way) looked to the place of Jews in Christian times for inspiration— sometimes as a model, sometimes merely as an effective rhetorical contrast.

This book does not tell a story about how we started out in a different time and space to arrive at our present. How could it do that when its actual goal is to show how tightly our rhetorics of different dimensions are bound to our rhetorics of dimensions of difference? Nor, as I hope is abundantly clear, does it claim a privileged metaphysical or foundational status for Jewish difference in the history of what it still pleases us to call the West, except insofar as that history is shaped, implicitly or explicitly, by the Christian sacred narrative. Nor again do I mean to suggest a new key for a universal history of modernity, suggestive as the panoptic and expansionist canons of Lateran IV may be; the ideological and political histories that made modern racial slavery possible, for example, are hardly touched upon in this story.

I do hope this book has helped articulate how the Christian saving narrative of growth out of and away from Jewishness shapes dominant notions of progress through time and ideals of universal unity. It is not merely that Christians and Christianity spent much energy in addressing the "Jewish" past, but that defining Christianity over against Jewishness fundamentally shaped Christian rhetorics of a transcended past, an embattled and imperfect future, and a longed-for future redemption—rhetorics that were applied, modified and sometimes rejected in the encounter with colonial and other forms of difference.

The time and space considered here is in any case critical to our current situation. In it, powers concentrated in the hands of Christian Europeans and managed through rhetorics and practices of identity and difference began an evolution in scope that, centuries later, has left our species in control of the conditions for its very existence and at risk of developing itself to death. Precisely because of that concentration of power, it is all too easy to forget the internal conflicts among Christian Europeans (and of course within individual Christian Europeans)—to forget, that is, that Christian European identity had always to be reclaimed, reinvented, and protected. It is not the least claim of this book that the frequent strain of that effort to sustain a dominant Christianness is inseparable from, and perhaps lies somewhere near the heart of, any explanation for the frequently murderous exercise of Christian European authority. To speak of Christian Europe, then, is at once to reexamine our conventional historical categories and to transform into a contingent, ambiguous, and fragile human project what might otherwise have been lauded as the most advanced moment in the human story or caricatured as an old world whose shackles might now be discarded. Much of what remains exploratory or tentative here is inseparable from the fact that I am working to be *charitable toward the dominant* without excusing what are understood to be, and which I am not denying as, the destructive effects of the exercise of domination.

The project of Christian Europe continues to shape our conditions—our imagination and constraints, our crises and our dreams. Exercising those conditions in favor of continued life, a common human task if there ever was one, surely mandates in turn that we recast our understandings of identity—individual, group-wide, and species-wide. In that task the interdisciplinary conversation known as cultural studies surely has a role to play, but those involved in the conversation have not yet agreed on the task, let alone how to share it amongst themselves.

Yet perhaps I, like others, have succeeded in keeping the past open, or reopening a chink in the past. And like others, I am convinced that the story—in time and space—can continue only if we work at setting aside the hard encrustations of our differences without falling prey to the illusion that we can all become one. Such a project can and should have no real conclusion. Consider, then, this book both a tribute to those who have undertaken the project, and an invitation to carry it on.

NOTES

PREFACE AND ACKNOWLEDGMENTS

1. Gil Anidjar, *The Jew, The Arab: A History of the Enemy* (Stanford, CA: Stanford University Press), xvii.

2. Talal Asad, *Formations of the Secular: Christianity, Islam, Modernity* (Stanford: CA: Stanford University Press, 2003), 15.

INTRODUCTION

1. An obvious flaw in this strategy is its occlusion of the existence of Jewish communities *outside* Western Christendom from the later Middle Ages through the earlier centuries of colonialism. Such an occlusion should not be allowed to stand for long. Nor, of course, by focusing on the Mexican moment in the colonial encounter do I intend to suggest that it is more important than any other such moment. To point this out is to articulate just one way in which this book is intended as a provocation, and not as a definitive statement. But it would perhaps be conceding too much to subtitle the book "Some Jews, Some Indians, and the Identity of Part of Christian Europe."

2. A loose methodological guide for my project at its outset years ago was the "New Historicist" group of cultural scholars—for example, Stephen Greenblatt's *Shakespearean Negotiations: The Circulation of Social Energy in Renaissance England* (Berkeley: University of California Press, 1988) and the essays in H. Aram Veeser's edited volume *The New Historicism* (New York: Routledge, 1989). Their work relates various genres of spoken and written discourse to considerations of power, legitimation, and the formation of collective identities in earlier periods.

3. J.H. Elliott, "A Europe of Composite Monarchies," *Past and Present* 137 (1992), 48–71, at 57.

4. See Walter D. Mignolo, "The Many Faces of Cosmo-Polis: Border Thinking and Critical Cosmopolitanism," *Public Culture* 12:3 (2000), 721–48.

5. Steven F. Kruger, *The Spectral Jew: Conversion and Embodiment in Medieval Europe* (Minneapolis: University of Minnesota Press, 2006).

6. Lucy Pick, *Conflict and Coexistence: Archbishop Rodrigo and the Muslims and Jews of Medieval Spain* (Ann Arbor: University of Michigan Press, 2004), 91–92.

7. Frederick W. Turner, *Beyond Geography* (New Brunswick, NJ: Rutgers University Press, 1980).

8. Peter Hulme, "European Ethnography and the Caribbean," in *Implicit Understandings: Observing, Reporting, and Reflecting on the Encounters between Europeans and Other Peoples in the Early Modern Era*, ed. Stuart B. Schwartz (New York: Cambridge University Press, 1994), 195.

9. Vassilis Lambropoulos documents the continuing appeal of this dichotomy in *The Rise of Eurocentrism: Anatomy of Interpretation* (Princeton, NJ: Princeton University Press, 1992).

10. José Faur, *In the Shadow of History: Jews and Conversos at the Dawn of Modernity* (Albany: State University of New York Press, 1992).

11. Ibid., 5–6.

12. Ibid., 6.

13. Compare the more moderated account by Lawrence G. Duggan, who reviews the instances of compulsion and exclusivism in the relation of Yahweh with his people, notes that "[f]orce also appears in the life of Jesus," and points to the "truly decisive step [that] was taken in the fourth century, when the Emperor Constantine (306–37) was inspired to adopt Christianity." Lawrence G. Duggan, " 'For Force is not of God?' Compulsion and Conversion from Yahweh to Charlemagne," in *Varieties of Religious Conversion in the Middle Ages*, ed. James Muldoon (Gainesville: University of Florida Press, 1991), 52–53.

14. Rolena Adorno, *Guaman Poma: Writing and Resistance in Colonial Peru* (Austin: University of Texas Press, 1986).

15. Stephen Greenblatt, "Kindly Visions," *The New Yorker*, October 11, 1993, 120.

16. Elisa Marie Narin van Court, "Critical Apertures: Medieval Anti-Judaisms and Middle English Narrative." Ph.d. diss., University of California, Berkeley, 1995, 3–4.

17. See, for example Ivan G. Marcus, "A Jewish-Christian Symbiosis: The Culture of Early Ashkenaz," in *Cultures of the Jews: A New History*, ed. David Biale (New York: Schocken Books, 2002), 478–84. For example, it is a commonplace of Jewish historiography that many of the best-known anti-Jewish polemics of the Middle Ages and after were written either by converts from Judaism or by authors informed by such converts. But the traffic of "informants" traveled both ways, as in the thirteenth-century Jewish polemic *Nizzahon vetus*, which, according to David Berger, reflects contact with converts from Christianity to Judaism. David Berger, *The Jewish-Christian Debate in the High Middle Ages* (Philadelphia: Jewish Publication Society, 1979), 31–32.

18. Lesley Bird Simpson, Translator's preface to *The Spiritual Conquest of Mexico*, by Robert Ricard (Berkeley: University of California Press, 1966), vii.

19. Robert Ricard, *The Spiritual Conquest of Mexico: An Essay on the Apostolate and the Evangelizing Methods of the Mendicant Orders in New Spain: 1523–1572*, trans. Lesley B. Simpson (Berkeley: University of California Press, 1966), 34.

20. Ibid., 52, 283.

21. Louise M. Burckhardt, *The Slippery Earth: Nahua-Christian Moral Dialogue in Sixteenth-Century Mexico* (Tucson: University of Arizona Press, 1989), 17.

22. Thus Avril Keely describes how, in his *Histories*, the sixth-century Gregory of Tours "employed Arians and Jews as agents of differentiation: their function in the *Histories* is to sharpen the self-identity of the Christians of sixth-century Gaul. If the Church clearly had problems in persuading the Christian community to think of itself in exclusive terms, then, surely, Gregory would use his narrative as a vehicle for shaping the self-identity of the Christians." Avril Keely, "Arians and Jews in the *Histories* of Gregory of Tours," *Journal of Medieval History* 23, no. 2 (1997), 103–4.

23. See Daniel Boyarin, *Border Lines: The Partition of Judaeo-Christianity* (Philadelphia: University of Pennsylvania Press, 2004), and Judith M. Lieu, *Christian Identity in the Jewish and Graeco-Roman World* (New York: Oxford University Press, 2004).

24. On this particular sense of the double nature of authority in medieval Christian Europe, see Charles Taylor, "Modes of Civil Society," *Public Culture* 3 (Fall 1990).

25. Lucy Pick, *Conflict and Coexistence: Archbishop Rodrigo and the Muslims and Jews of Medieval Spain* (Ann Arbor: University of Michigan Press, 2004), 172.

26. See Robert Chazan, *Daggers of Faith: Thirteenth-Century Christian Missionizing and Jewish Response* (Berkeley: University of California Press, 1989), 13.

27. Jeremy Cohen, *Living Letters of the Law: Ideas of the Jew in Medieval Christianity* (Berkeley: University of California Press, 1999), 33. Now see Paula Fredriksen's *Augustine and the Jews: A Christian Defense of Jews and Judaism* (New York: Doubleday, 2008).

28. Cohen, *Living Letters of the Law*, 220; see also 286. Meanwhile, for Thomas Aquinas, "Jewish observance of the Mosaic commandments now amount[ed] to nothing less than a repudiation of their literal sense, which limited their appropriateness to a particular period in the past. Although Thomas's Jewish policy stood squarely within Augustinian tradition, the Jew who emerged from his biblical hermeneutic and his theology challenged the very rationale for that policy. . . . Thomas proceeded to characterize Judaism as a variety of *infidelitas*, not as sui generis." Ibid., 388. Compare, however, Anna Sapir Abulafia's view that Rupert of Deutz and Peter the Venerable were ready to define Jews out of humanity. Anna Sapir Abulafia, *Christians and Jews in the Twelfth-Century Renaissance* (London: Routledge, 1995), 132–33.

29. Jonathan Elukin, "From Jew to Christian? Conversion and Immutability in Medieval Europe," in *Varieties of Religious Conversion in the Middle Ages*, ed. James

Muldoon (Gainesville: University Press of Florida, 1997),172; Cohen, *Living Letters of the Law*, 16.

30. Miri Rubin, *Gentile Tales: The Narrative Assault on Late Medieval Jews* (New Haven: Yale University Press, 1999), 141.

31. Lester K. Little, *Benedictine Maledictions: Liturgical Cursing in Romanesque France* (Ithaca, NY: Cornell University Press, 1993), 67.

32. Claudine Fabre-Vassas, *The Singular Beast: Jews, Christians, and the Pig*, trans. Carol Volk (New York: Columbia University Press, 1997), 151.

33. Gilbert Dahan, *Les intellectuels chrétiens et les Juifs au Moyen Âge* (Paris: Le Cerf, 1990), 22–23. Robert Chazan, surveying "Western Christendom" as a whole, concurs. Chazan, *Daggers of Faith*, 4. Frank Manuel, on the other hand, describes Spain as aberrant, rather than delayed: "Events south of the Pyrenees appeared to take place in a spiritual landscape alien to other countries of Western Europe." Frank Manuel, *The Broken Staff: Judaism Through Christian Eyes* (Cambridge, MA: Harvard University Press, 1992), 23. In his summary of a period before the centuries that are Manuel's primary topic, and given his subtitle for that section ("Iberia: the Facade of Coexistence"), Manuel may be reflecting the historical *English* representation of "the Spanish horror." See Michael Ragussis, "The Birth of a Nation in Victorian Culture: The Spanish Inquisition, the Converted Daughter, and the 'Secret Race,'" *Critical Inquiry* 20, no 3 (1994).

34. John Edwards, *The Jews in Christian Europe, 1400–1700* (1988; New York: Routledge, 1991), 12. In the case of the Spanish expulsion, Edwards observes straightforwardly that the immediate cause of Ferdinand and Isabella's decree to expel the Jews has never been clarified, although he does make a strong case that the major determinant was the desire for churchmen to remove recent *conversos* from the ideological danger of continued contact with unbaptized Jews. Albert Sicroff concurs with Edwards on this, as does Henry Kamen. See Albert A. Sicroff, *Les controverses des statuts de "pureté de sang" en Espagne du 15e au 17e siècle* (Paris: Didier, 1960), 62; Henry Kamen, *Inquisition and Society in Spain in the Sixteenth and Seventeenth Centuries* (Bloomington: Indiana University Press, 1982), 14; and Henry Kamen, *The Spanish Inquisition: A Historical Revision* (New Haven: Yale University Press, 1997), 17. Jane Gerber does not point to the clergy, though she does paraphrase the expulsion order that claimed that "it was necessary . . . to remove the pernicious presence of the Jews and their living Judaism because they were having a corrupting influence on 'bad Christians.'" Jane Gerber, *The Jews of Spain: A History of the Sephardic Experience* (New York: The Free Press, 1992), 137. Meanwhile, *conversos* had already been excluded from mendicant orders. See Judith Laikin Elkin, "Imagining Idolatry: Missionaries, Indians, and Jews," in *Religion and the Authority of the Past*, ed. Tobin Siebers (Ann Arbor: University of Michigan Press, 1993), 81. So the question might be asked: "Whose ideological safety was at stake here?" The answer, explored further in my first chapter, appears to be: everyone's. At least some of the missionaries in the Spanish Americas seem to have understood this, as did the rector of Cracow Univer-

sity, who criticized forced conversion of non-Christians at the Council of Constance in 1417. Denys Hay, *Europe: The Emergence of an Idea* (Edinburgh: Edinburgh University Press, 1957), 82.

35. See the introduction to *Rereading the Black Legend: The Discourses of Religions and Racial Difference in the Renaissance Empires*, ed. Margaret R. Greer, Walter D. Mignolo, and Maureen Quilligan (Chicago: University of Chicago Press, 2007), 1-24.

36. Enrique Dussel, "Beyond Eurocentrism: The World-System and the Limits of Modernity," in *The Cultures of Globalization*, ed. Fredric Jameson and Masao Miyoshi (Durham and London: Duke University Press, 1998), 3-31, at 15. Compare the formulation of Homi Bhabha: "Thus the political and theoretical genealogy of modernity lies. . . . in this history of the colonial moment. It is to be found in the resistance of the colonized populations to the Word of God and Man—Christianity and the English language." Homi K. Bhabha, *The Location of Culture* (New York: Routledge, 1994), 32.

37. Geoffrey Galt Harpham, "So . . . What *Is* Enlightenment? An Inquisition into Modernity." *Critical Inquiry* 20:3 (1994), 524-56.

38. Irene Silverblatt, "The Black Legend and Global Conspiracies: Spain, the Inquisition, and the Emerging Modern World," in *Rereading the Black Legend: The Discourses of Religions and Racial Difference in the Renaissance Empires*, ed. Margaret R. Greer, Walter D. Mignolo, and Maureen Quilligan (Chicago: University of Chicago Press, 2007), 99-116, at 100.

39. Mignolo, "The Many Faces of Cosmo-Polis," 721.

40. Mignolo, Walter D. "Globalization, Civilizing Processes, and the Relocation of Languages and Cultures," in *The Cultures of Globalization*, 32-53, at 35.

41. See, for example, his statement that "The debates [at Valladolid] broke out several decades after the triumph of Christianity over the Moors and the Jews, which was followed by the expulsion of both groups from the Iberian Peninsula." "The Many Faces of Cosmo-Polis," 728. In itself this statement implies that Moors and Jews are comparable not only to each other but to some collective agent called Christianity, that they were adversaries of Christianity in the same way, and that the end of the last vestige of Muslim dominion in Iberia and the expulsion of the Jews from Spain were analogous triumphs. A history of the politics of difference, incontestably relevant to the colonial encounter, is obliterated here. Elsewhere, Mignolo references Hebrew as though it were the vernacular of a thriving early modern, non-Western nation or empire: "Certainly, well-established languages such as Chinese, Japanese, Arabic, and Hebrew were not suppressed by modern colonial languages, as was the case of less-established ones such as Quechua, Aymara, or Nahuatl, which suffered the impact of Latin and Spanish . . ." "Globalization, Civilizing Processes, and the Relocation of Languages and Cultures," 40. I have no idea what to make of this, except to take it as a mark of inattention. Nor, *pace* Mignolo, were *conversos* and *moriscos* "ex-Jews and ex-Moors who had converted to Christianity," but such people *and their descendants*; the difference is quite consequential. Mignolo, "Afterword: What Does the Black Legend Have to Do With Race?" in *Rereading the Black Legend*, 312-24, at 318.

42. Mignolo, "Afterword," at 318.

43. Patricia Seed has neatly articulated the various solutions different "European" colonial powers applied to the problem of formally marking and legitimating the process of conquest, as well as the contrast between, for example, the English concern with title to land and the Iberian's concern with dominion over "souls." Patricia Seed, *Ceremonies of Possession in the New World, 1492–1640* (Cambridge: Cambridge University Press, 1995), and *American Pentimento: The Invention of Indians and the Pursuit of Riches* (Minneapolis: University of Minnesota Press, 2001).

44. Though Benzion Netanyahu's massive and massively researched study *The Origins of the Inquisition* must be mentioned, it is difficult to make use of here because his careful analysis of social, economic, and political motives is predicated on the assumption of a Jew hatred that is transhistorical, universal among Christians, racialist, and national. See, for example, Benzion Netanyahu, *The Origins of the Inquisition in Fifteenth-Century Spain* (New York: Random House, 1995), 1047. By contrast, my own point of departure views the figure of Jewish difference as foundational in the discourses of Western identity, but also as highly contingent and ambivalent in its effects on relations with living Jews.

45. Charles Tilly summarizes the advantages and disadvantages to rulers of having a culturally homogeneous population in *Coercion, Capital and European States, 990–1992* (Cambridge, MA: Basil Blackwell, 1992), 106–7. Kenneth Stow, for example, acknowledges the difficulty of explaining the phenomenon of expulsions, but attempts such explanation all the same. Regarding England, Stow sees the root cause as being the progressive collapse of the system of using Jews as financial intermediaries, resolved by a deal freeing the nobility from the perceived threat of ruinous usury in return for a large one-time subsidy and increased royal judiciary control, leading in turn to the enhancement of the overall reach of the royal state. In the case of France, while once again Stow focuses on the royalty, the explanation has much more to do with royal personal initiative. In the case of Spain, Stow's explanation emphasizes the fear of ideological "contamination" of *conversos* by unconverted Jews. In the Holy Roman Empire, the situation was one of more protracted "instability and decline." In mid-sixteenth century Italy, on the other hand, the Roman ghetto was established by the pope as "an anchor of rigorous canonical regulation." Kenneth R. Stow, *Alienated Minority: The Jews of Medieval Latin Europe* (Cambridge, MA: Harvard University Press, 1992), 285–95, 297, 299, 305.

46. Rubin, *Gentile Tales*, 47.

47. Robert Bartlett, *The Making of Europe: Conquest, Colonization and Cultural Change, 950–1350* (Princeton, NJ: Princeton University Press, 1993), 2. María Menocal argues further for the difference between the fourteenth and fifteenth centuries and the earlier centuries, emphasizing the disastrous influence of the Black Death on the "intercultural" character of medieval life: "these two centuries, the fourteenth and the fifteenth, are the most 'medieval' in some of the worst senses of the stereotype. It is the time of the catastrophic effects of the Black Death, which reigned over much

of Europe during those centuries and created palpable darkness and a host of cruel repressions where there once had been tolerance. And precisely because this period constitutes *at least* as severe a break from the ethos of the previous centuries as it does from the later ones I specifically exclude it from my own axiomatic definitions of 'medieval' in this study." María Rosa Menocal, *Shards of Love: Exile and the Origins of the Lyric* (Durham, NC: Duke University Press, 1994), 40. Although the juridical forms and ideological rationale for repressions had certainly been developed before the fourteenth century, her argument is an important reminder that they did not lead inevitably or of themselves to the realization of a full-blown "persecuting society" in the fifteenth and sixteenth centuries.

48. R.I. Moore, *The Formation of a Persecuting Society: Power and Deviance in Western Europe, 950–1250* (New York: Basil Blackwell, 1987), 43. As Moore specifies his thesis, "deliberate and socially sanctioned violence began to be directed, *through established governmental, judicial and social institutions*, against groups of people defined by general characteristics such as race, religion or way of life; and that membership of such groups in itself came to be regarded as justifying these attacks." "Preface to the First Edition," in the second edition of *The Formation of a Persecuting Society* (Blackwell, 2000), 4.

49. Ibid., 135.

50. As pointed out by Jonathan Elukin, *Living Together, Living Apart: Rethinking Jewish-Christian Relations in the Middle Ages* (Princeton and Oxford: Princeton University Press, 2007), 4.

51. See Cary J. Nederman, "Introduction: Discourses and Contexts of Tolerance in Medieval Europe," in *Beyond the Persecuting Society: Religious Toleration Before the Enlightenment*, ed. John Christian Laursen and Cary J. Nederman (Philadelphia: University of Pennsylvania Press, 1998), 13–14.

52. Elukin, *Living Together, Living Apart.*

53. R.I. Moore, *The First European Revolution, c. 970–1215* (Oxford and Malden, MA: Blackwells, 2000), 155.

54 . Accordingly, this book is not intended primarily as a contribution to the debate over the "persecuting society" thesis. For Moore's own response to that debate, see the second edition of *The Formation of a Persecuting Society*, 172–96.

55. Barbara H. Rosenwein and Lester K. Little, "Social Meaning in the Monastic and Mendicant Spirituality," *Past and Present* 63 (1974), 24–25.

56. Ibid., 32.

57. Ibid.

58. An early work by Jeremy Cohen focusing on the role of the Dominicans and Franciscans emphasizes how their generally urban and middle-class orientation contributed to both their particular awareness of and their perception of threat coming from Jews. Yet Cohen places a much greater emphasis on ideological factors per se, and indeed on the shaping force of the monks' preaching, than even R.I. Moore. Thus, he prefaces his summaries of the anti-Jewish sermonizing of Berthold of Regensburg

and Giordano da Rivalto with the sentence, "Precisely how the friars may have conditioned the European mind to reject the legitimacy of Jewish life in Western Christendom becomes apparent in the extant sermons of two of the greatest mendicant preachers of the period." Jeremy Cohen, *The Friars and the Jews: The Evolution of Medieval Anti-Judaism* (Ithaca, NY: Cornell University Press, 1982), 229. Whereas Moore is at considerable pains to dismiss the notion that the reason for vigorous campaigns against heresy had to do with a sudden increase in the number of heretics (or that new restrictions were being placed on Jews because Jews were becoming newly powerful), Cohen appears to give much greater credence to the objective presence of "centrifugal forces that threatened Christian unity." Ibid., 263.

59. Bartlett, *The Making of Europe*, 232.

60. Ibid., 237. Bartlett identifies this source as *De Theutonicis bonum dictamen*, probably written by an educated Czech-speaking townsman, possibly a notary or some other official (236).

61. Heiki Valk, "Christianisation in Estonia: A Proces of Dual-Faith in Syncretism," in *The Cross Goes North: Processes of Conversion in Northern Europe, AD 300–1300* (York, UK: York Medieval Press, 2003), 571–79.

62. Daniel T. Reff, "Making the Land Holy: The Mission Frontier in Early Medieval Europe and Colonial Mexico," in *The Spiritual Conversion of the Americas*, ed. James Muldoon (Gainesville: University Press of Florida, 2004), 17–35.

63. See Cohen, *The Postcolonial Middle Ages*.

64. Anna Sapir Abulafia, "The Intellectual and Spiritual Quest for Christ and Central Medieval Persecution of Jews," in *Religious Violence between Christians and Jews: Medieval Roots, Modern Perspectives*, ed. Anna Sapir Abulafia (New York: Palgrave, 2002), 74–75.

65. Abulafia, *Christians and Jews in the Twelfth-Century Renaissance*, 116.

66. Quoted in Cohen, *Living Letters of the Law*, 14.

67. By as much as anything, I was led years ago to embark on this parlous venture by the wonderful literature—grounded in historiography, but bringing anthropological and literary-critical perspectives as well—on the colonial encounter in Latin America. I was especially impressed by the work of people like Anthony Pagden, Inga Clendinnen, Rolena Adorno, and Sabine MacCormack, which I cite throughout.

68. See María Rosa Menocal, *Shards of Love: Exile and the Origins of the Lyric* (Durham, NC: Duke University Press, 1994), 27.

69. Tzvetan Todorov, *The Conquest of America: The Question of the Other* (New York: Harper and Row, 1984), 50. Walden Browne suggests that, rather than modernity being exported to the New World, it is rather the site—or at least, one site—where modernity was produced: the missionary Nahua scholar "Sahagún was forced to produce his own 'modernity'—a modern view of the world that is unique to his situation in the Americas. This notion runs counter to the commonly held belief that Europe invented modernity and then—and only then—exported it to the New World." Walden Browne,

Sahagún and the Transition to Modernity (Norman: University of Oklahoma Press, 2000), 9. Compare the provocative thesis of Nathan Wachtel, put forth as a matter of common knowledge, that "the transformation of a Spain characterized by its situation at the frontier of Christianity to a Spain situated at the center of a vast empire stimulated the emergence of an internal frontier, excluding an 'Other' who had become too similar, that is, these 'new Christians' of Jewish origin, victims of an overly successful integration." Nathan Wachtel, introduction to *Le Nouveau Monde, mondes nouveaux*, ed. Serge Gruzinski and Natan Wachtel (Paris: Éditions Recherche sur les Civilisations; Éditions de l'École des Hautes Études en Sciences Sociales, 1996), 465–66.

70. One reason for focusing precisely on the connections between the exclusion of Jews and of pre-Columbian Americans is that it should help us to avoid this kind of Eurocentric bias. See the discussions in Inga Clendinnen, " 'Fierce and Unnatural Cruelty': Cortés and the Conquest of Mexico", *Representations* 33 (1991), 66, and Gananath Obeyesekere, *The Apotheosis of Captain Cook* (Princeton, NJ: Princeton University Press, 1992), 16–19. See also the careful reconsideration of the question of Aztec time by Ross Hassig, who suggests that the Aztecs "did not have a cyclical notion of time, but a linear one, and that their temporal concepts as embodied in the calendar were manipulated for political purposes." Ross Hassig, *Time, History, and Belief in Aztec and Colonial Mexico* (Austin: University of Texas Press, 2000), xiii.

71. Todorov, *The Conquest of America*, 15. Ian McLean goes Todorov one better, totally dissolving the distinctions in power between Columbus and those whom he encounters and enthusiastically endorsing Todorov's claim that "we are all the descendants of Columbus." Ian McLean, " 'The Circumference Is Everywhere and the Centre Nowhere': Modernity and the Diasporic Discovery of Columbus as Told by Tzvetan Todorov," *Third Text* 24 (1992–93). For Todorov and McLean, Columbus is a paradigmatic figure for "Western" consciousness.

72. David E. Stannard, *American Holocaust: Columbus and the Conquest of the New World* (New York: Oxford University Press, 1992), 6.

73. Krister Stendahl, *Paul among Jews and Gentiles* (Philadelphia: Fortress Press, 1976), 7.

CHAPTER ONE

1. Even a book devoted to questioning fixed markers of difference must often resort to labels such as "Jew," "Indian," and "Christian" as if they represented identities that were stable through time and among persons.

2. Gayatri Chakravorti Spivak, "Can the Subaltern Speak?" in *Marxism and the Interpretation of Culture*, ed. Cary Nelson and Lawrence Grossberg (Urbana: University of Illinois Press, 1988); Miguel Léon-Portilla, *Vision de los Vencidos: Cronicas Indigenas* (Madrid: Historia, 1985); Natan Wachtel, *The Vision of the Vanquished: The Spanish Conquest of Peru Through Indian Eyes* (New York: Barnes and Noble, 1977).

3. José Rabasa's *Inventing America: Spanish Historiography and the Formation of Eurocentrism* (Norman: University of Oklahoma Press, 1993) is an exemplary text that traces ways in which "knowledge of other cultures" was connected to the justification of Spanish conquest and conversion.

4. Thomas H. Luxon, *Literal Figures: Puritan Allegory and the Reformation Crisis in Representation* (Chicago: University of Chicago Press, 1993).

5. Caroline Walker Bynum, *Jesus as Mother: Studies in the Spirituality of the High Middle Ages* (Berkeley: University of California Press, 1982). For cases of voluntary martyrdom by Christian missionaries in Muslim Spain *before* the *Reconquista*, see Edward P. Colbert, *The Martyrs of Cordoba (850–859): A Study of the Sources* (Washington, D.C.: Catholic University of America Press, 1962) and A. Cutler, "The Ninth-Century Spanish Martyrs' Movement and the Origins of Western Christian Missions to the Muslims," *Muslim World* 58 (1968): 57–71, 155–64. In the sixteenth century Las Casas, the defender of the Indians, argued against punitive wars against them for having killed missionaries: "The missionaries who are sacrificed in this way by the Indians obtain the palm of martyrdom and go directly to Heaven, an immense benefit for which they must thank the Indians." Cited in Angel Losada, "The Controversy between Sepúlveda and Las Casas in the Junta of Valladolid," in *Bartolomé de Las Casas in History*, ed. Juan Friede and Benjamin Keen (DeKalb, IL: Northern Illinois University Press, 1971), 293.

6. Talal Asad, *Genealogies of Religion: Discipline and Reasons of Power in Christianity and Islam* (Baltimore: Johns Hopkins University Press, 1993), 157.

7. Peter Brown, *The Rise of Western Christendom: Triumph and Diversity, A.D. 200–1000*, 2d ed. (Malden, MA: Blackwell Publishing), 29.

8. Karl F Morrison, *Understanding Conversion* (Charlottesville: University of Virginia Press, 1992), 73.

9. Daniel Boyarin, *Border Lines: The Partition of Judaeo-Christianity* (Philadelphia: University of Pennsylvania Press, 2004).

10. Claudine Fabre-Vassas, *The Singular Beast: Jews, Christians and the Pig*, trans. Carol Volk (New York: Columbia University Press, 1997), 8.

11. Quoted in Jeremy Cohen, *Living Letters of the Law: Ideas of the Jew in Medieval Christianity* (Berkeley: University of California Press, 1999), 203.

12. Jonathan Elukin, "The Discovery of the Self: Jews and Conversion in the Twelfth Century," in *Jews and Christians in Twelfth-Century Europe*, ed. Michael A. Singer and John van Engen (Notre Dame, IN: Notre Dame University Press, 2001).

13. Quoted in Tomaž Mastnak, *Crusading Peace: Christendom, the Muslim World, and Western Political Order* (Berkeley: University of California Press, 2002), 221.

14. David Nirenberg, "Conversion, Sex, and Segregation: Jews and Christians in Medieval Spain," *American Historical Review* 107 (October 2002):1065–93.

15. Louise M. Burckhardt, *The Slippery Earth: Nahua-Christian Moral Dialogue in Sixteenth-Century Mexico* (Tucson: The University of Arizona Press, 1989), 11.

16. Hohmi K. Bhabha, Introduction to *Nation and Narration*, ed. Homi K. Bhabha (New York: Routledge), 4.

17. See Hohmi K. Bhabha, "Call for Proposals: Frontlines/Borderposts," *Critical Inquiry* 19, no. 3 (1993): 595–98.

18. Indeed, the Western discourse of group identity extends at least as far back as the ancient Greek historians. See François Hartog, *The Mirror of Herodotus: The Representation of the Other in the Writing of History*, trans. Janet Lloyd (Berkeley: University of California Press, 1988).

19. María Rosa Menocal, in *Shards of Love: Exile and the Origins of the Lyric* (Durham, NC: Duke University Press, 1994), is one recent scholar who has lucidly questioned this conventional view. See also Gil Anidjar, "Postscript: Futures of Al-Andalus," in *In the Light of Medieval Spain: Islam, the West, and the Relevance of the Past*, ed. Simon R. Doubleday and David Coleman (New York: Palgrave Macmillan, 2008), 189–208.

20. See, for several examples, *The Postcolonial Middle Ages*, ed. Jeffrey Jerome Cohen, New York: St. Martin's Press, 2000; *Postcolonial Approaches to the European Middle Ages: Translating Cultures*, ed. Ananya Jahanara Kabir and Deanne Williams (Cambridge: Cambridge University Press, 2005); "Postcolonialism and the Past," a special issue of Modern Language Quarterly 65:3 (2004), ed. Barbara Fuchs and David J. Baker; *Under the Influence: Questioning the Comparative in Medieval Castile*, ed. Cynthia Robinson and Leila Rouhi (Leiden: Brill, 2005); the special issue of *Medieval Encounters*, "Interrogating Medieval Encounters," 12:3 (2006), ed. Maria Judith Feliciano and Cynthia Robinson; the special issue of *The Journal of Medieval and Early Modern Studies*, "Medieval/Renaissance: After Periodization" 37:3 (2007), ed. Jennifer Summit and David Wallace; and *Coloniality at Large: Latin America and the Postcolonial Debate*, ed. Mabel Moraña, Enrique Dussel, and Carlos A. Jáuregui (Durham: Duke University Press, 2008).

21. J.H. Elliott, "The Spanish Conquest and Settlement of America," in *The Cambridge History of Latin America*, vol. 1 (Cambridge: Cambridge University Press, 1984), 158.

22. Caroline Walker Bynum, *The Resurrection of the Body in Western Christianity, 200–1336* (New York: Columbia University Press, 1995), 215.

23. Ibid.

24. Anna Sapir Abulafia, *Christians and Jews in the Twelfth-Century Renaissance* (London: Routledge, 1995), 44.

25. Morrison, *Understanding Conversion*, 144.

26. Elliott, "The Spanish Conquest and Settlement of America," 180.

27. Jacques Derrida, *The Other Heading: Reflections on Today's Europe* (Bloomington: Indiana University Press, 1992).

28. Stephen Greenblatt, *Marvelous Possessions: The Wonder of the New World* (Chicago: University of Chicago Press, 1991), 9.

29. A similar question can be asked about J.H. Elliott's statement that by the seventeenth century, there came into being "a Europe whose triumphs over the Islamic peoples of the East and the heathen peoples of the West had made it arrogantly self-assured." J.H. Elliott, *The Old World and the New, 1492–1650* (Cambridge: Cambridge University Press, 1970), 103. It is not so clear that "arrogance" and confident identity commonly coexist.

30. For a more extended contemporary deployment of this technique, see Gananath Obeyesekere's essay " 'British Cannibals': Contemplation of an Event in the Death and Resurrection of James Cook, Explorer," *Critical Inquiry* 18 (Summer, 1992): 630–54.

31. The mendicant missionaries were, in any case, barred from shares in the treasure of the New World expeditions, unlike members of the secular clergy. Robert Himerich y Valencia, *The Encomenderos of New Spain, 1521–1555* (Austin: University of Texas Press, 1991), 97.

32. Doris Heyden, translator's introduction to Fray Diego Durán, *The History of the Indies of New Spain* (Norman: University of Oklahoma Press, 1994), xxi.

33. See Johannes Fabian, *Time and the Other* (New York: Columbia University Press, 1983). Sometimes the focus on missionary cultural curiosity undergirds arguments that are avowedly sympathetic toward the missionaries, as in Rubert de Ventós's discussion of the "universalist anthropology" of Spanish colonial chroniclers. Xavier Rubert de Ventós, *The Hispanic Labyrinth: Tradition and Modernity in the Colonization of the Americas*, trans. Mary Ann Newman (New Brunswick, NJ: Transaction Books, 1991), 65. As in the case of Durán, it is difficult to determine what element of this "universalism" has to do with Christian charity toward those who have not yet heard the Gospel and what might be attributed to principled respect for the other as such.

Anthony Pagden has a somewhat more sober take on this subject of Spanish missionary as anthropologist. Like de Ventós, he notes the religious origins of liberal universalism. Anthony Pagden, *The Fall of Natural Man* (New York: Columbia University Press, 1986), 134. Yet when Pagden says that missionaries were substantially like anthropologists he aims not merely to emphasize their humanism, but to identify certain shared problems inherent in both enterprises. He notes that "for the cultural historian [e.g. Las Casas]—who had inherited from the theologians that project which in the nineteenth century came to be 'anthropology'—differences in place may be identical to differences in time." Ibid., 2. Pagden thus identifies the reliance of some missionaries' tolerance toward the Indians on spatialized supersessionism. He likewise marks the ambivalent situation shared by colonial missionaries and by anthropologists: professionally aligned with and dependent on the colonizers, yet with a professional interest in defending the humanity of the colonized. What is worth adding here is that for both colonial missionaries and later anthropologists, this professional tension was balanced by an ideology which sometimes bridged their alliances with colonizer and colonized. For the earlier missionaries that ideology was Catholic universalism. For the later anthropologists it was a progressive and Eurocentric humanism. Most recently,

Walden Browne has argued that the entire effort to see a missionary scholar such as Fray Bernardino de Sahagún as a proto-ethnographer is misguided. Rather, he argues, "Sahagún was trying to write a summa of Nahua culture. The days of summae, however, were drawing to an end." Walden Browne, *Sahagún and the Transition to Modernity* (Norman: University of Oklahoma Press, 2000), 130.

34. Jacque Derrida, *Specters of Marx: The State of the Debt, the Work of Mourning, and the New International*, trans. Peggy Kamuf; intro. Bernd Magnus and Stephen Cullenberg (New York: Routledge, 1994); Steven F. Kruger, *The Spectral Jew: Conversion and Embodiment in Medieval Europe* (Minneapolis: University of Minnesota Press, 2006).

35. Even studies explicitly concerned with Christian schemata of salvation in the articulated fullness of time may sometimes slip toward the suggestion that the entire world—and all of time—have indeed fallen under the sway of those schemata. Thus, the chapter on the Book of Revelation in Steven Goldsmith's study of romantic apocalypse concludes that Revelation "stands as a permanent reminder that a once significant historical difference [between Hebrew and Christian scriptures] ended in a timeless literary unity." Steven Goldsmith, *Unbuilding Jerusalem: Apocalypse and Romantic Representation* (Ithaca, NY: Cornell University Press, 1993). Timeless for whom, and for what ends? Evidently it is extraordinarily difficult to remain aware of a continuing tradition of Jewish textual study that is not subsumed under the rubric of the Bible as designated by Christians. See Kathleen Biddick's careful articulation of the difficulty of escaping the supersessionist schema. Kathleen Biddick, *The Typological Imaginary: Circumcision, Technology, History* (Philadelphia: University of Pennsylvania Press, 2003).

36. Homi Bhabha, *The Location of Culture* (New York: Routledge, 1994), 196.

37. Talal Asad, *Genealogies of Religion: Discipline and Reasons of Power in Christianity and Islam* (Baltimore: Johns Hopkins University Press, 1993).

38. Stephen Greenblatt, *Renaissance Self-Fashioning* (Chicago: University of Chicago Press, 1980), 9.

39. To be sure, even as a stereotype this characterization might be more generally true for English than for Spanish responses to the people they found in the New World. From the beginning, colonizers' accounts of Mexico acknowledged, for example, the greatness of Montezuma's capital in Mexico: "The city is as large as Sevillle or Cordoba [and] there is one square twice as large as that of Salamanca." Hernan Cortés, *Conquest: Dispatches from the New World*, intro and commentaries by Irwin R. Blacker, texts ed. by Harry M. Rosen (New York: Grosset & Dunlap, 1962), 54–55. The eyewitness Bernal Díaz likewise testified that he was "astounded" on first sight of the cities and villages of Mexico. *The Conquest of New Spain*, trans. and intro. by J.M. Cohen (Baltimore: Penguin, 1963), 216.

40. John E. Benton, "Consciousness of Self and Perceptions of Individuality," in *Culture, Power and Personality in Medieval France*, ed. Thomas N. Bisson (London: The Hambildon Press, 1991), 336, 343.

41. Bynum, *Jesus as Mother*, 109.

42. Burckhardt, *The Slippery Earth*, 33.

43. Richard M. Fraher, "IV Lateran's Revolution in Criminal Procedure: The Birth of *Inquisitio*, the End of Ordeals, and Innocent III's Vision of Ecclesiastical Politics," in *Studia in Honorem Eminentissimi Cardinalis Alphonsi M. Stickler*, Studia et Textus Historiae Iuris Canonici 7 (Rome: LAS, 1992).

44. Jaroslav Pelikan describes this last point as "the doctrinal achievement more of the twelfth than of the thirteenth century." Jaroslav Pelikan, *The Growth of Medieval Theology (600–1300)* (Chicago: University of Chicago Press, 1978), 268–69.

45. John Howe, "The Nobility's Reform of the Medieval Church," *The American Historical Review* 93 (1988), 321.

46. G. Tellenbach, *Church, State, and Christian Society at the Time of the Investiture Contest*, trans. R.F. Bennett (Toronto: University of Toronto Press, 1991), 164.

47. Michael Costen, *The Cathars and the Albigensian Crusade* (Manchester: Manchester University Press, 1997), 168.

48. Daniel T. Reff, "Making the Land Holy: The Mission Frontier in Early Medieval Europe and Colonial Mexico," in *The Spiritual Conversion of the Americas*, ed. James Muldoon (Gainesville: University Press of Florida, 2004), 17–35.

49. Mary Douglas, *Purity and Danger: An Analysis of the Concepts of Pollution and Taboo* (London: Routledge, 1992).

50. R.I. Moore, *The Formation of a Persecuting Society: Power and Deviance in Western Europe, 950–1250* (New York: Basil Blackwell, 1987), 101.

51. See also the critique by David Nirenberg, on other grounds, of what he calls Moore's "scapegoating paradigm." David Nirenberg, *Communities of Violence: Persecution of Minorities in the Middle Ages* (Princeton, NJ: Princeton University Press, 1996), 242.

52. R.W. Southern, *Scholastic Humanism and the Unification of Europe, Vol. 1: Foundations* (Oxford: Blackwells, 1995) 34–35; Robert Chazan, *Fashioning Jewish Identity in Medieval Christendom* (Cambridge: Cambridge University Press, 2004), 3–4.

53. Ascetic self-denial need not lead to an absence of self, but rather can be encompassed within the poetics of self-making as one of its possible modes. See Debbora Battaglia, ed., *Rhetorics of Self-Making* (Berkeley: University of California Press, 1995). Dominic comes across in most accounts as self-effacing. Yet this is also understood as a problem for his followers: how is it possible to mold an identity according to an effaced model? Francis, by contrast, is an elaborated self, a dramatic character. Rosalind B. Brooke, *The Coming of the Friars* (New York: Barnes and Noble, 1975). Following in his footsteps, Franciscan tracts "emphasized the fact that the friars were to arouse men to repent and prepare for the coming judgment by example more than by preaching." E. Randolph Daniel, *The Franciscan Concept of Mission in the High Middle Ages* (Lexington: University Press of Kentucky, 1975), 104. In order for the individual Franciscan to serve as an example, his "self" clearly had to be molded some-

how, and the life of Francis was intended to show the way; only the accoutrements of selfhood constituted by personal dominion were in fact denied.

54. Daniel, *The Franciscan Concept of Mission*, 40.

55. Barbara H. Rosenwein and Lester K. Little, "Social Meaning in the Monastic and Mendicant Spirituality," *Past and Present* 63 (1974), 13.

56. Daniel, *The Franciscan Concept of Mission*, 40.

57. J-P. Migne, ed., *Burchardi vormatiensis episcopi opera omnia*, Patrologiae cursus completus ... series Latina, vol. 140 (Paris: Garnier, 1880), column 952.

58. Ibid., column 772.

59. R.B.C. Huygens, ed., *Guibert de Nogent: Dei gesta per Francos et cinq autres textes*, Corpus Christianorum: Continuatis medievalis 12A (Turnholt: Brepols, 1996), 7, 221. See discussion cited in D.E. Luscombe and G.R. Evans, "The Twelfth-Century Renaissance," in *The Cambridge History of Medieval Political Thought: C. 350–C.1450*, ed. J. H. Burns (New York: Cambridge University Press), 309. Thus, in a topos dating back at least to Augustine, the church is defined not only as spiritual but also by diametrical contrast to "Israel according to the flesh" (1 Cor. 10:18). See Daniel Boyarin, *Carnal Israel: Reading Sex in Talmudic Culture* (Berkeley: University of California Press, 1993), 1. This traditional emphasis on Israelite carnality is quite different from the critique of Old Testament chauvinism or intolerance mounted by post-Enlightenment commentators such as Frederick Turner, yet the two are linked in the shared critique of Jewishness as a religion with an explicitly "ethnic" genealogical structure of identification.

60. Huygens, ed., *Guibert de Nogent*, 37: "Instituit nostro tempore prelia sancta deus, ut ordo equestris et vulgus oberrans, qui vetustae paganitatis exemplo in mutuas versebantur cedes, novum repperirent salutis promerendae genus." See Robert Levine, *The Deeds of God Through the Franks: A Translation of Guibert de Nogent's "Gesta Dei per Francos"* (Rochester, NY: Bordell and Brewer, 1997), 28; see also Luscombe and Evans, "The Twelfth-Century Renaissance," 309.

61. Rosenwein and Little, "Social Meaning in the Monastic and Mendicant Spirituality," 15.

62. Brooke, *The Coming of the Friars*, 101.

63. See J. A. Watt, "The Separation of Spiritual and Temporal Powers," in *The Cambridge History of Medieval Political Thought*, ed. J. H. Burns (New York: Cambridge University Press, 1988).

64. Quoted in Cohen, *Living Letters of the Law*, 37.

65. Brooke, The Coming of the Friars, 94.

66. Adhémar Esmein, *A History of Continental Criminal Procedure: With Special Reference to France*, trans. John Simpson (London: John Murray, 1914), 9, cited in Talal Asad, *Genealogies of Religion: Discipline and Reasons of Power in Christianity and Islam* (Baltimore: Johns Hopkins University Press, 1993), 85.

67. Asad, *Genealogies of Religion*, 85.

68. Talal Asad, *The Idea of an Anthropology of Islam*, Occasional Papers Series, (Washington, DC: Center for Contemporary Arab Studies, Georgetown University, 1986).

69. See Miriam Bodian, *Hebrews of the Portuguese Nation: Conversos and Community in Early Modern Amsterdam* (Bloomington: Indiana University Press, 1997), 102.

70. Jorge Klor de Alva, "Colonizing Souls: The Failure of the Indian Inquisition and the Rise of Penitential Discipline," in *Cultural Encounters: The Impact of the Inquisition in Spain and the New World*, ed. Mary Elizabeth Parry and Anne J. Cruz (Berkeley: University of California Press. 1991), 12.

71. Richard E. Greenleaf, *The Mexican Inquisition of the Sixteenth Century* (Albuquerque: University of New Mexico Press, 1969).

72. Greenleaf, *The Mexican Inquisition*, 74–75. Although Klor de Alva argues in "Colonizing Souls" that "the Holy Office was ill suited to discipline a people who did not share its basic cultural or penal assumptions" (12, 15), another scholar has documented the existence of a similar institution directed against Indian heresy that "generated an enormous number of trials, very few of which have come to light." Roberto Moreno de los Arcos, "New Spain's Inquisition for Indians from the Sixteenth to the Nineteenth Century," in *Cultural Encounters: The Impact of the Inquisition in Spain and the New World*, ed. Mary Elizabeth Perry and Anne J. Cruz (Berkeley: University of California Press, 1991), 23.

73. Geoffrey Galt Harpham, "So . . . What *Is* Enlightenment? An Inquisition into Modernity," *Critical Inquiry* 20, no. 3 (1994): 550–51. For more on *conversos* and modernity, see Yosef Kaplan, ed., *Jews and Conversos* (Jerusalem: Magnes Press, 1985); Yermiyahu Yovel, *Spinoza and Other Heretics: The Marrano of Reason* (Princeton, NJ: Princeton University Press, 1992); and José Faur, In the Shadow of History: Jews and Conversos at the Dawn of Modernity (Albany: State University of New York Press, 1992).

74. Harpham, "So . . . What *Is* Enlightenment?" 542.

75. Robert Chazan, *European Jewry and the First Crusade* (Berkeley: University of California Press, 1987), 100.

76. Caroline Walker Bynum, *The Resurrection of the Body in Western Christianity, 200–1336* (New York: Columbia University Press, 1995), 97.

77. See Daniel Boyarin, *A Radical Jew: Paul and the Politics of Identity* (Berkeley: University of California Press, 1994).

78. Denise Kimber Buell, *Making Christians: Clement of Alexandria and the Rhetoric of Legitimacy* (Princeton, NJ: Princeton University Press, 1999), 80; see also idem, *Why This New Race: Ethnic Reasoning in Early Christianity* (New York: Columbia University Press, 2005).

79. Bynum, *The Resurrection of the Body in Western Christianity*, 12.

80. Jeremy Cohen, *The Friars and the Jews: The Evolution of Medieval Anti-Judaism* (Ithaca, NY: Cornell University Press 1982), 246.

81. For a comparison case in a very different part of the world, see Willard J. Peterson, "What to Wear? Observation and Participation by Jesuit Missionaries in Late Ming Society," in *Implicit Understandings: Observing, Reporting, and Reflection on the Encounters between Europeans and Other Peoples in the Early Modern Era*, ed. Stuart B. Schwartz (New York: Cambridge University Press, 1994).

82. John Leddy Phelan, *The Millennial Kingdom of the Fransciscans in the New World*, 2nd ed. (Berkeley: University of California Press, 1970).

83. Elliott, *The Old World and the New*, 25.

84. Ibid.

85. See Cemal Kadafar, *Between Two Worlds: The Construction of the Ottoman State* (Berkeley: University of California Press, 1995).

CHAPTER TWO

1. John Tolan, *Saracens: Islam in the Medieval European Imagination* (New York: Columbia University Press, 2002), 269.

2. Michael Frassetto, "The Image of the Saracen as Heretic in Sermons of Ademar of Chabannes," in *Western Views of Islam in Medieval and Early Modern Europe: Perception of Other*, ed. David R. Blanks and Michael Frassetto (New York: St. Martin's Press, 1999), 83–96.

3. Ana Echevarría, *The Fortress of Faith: The Attitude towards Muslims in Fifteenth-Century Spain* (Leiden: Brill, 1999), 102, 162.

4. Tolan, *Saracens*, 117.

5. Barbara Fuchs, "The Spanish Race," in *Rereading the Black Legend: The Discourses of Religions and Racial Difference in the Renaissance Empires*, ed. Margaret R. Greer, Walter D. Mignolo, and Maureen Quilligan (Chicago: University of Chicago Press, 2007), 88–98.

6. Ibid., 3. Medieval accounts of Muslims as heretics and of Muhammad as heresiarch are described in both Tolan's *Saracens* and Debra Strickland's *Saracens, Demons, and Jews: Making Monsters in Medieval Art* (Princeton, NJ: Princeton University Press, 2003).

7. Quoted in Tolan, *Saracens*, 244.

8. Ibid., 251, 117, 121, 130, 131; Strickland, *Saracens, Demons, and Jews*, 166; Mary Elizabeth Perry, *The Handless Maiden: Moriscos and the Politics of Religion in Early Modern Spain* (Princeton, NJ: Princeton University Press, 2005), 47.

9. On the confusion of "Indio" and "Iudio" in Spanish colonial texts, see Judith Laikin Elkin, "Imagining Idolatry: Missionaries, Indians, and Jews," in *Religion and the Authority of the Past*, ed. Tobin Siebers (Ann Arbor: University of Michigan Press 1993), as well as Yakov Malkiel and María-Rosa Lida Malkiel, "The Jew and the Indian: Traces of a Confusion in the Hispanic Tradition," in *For Max Weinreich on His Seventieth Birthday: Studies in Jewish Languages, Literature, and Society* (The

Hague: Mouton, 1964), who point out the remarkable convergence of typographical and cultural slippage. The confusion of Muslims and Jews, on the other hand, had significant echoes in early nineteenth-century England, where the move to reject Catholic emancipation fed into an English historiography that stressed the evils of the Spanish Catholic Church and monarchy. At the same time, anti-Catholics did not want to arouse sympathy for Jews. This dilemma led a historian such as John Stockdale sometimes to substitute " 'Moor' when 'Jew' would be historically correct" in identifying victims of Spanish Catholic persecution. See Michael Ragussis, "The Birth of a Nation in Victorian Culture: The Spanish Inquisition, the Converted Daughter, and the 'Secret Race,' " *Critical Inquiry* 20:3 (1994), 481. Indeed, the nineteenth-century fight over Jewish emancipation in England and the way the Spanish Inquisition was represented in England at that time provide a multiply reflecting "mirror chain" connecting the late medieval history of Catholics, Jews, and Muslims to the nineteenth-century and twentieth-century "post-Enlightenment" question of the linked situation of Jews and Muslims in "Europe." Ibid.

10. See Michael Rothberg, *Multidirectional Memory: Remembering the Holocaust in the Age of Decolonization* (Stanford, CA: Stanford University Press, 2009).

11. Quoted in Jeremy Cohen, *Living Letters of the Law: Ideas of the Jew in Medieval Christianity* (Berkeley: University of California Press, 1999), 221; see also Gil Anidjar, *The Jew, the Arab: A History of the Enemy* (Stanford, CA: Stanford University Press, 2003), xv.

12. Geraldine Heng, "The Romance of England: Richard Coeur de Lyon, Saracens, Jews, and the Politics of Race and Nation," in *The Postcolonial Middle Ages*, ed. Jeffrey Jerome Cohen (New York: St. Martin's Press, 2000), 143.

13. Tomaž Mastnak, *Crusading Peace: Christendom, the Muslim World, and Western Political Order* (Berkeley: University of California Press, 2002), 40–41.

14. Anwar G. Chejne, *Islam and the West: The Moriscos, a Cultural and Social History* (Albany: State University of New York Press, 1983), 12.

15. Gonazol Lamana, "Of Books, Popes, and *Huacas*: Or, the Dilemmas of Being Christian," in *Rereading the Black Legend*, 125.

16. Andrée Collard, "Introduction," *History of the Indies: Bartolomé de Las Casas* (New York: Harper & Row, 1971), xv.

17. Max Harris, *Aztecs, Moors, and Christians: Festivals of Reconquest in Mexico and Spain* (Austin: University of Texas Press, 2000), 136–47. On the analogies between Moriscos and Indians in the area of evangelization, see Antonio Garrido Aranda, *Moriscos e Indios: Precedentes Hispanicos de la Evangelización en México* (Mexico: Universidad Nacional Autónoma de México, 1980).

18. Harris, *Aztecs, Moors, and Christians*, 206–8.

19. Mikel de Epalza, "Principes chrétiens et principes musulmans face au problème morisque," in *Les Morisques et l'Inquisition*, ed. Louis Cardaillac (Paris: Publisud, 1990), 47; Rolena Adorno, "La *Ciudad Letrada* y los Discursos Coloniales," *Hispamerica* 48 (December 1987), 5.

20. James B. Tueller, *Good and Faithful Christians: Moriscos and Catholicism in Early Modern Spain* (New Orleans: University Press of the South, 2002), 154.

21. Barbara Fuchs, "Imperium Studies: Theorizing Early Modern Expansion," in *Postcolonial Moves: Medieval Through Modern*, ed. Patricia Clare Ingham and Michelle R. Warren (New York: Palgrave MacMillan, 2003), 74.

22. Tolan, *Saracens*, 163.

23. John V. Tolan, *Sons of Ishmael: Muslims Through European Eyes in the Middle Ages* (Gainesville: University Press of Florida, 2008), xii, 45, 51,63.

24. Echevarría, *The Fortress of Faith*, 60.

25. See the astute analysis in Kathleen Davis, "Time Behind the Veil: The Media, The Middle Ages, and Orientalism Now," in *The Postcolonial Middle Ages*, ed. Jeffrey Jerome Cohen (New York: St. Martin's Press, 2000), 105–122.

26. Thomas E. Burman, *Reading the Qur'an in Western Christendom, 1140–1560* (Philadelphia: University of Pennsylvania Press, 2007).

27. See, for example, Echevarría, *Fortress of Faith*, 129, 69.

28. Thomas E. Burman, *Religious Polemic and the Intellectual History of the Mozarabs, c. 1050–1200* (Leiden: Brill, 1994),16.

29. Editor's introduction to *Under the Influence: Questioning the Comparative in Medieval Castile*, ed. Cynthia Robinson and Leyla Rouhi (Leiden: Brill, 2005), 1–18. A more concentrated instance of the effort to move beyond the rhetoric of "'influence'" is contained in the special issue of *Medieval Encounters*, "Interrogating Iberian Frontiers." It is noteworthy that while the introduction by María Judith Feliciano and Leyla Rouhi calls for problematization of "the notion of 'hybridity,'" they still refer to "the formation and development of a hybrid Iberia." "Introduction: Interrogating Iberian Frontiers," *Medieval Encounters* 12:3 (2006), 317–28, at 325. To which, citing the question of the historian Moshe Rosman, we might respond: "[What here is] Hybrid with What?" See Rosman, *How Jewish Is Jewish History?* (Oxford: The Littman Library of Jewish Civilization, 2007), 82–110. The present book, of course, displays the same terminological handicap: how to speak of interactions (between idioms? between worlds?) without once again reifying fixed group identities.

30. Perry, *The Handless Maiden*, 26.

31. Robinson, Cynthia. "Trees of Love, Trees of Knowledge: Toward the Definition of a Cross-Confessional Current in Late Medieval Spirituality." *Medieval Encounters* 12:3 (2006), 388–43, at 394.

32. Patricia Seed, *Ceremonies of Possession in the New World, 1492–1640* (Cambridge,: Cambridge University Press, 1995), 75.

33. L.P. Harvey, *Muslims in Spain, 1500 to 1614* (Chicago: University of Chicago Press, 2005), 138.

34. See Mastnak, *Crusading Peace*, 92.

35. Tolan, *Saracens*, 103, 126–27.

36. Steven F. Kruger, *The Spectral Jew: Conversion and Embodiment in Medieval Europe* (Minneapolis: University of Minnesota Press, 2006), 30.

37. Lucy Pick, *Conflict and Coexistence: Archbishop Rodrigo and the Muslims and Jews of Medieval Spain* (Ann Arbor: University of Michigan Press, 2004), 25.

38. For a powerful evocation of an alternative articulation, by Jewish literati of Arab culture, of Iberian timespace long before the sporadic Muslim retreat became the accomplished Christian reconquest, see Gil Anidjar, *Our Place in al-Andalus: Kabbalah, Philosophy, Lliterature in Arab Jewish Letters* (Stanford, CA: Stanford University Press, 2002).

39. Bernard F. Reilly, *The Medieval Spains* (Cambridge: Cambridge University Press, 1993), 115.

40. Burman, *Religious Polemic and the Intellectual History of the Mozarabs*, 4.

41. Harvey, *Muslims in Spain*, 19–20.

42. Perry, *The Handless Maiden*, 22.

43. Joseph F. O'Callaghan, *Reconquest and Crusade in Medieval Spain* (Philadelphia: University of Pennsylvania Press, 2003), 8.

44. Tolan, *Saracens*, xix.

45. Louise Mirrer, *Women, Jews and Muslims in the Texts of Reconquest Castile* (Ann Arbor: University of Michigan Press, 1996), 9.

46. Steven Epstein, *Genoa and the Genoese, 958–1528* (Chapel Hill: University of North Carolina Press, 1996), 310. In *Crusade and Mission: European Approaches Toward the Muslims*, Princeton, NJ: Princeton University Press, 1984), Benjamin Z. Kedar has patiently unraveled and rewoven the twin themes of conquest and conversion as medieval Christian European approaches to Muslim power and religious difference. See his *Crusade and Mission: European Approaches toward the Muslims* (Princeton, NJ: Princeton University Press, 1984). Norman Daniel's pioneering *Islam and the West: The Making of an Image* (Edinburgh: The University Press, 1960) must be mentioned here as well.

To some extent, the relation between mission and crusade was also one of sequence, since there was a gradual "disillusion with the prospects of missionizing, [and] growing emphasis on the crusade." Kedar, *Crusade and Mission*, 154. Broadly similar processes—an initial wave of enthusiasm for the possibilities of conversion, followed by demonization—can be seen in the New World. For Mexico, see John Leddy Phelan, *The Millennial Kingdom of the Franciscans in the New World*, 2nd ed (Berkeley: University of California Press, 1970), and Stafford Poole, C.M., "The Declining Image of the Indian Among Churchmen in Sixteenth-Century Spain," in *Indian-Religious Relations in Colonial Spanish America*, ed. Susan E. Ramírez (Syracuse, NY: Maxwell School of Citizenship and Public Affairs, 1989). For the British in North America, see Roy Harvey Pearce, *Savagism and Civilization: The Indian and the American Mind* (Berkeley: University of California Press, 1988; originally published 1953).

47. Kedar, *Crusade and Mission*, 141–45, 109.

48. Ibid., 159–60; see also Robert A. Williams, *The American Indian in Western Legal Thought: The Discourses of Conquest* (New York: Oxford University Press, 1990)

and J. Muldoon, *Popes, Lawyers and, Infidels: The Church and the Non-Christian World, 1250-1550* (Philadelphia: University of Pennsylvania Press, 1979).

49. Xavier Rubert de Ventós, *The Hispanic Labyrinth: Tradition and Modernity in the Colonization of the Americas*, trans. Mary Ann Newman (New Brunswick, NJ: Transaction Books, 1991), 12.

50. Diana Wood, "Infidels and Jews: Clement VI's Attitude to Persecution and Toleration," in *Persecution and Toleration*, ed. W.J. Sheils, Studies in Church History 21 (London: Basil Blackwell, 1984), 116-17.

51. The Peruvian colonial writer Guaman Poma argued, consistently with the argument of Clement VI, that the Gospel had been revealed in the Americas in apostolic times, long before the arrival of the Spanish. He drew a conclusion diametrically opposite to that of the pope, however: "And thus we Indians are Christians, [thanks to] the apostles of Jesus Christ, St. Bartholomew, St. James the Greater, and by the holy cross of Jesus Christ, all of which arrived in this kingdom before the Spaniards. Because of this we are Christian and we believe in only one God of the Holy Trinity." Quoted in Rolena Adorno, *Guaman Poma: Writing and Resistance in Colonial Peru* (Austin: University of Texas Press, 1986), 27, 29. Therefore, according to Guaman Poma, the Spanish conquest could not be justified in the name of proselytizing.

52. Kedar, *Crusade and Mission*, 14.

53. Tolan, *Saracens*, 88-89, 232, 216.

54. Kruger, *The Spectral Jew*, 80.

55. Sabine MacCormack, *Religion in the Andes: Vision and Imagination in Early Colonial Peru* (Princeton, NJ: Princeton University Press, 1991), 127.

56. Marc Shell, "Marranos (Pigs), or from Coexistence to Toleration," *Critical Inquiry* 17 (1991): 306-35. The gloss of "marranos" in the title of Shell's essay is quite pointed: if we accept that the word not only means "pig," but derives from the Arabic *moharram*, "forbidden" or "dangerous" (see Claudine Fabre-Vassas, *The Singular Beast: Jews, Christians, and the Pig*, trans. Carol Volk [New York: Columbia University Press, 1997,] 123), we could come to the conclusion that the exclusion of those who did not eat pig was central to the identity of Catholic Spain.

57. Barbara Fuchs, "The Spanish Race," in *Rereading the Black Legend*, 93.

58. Robert Chazan, *Daggers of Faith: Thirteenth-Century Christian Missionizing and Jewish Response* (Berkeley: University of California Press, 1989), 5.

59. Catlos, Brian A. *Victors and the Vanquished: Christians and Muslims of Catalonia and Aragon, 1050-1300* (West Nyack, NY: Cambridge University Press, 2004), 407.

60. Quoted in Frank Manuel, *The Broken Staff: Judaism Through Christian Eyes* (Cambridge, MA: Harvard University Press, 1992), 1.

61. Ibid., 19.

62. Tolan, *Saracens*, 27-28.

63. Gilbert Dahan, *Les intellectuels chrétiens et les Juifs au Moyen Âge* (Paris: Le Cerf, 1990), 117; Kedar, *Crusade and Mission*, 210. In *Medieval Identity Machines*

(Minneapolis: University of Minnesota Press, 2003), Jeffrey Cohen concludes that in late medieval rhetoric, the "Saracen is a monster, an abject and phantasmatic body produced through category violation in order to demarcate the limits of the Christian possible" (202).

64. O'Callaghan, *Reconquest and Crusade*, 12.

65. Quoted in Adorno, *Guaman Poma*, 167.

66. Anthony Pagden, "*Ius et Factum*: Text and Experience in the Writings of Bartolomé de Las Casas," *Representations* 33 (1991): 156.

67. Barbara Fuchs, *Mimesis and Empire: The New World, Islam, and European Identities* (Cambridge: Cambridge University Press, 2001), 74–75.

68. Bernardino Vérastique, *Michoacán and Eden: Vasco de Quiroga and the Evangelization of Western Mexico* (Austin: University of Texas Press, 2000), 92.

69. Phelan, *The Millennial Kingdom of the Fransciscans*, 6.

70. Pick, *Conflict and Coexistence*, 133–34; Tolan, *Saracens*, 172–73.

71. Mary Elizabeth Perry, "Memory and Mutilation: The Case of the Moriscos," in *In the Light of Medieval Spain: Islam, the West, and the Relevance of the Past*, ed. Simon R. Doubleday and David Coleman (New York: Palgrave MacMillan, 2008), 75–76.

72. Iogna-Prat, *Order and Exclusion*, 348–49. The internal citation is to textual divisions in Reinhold Glei, ed., *Petrus Venerabilis Schriften zum Islam*, Corpus Islamico-Christianum, Series Latina, 1 (Altenberge: CIS-Verlag, 1985).

73. It has been suggested that the Inquisition moved on to surveillance of suspected former Muslim backsliders as Judaizers became unavailable; see Teofilo Ruiz, *Spanish Society, 1400–1600* (Harlow, UK: Longmans, 2001), 106.

74. Perry, *The Handless Maiden*, 3.

75. Ibid., 118.

76. Seed, *Ceremonies of Possession*, 85.

77. On the events of 1391, see Henry Kamen, *The Spanish Inquisition: A Historical Revision* (New Haven: Yale University Press, 1997), 11; for Muslims in the sixteenth century, see Harvey, *Muslims in Spain*, and Perry, *The Handless Maiden*; for Mexicans in the sixteenth century, see Osvaldo F. Pardo, *The Origins of Mexican Catholicism: Nahua Rituals and Christian Sacraments in Sixteenth-Century Mexico* (Ann Arbor: University of Michigan Press, 2004), especially 38–43.

78. Chejne, *Islam and the West*, 23–24.

79. Pardo, *The Origins of Mexican Catholicism*, 51.

80. Inga Clendinnen, " 'Fierce and Unnatural Cruelty': Cortés and the Conquest of Mexico," *Representations* 33 (1987): 72–92.

81. Pardo, *The Origins of Mexican Catholicism*, 37–43; Kamen, *The Spanish Inquisition*, 223.

82. Perry, *The Handless Maiden*, 38.

83. Pardo, *The Origins of Mexican Catholicism*, 59.

84. Fuchs, *Mimesis and Empire*, 104.

85. Harvey, *Muslims in Spain*, 112–13.

86. Perry, *The Handless Maiden*, 51, 69.

87. Harvey, *Muslims in Spain*, 76, 94, 103.

88. Tueller, *Good and Faithful Christians*, 205.

89. Cohen, *Medieval Identity Machines*, 202.

90. Strickland, *Saracens, Demons, and Jews*, 202.

91. Kathleen Biddick, *The Typological Imaginary: Circumcision, Technology, History* (Philadelphia: University of Pennsylvania Press, 2004), 11–12.

92. Pope Benedict XVI, "Prepolitical Moral Foundations of a Free Republic," in *Political Theologies*, ed. Hent de Vries and Lawrence E. Sullivan (New York: Fordham University Press, 2006), 265–66.

CHAPTER THREE

1. Augustine, *Confessions* 2:8, cited in Sarah Beckwith, *Christ's Body: Identity, Culture and Society in Late Medieval Writings* (New York: Routledge, 1993), 22.

2. Jeremy Cohen, *Living Letters of the Law: Ideas of the Jew in Medieval Christianity* (Berkeley: University of California Press), 93.

3. Lucy Pick, citing Peter Linehan, points out that "during the 1180s . . . Alfonso VIII began to depict himself as the defender of Christendom and the Christian religion, not just of Spain and its Christians." Lucy Pick, *Conflict and Coexistence: Archbishop Rodrigo and the Muslims and Jews of Medieval Spain* (Ann Arbor: University of Michigan Press, 2004), 26.

4. Missionaries per se, as opposed to Spanish priests ministering to the colonists, began arriving in mainland New Spain in the 1520s: the Franciscans in 1524, the Dominicans in 1526, the Augustinians in 1533, and eventually the Jesuits in 1572. Jerry M. Williams and Robert E. Lewis, eds., *Early Images of the Americas: Transfer and Invention* (Tucson: University of Arizona Press), xx. See also Robert Ricard, *The Spiritual Conquest of Mexico: An Essay on the Apostolate and the Evangelizing Methods of the Mendicant Orders in New Spain: 1523–1572*, trans. Lesley B. Simpson (Berkeley: University of California Press, 1966), 3, and Doris Heyden, translator's introduction, *The History of the Indies of New Spain: Fray Diego Durán* (Norman: University of Oklahoma Press, 1994), xxv.

5. This image is exploited, for instance, on the cover illustration of Derrida's *The Other Heading*. Jacques Derrida, *The Other Heading: Reflections on Today's Europe* (Bloomington: Indiana University Press, 1992).

6. Pick, *Conflict and Coexistence*, 57, 46, 125.

7. Robin Wright, *Stolen Continents: The "New World" Through Indian Eyes* (Boston: Houghton Mifflin, 1992), 12.

8. Miguel Ladero Quesada, "Spain, Circa 1492: Social Values and Structures," in *Implicit Understandings: Observing, Reporting, and Reflecting on the Encounters between Europeans and Other Peoples in the Early Modern Era*, ed. Stuart B. Schwartz (New York: Cambridge University Press, 1994), 106.

9. María Rosa Menocal, *Shards of Love: Exile and the Origins of the Lyric* (Durham, NC: Duke University Press, 1994), 43.

10. Judith Herrin, *The Formation of Christendom* (Princeton, NJ: Princeton University Press, 1987); Herbert Eugene Bolton, *Rim of Christendom: A Biography of Eusebio Francisco Kino, Pacific Coast Pioneer* (Tucson: University of Arizona Press, 1974; originally published 1936).

11. "Tactics and strategies deployed through implantations, distributions, demarcations, control of territories and organisations of domains . . . could well make up a sort of geopolitics." Michel Foucault, "Questions on Geography," in *Power/Knowledge: Selected Interviews and Other Writings, 1972–1977*, ed. Colin Gordon (New York: Pantheon, 1980), 77.

12. "Newfound lands were considered *terrae nullius* . . . because they did not belong to a Christian prince. . . . Pedro Mártir de Anglería . . . at the beginning of the fifteenth century defended European hegemony over every place in the New World that is 'empty of Christians.'" Luis N. Rivera, *A Violent Evangelism: The Political and Religious Conquest of the Americas* (Louisville, KY: Westminster/John Knox Press, 1992), 11. Very early in the expansion of Europe, the idea that land was empty if its occupants were not Christians was combined with the notion that it was empty if it was not being effectively husbanded. Lands in eastern Europe settled by Cistercians in the late Middle Ages were described in this way. As Robert Bartlett notes, "The spread of cult and the spread of [cereal] cultivation went hand in hand." Even more remarkable was the propagation of a revisionist historical memory by Cistercian settlers in the Polish region of Henryków, where there had in fact been earlier settlement: "The monks progressively obliterated the memory of these earlier settlers in favor of a founding myth of pioneers in an empty land." Robert Bartlett, *The Making of Europe: Conquest, Colonization and Cultural Change, 950–1350* (Princeton, NJ: Princeton University Press, 1993), 153–54. The parallels with the ideological history of European settlement in North America are striking. See, for example, Henry Nash Smith, *Virgin Land: The American West as Symbol and Myth* (Cambridge, MA: Harvard University Press, 1970; originally published 1950), Perry Miller, *Errand into the Wilderness* (Cambridge, MA: Belknap Press of Harvard University Press, 1956), and Myra Jehlen, *American Incarnation: The Individual, the Nation, and the Continent* (Cambridge, MA: Harvard University Press, 1986).

13. Bartlett, *The Making of Europe*, 5.

14. Bernard F. Reilly, *The Medieval Spains* (Cambridge: Cambridge University Press, 1993), 92.

15. Talal Asad, *Genealogies of Religion: Discipline and Reasons of Power in Christianity and Islam* (Baltimore: Johns Hopkins University Press, 1993), 160.

16. Gustavo Gutiérrez, *Las Casas: In Search of the Poor of Jesus Christ*, trans. Robert E. Barr (Maryknoll, NY: Orbis Books, 1993); Osvaldo F. Pardo, *The Origins of Mexican Catholicism: Nahua Rituals and Christian Sacraments in Sixteenth-Century Mexico* (Ann Arbor: University of Michigan Press, 2004), 19.

17. See Xavier Rubert de Ventós, *The Hispanic Labyrinth: Tradition and Modernity in the Colonization of the Americas*, trans. Mary Ann Newman (New Brunswick, NJ: Transaction Books, 1991), 40 ff.; Bernardino Vérastique, *Michoacán and Eden: Vasco de Quiroga and the Evangelization of Western Mexico* (Austin: University of Texas Press, 2000), 124. The reductions did not last, and the experiment was a failure. See Nancy M. Farriss, *Maya Society under Colonial Rule: The Collective Enterprise of Survival* (Princeton, NJ: Princeton University Press, 1984), 206.

18. William L. Merrill, "Conversion and Colonialism in Northern Mexico: The Tarahumara Response to the Jesuit Mission Program, 1601–1767," in *Conversion to Christianity: Historical and Anthropological Perspectives on a Great Transformation* (Berkeley: University of California Press, 1993); Donald K. Pollock, "Conversion and 'Community' in Amazonia," in *Conversion to Christianity*, 166.

19. Merrill, "Conversion and Colonialism," 135.

20. L.P. Harvey, *Islamic Spain, 1250–1500* (Chicago: University of Chicago Press, 1990), 64.

21. Bartlett, *The Making of Europe*, 23.

22. Kenneth R. Stow, *Alienated Minority: The Jews of Medieval Latin Europe* (Cambridge, MA: Harvard University Press, 1992), 304.

23. Max Weinreich, "The Reality of Jewishness versus the Ghetto Myth: The Sociolinguistic Roots of Yiddish," in *To Honor Roman Jakobson*, vol. 3 (The Hague: Mouton, 1967), 2199–2212. The situation was similar in Muslim Spain. See the schematic maps of the Jewish quarters of several Iberian cities in the ninth and tenth centuries provided in Eliyahu Ashtor, *The Jews of Moslem Spain*, vol. 1, trans. Aaron Klein and Jenny Machlowitz Klein (Philadelphia: Jewish Publication Society, 1973), 293, 301, 311, 322, 329, 333.

24. Stow, *Alienated Minority*, 305.

25. Peter Brown, *Authority and the Sacred: Aspects of the Christianization of the Roman World* (Cambridge: Cambridge University Press, 1995), 10–11.

26. *Encyclopaedia Britannica*, 15th ed. (1992), vol. 16, s.v. Christianity at 253b; see also Jaroslav Pelikan, *The Growth of Medieval Theology (600–1300)* (Chicago: University of Chicago Press, 1978), 11.

27. Averil Cameron, *Christianity and the Rhetoric of Empire* (Berkeley: University of California Press, 1991), 136.

28. Peter Brown, *The Rise of Western Christendom: Triumph and Diversity, A.D. 200–1000*, 2nd ed. (Malden, MA: Blackwell, 2003), 4. The somewhat defensive and resentful undercurrent that lurks beneath the surface of the fourth-century military oath just quoted might well reflect relatively recent Christian memories of having been persecuted within this same Roman empire. The claim by which the fifth-century Vincent of Lérins, a Gallic theologian, provided a formula according to which Christianity expressed a faith that "has been believed everywhere, always, and by all" (quoted in *Encyclopaedia Britannica*, 15th ed. (1992), vol. 16, s.v. Christianity at 253b) should of course not be taken to indicate that by the time the oath was uttered, everyone in the

Roman Empire was already Christian. Peter Brown, *Power and Persuasion in Late Antiquity: Towards a Christian Empire* (Madison: University of Wisconsin Press, 1992), 128–29.

29. Alfred Hiatt, "Mapping the Ends of Empire," in Ananya Jahanara Kabir and Deanne Williams, eds., *Postcolonial Approaches to the European Middle Ages: Translating Cultures* (Cambridge: Cambridge University Press, 2005), 48–76.

30. Harvey, *Islamic Spain*, 64.

31. James Muldoon, ed., *The Expansion of Europe* (Philadelphia: University of Pennsylvania Press, 1977), viii.

32. Contrast the careful distinctions drawn by Barbara Fuchs, discussing Torquato Tasso's poem *Gerusalemme liberata* (1581) and *Gerusalemme conquistata* (1593), treated by Fuchs as one work. As she notes, Tasso's "imaginary Europe—unproblematically and univocally identified with Christendom—dissimulates the bitter imperial and religious rivalries that marked the poet's era." Barbara Fuchs, *Mimesis and Empire: The New World, Islam, and European Identities* (Cambridge: Cambridge University Press, 2001), 25. John van Engen makes a similar albeit more general point: "Medieval religious life included a constant struggle to establish or renew Christian religious culture in the face of various other religious practices." John Van Engen, "The Christian Middle Ages as an Historiographic Problem," *American Historical Review* 91, no. 3 (1986): 537–38. Christendom was constituted not, or certainly not only, by the fact of unity but against difference.

33. Williams and Lewis, *Early Images of the Americas*, xiv, xxi. In her contribution to the same volume, Patricia Seed refers more succinctly to "Christian (that is, European) rulers," a much more defensible equivalence than that between Christianity and European society. Patricia Seed, "Taking Possession and Reading Texts: Establishing the Authority of Overseas Empires," in *Early Images of the Americas*, 115.

34. The awkward place of Jews in this discourse, early and late, is thus an unexpectedly literal illustration of the point that Eurocentrism should not be understood simply as a geographical standpoint. As Josè Rabasa puts it, "Eurocentrism is not an 'out there' that we can identify, but the locus where minor discourses intervene." José Rabasa, "Dialogue as Conquest: Mapping Spaces for Counter-Discourse," in *The Nature and Context of Minority Discourse*, ed. Abdul R. JanMohamed and David Lloyd (New York: Oxford University Press, 1990), 213. But Jewish difference is again effaced by his reference to "the inner Other—that all too Eurocentric Self that haunts the ethnographer's most venerable intentions." (Ibid.) This formulation aptly expresses the element of doubt and doubling that helps to drive the dominant construction of Otherness. In psychologizing internal difference, however, it calls for a reminder about the historical inner Others of Christian Europe.

35. Perhaps the most famous example is Hugh Trevor-Roper, *The Rise of Christian Europe* (New York: Harcourt Brace and World, 1965).

36. Herrin, *The Formation of Christendom*, 477.

37. Ibid., 479.

38. Jacques Le Goff, *Intellectuals in the Middle Ages* (Cambridge, MA: Blackwell, 1993), xiv, xxiv.

39. Robert F. Berkhofer, *The White Man's Indian* (New York: Alfred A. Knopf, 1978), 24.

40. Denys Hay, *Europe: The Emergence of an Idea* (Edinburgh: Edinburgh University Press, 1957), x.

41. Charles Taylor, "Modes of Civil Society," *Public Culture 3* (Fall 1990), 102.

42. John Milbank, *Theology and Social Theory: Beyond Secular Reason* (New York: Blackwell, 1990), 9.

43. Hans J. Hillenbrand, *The Division of Christendom: Christianity in the Sixteenth Century* (Louisville: Westminster/John Knox Press, 2007), 343.

44. K.J. Leyser, "Concepts of Europe in the Early and High Middle Ages," Past and Present 137 (1992), 25–47, at 37.

45. Jeremy Cohen, *The Friars and the Jews: The Evolution of Medieval Anti-Judaism* (Ithaca, NY: Cornell University Press, 1982), 248, 252.

46. Bartlett, *The Making of Europe*, 7–9.

47. Miri Rubin, *Gentile Tales: The Narrative Assault on Late Medieval Jews* (New Haven: Yale University Press, 1999), 28–29. Conversely, Israel Jacob Yuval, pointing to reports (which he finds credible) of "Jews pour[ing] the milk [of Christian wet nurses] into the latrine so that their children would not drink milk derived from the host," has argued that medieval Jewish polemicists and liturgical poets (*paytanim*) "internalized the Christian notion of the Eucharist as it is expressed in the eating of the host by the congregation and the drinking of the wine by the priest." Israel Jacob Yuval, " 'They Tell Lies: You Ate the Man': Jewish Reactions to Ritual Murder Accusations," in *Religious Violence between Christians and Jews: Medieval Roots, Modern* Perspectives, ed. Anna Sapir Abulafia (New York: Palgrave, 2002), 97.

48. Kilgour, *From Communion to Cannibalism*, 4–19.

49. Rubin, *Gentile Tales*, 54.

50. The significance of the Inquisition in particular as a technique serving the ideological unification of Catholic Europe is worth insisting on here, especially since we still tend to think of the Inquisition in terms of its later revival in Spain. Jean-Pierre Guicciardi argues for this view of the medieval Inquisition: "Through its unity, its centralized structure, the veritable *web* that it wove throughout all of Europe, the Inquisition doubtless constituted a powerful factor of ideological and perhaps political unification, whose effects have not yet been thoroughly measured." Jean-Pierre Guicciardi, Introduction to *Abrégé du manuel des inquisiteurs*, ed. André Morellete (Grenoble: Jérôme Millon, 1990), 31–32.

51. Henri Baudet, *Paradise on Earth: Some Thoughts on European Images of Non-European Man* (New Haven: Yale University Press, 1965), 30.

52. See Daniel Boyarin and Jonathan Boyarin, "Diaspora: Generation and the Ground of Jewish Identity." *Critical Inquiry* 19, no. 4 (1993), 709.

53. Merrill, "Conversion and Colonialism," 138, 139.

54. See Daniel Boyarin, *Carnal Israel: Reading Sex in Talmudic Culture* (Berkeley: University of California Press, 1993) and *A Radical Jew: Paul and the Politics of Identity* (Berkeley: University of California Press, 1994).

55. Anthony Pagden, *The Fall of Natural Man* (New York: Columbia University Press, 1986), 143. Meanwhile, Spanish writers could also employ the reference to the inferior moral character of Jewish carnal practice in ways unflattering to the Spanish themselves. Thus, Gerónimo de Mendieta declared that "the Spaniards, like the Jews in Paul's time . . . glory in the 'outward circumcision'; whereas the recently converted Indians, like the Gentiles of antiquity, understand that 'true circumcision is achieved in the heart, according to the spirit, not the letter of the law, for God's not man's approval.'" Quoted in Phelan, *The Millennial Kingdom of the Franciscans*, 88.

56. Stafford C. M. Poole, "The Declining Image of the Indian among Churchmen in Sixteenth-Century Spain," in *Indian-Religious Relations in Colonial Spanish America*, ed. Susan E. Ramírez (Syracuse, NY: Maxwell School of Citizenship and Public Affairs, 1989), 15.

57. MacCormack, *Religion in the Andes*, 16.

58. Ibid., 26.

59. J.H. Burns, ed., *The Cambridge History of Medieval Political Thought: C. 350–C. 1450* (New York: Cambridge University Press, 1988), 659.

60. Howard Eilberg-Schwartz, *The Savage in Judaism* (Bloomington: Indiana University Press, 1990).

61. R.I. Moore, *The Formation of a Persecuting Society: Power and Deviance in Western Europe, 950–1250* (New York: Basil Blackwell, 1987).

62. Cited in Pierre Vidal-Nacquet, "Herodote et l'Atlantide: Entre les Grecs et les Juifs. Reflexions sur l'historiographie du siècle des Lumieres," *Quaderni di storia* 16 (1982), 5–74, at 30–31.

CHAPTER FOUR

1. "A few decades before the emergence of an unknown (from the perspective of European observers) continent and unknown people inhabiting it, geographical boundaries coincided with the boundaries of humanity." Walter D.Mignolo, "Globalization, Civilizing Processes, and the Relocation of Languages and Cultures," in *The Cultures of Globalization*, ed. Fredric Jameson and Masao Miyoshi (Durham and London: Duke University Press, 1998), 35.

2. Anthony Pagden, *The Fall of Natural Man: The American Indian and the Origins of Comparative Ethnology* (New York: Columbia University Press, 1986), 119.

3. Patricia Seed, *American Pentimento: The Invention of Indians and the Pursuit of Riches* (Minneapolis: University of Minnesota Press, 2001), 66.

4. Denise Kimber Buell, *Why This New Race: Ethnic Reasoning in Early Christianity* (New York: Columbia University Press, 2005).

5. Denise Kimber Buell, "Race and Universalism in Early Christianity," *Journal of Early Christian Studies* 10, no. 4 (2002): 430.

6. *Strōmateis* 7.93.4–5, cited in Denise Kimber Buell, *Making Christians: Clement of Alexandria and the Rhetoric of Legitimacy* (Princeton, NJ: Princeton University Press, 1999), 98.

7. Buell, "Race and Universalism," 430–31.

8. Buell, *Why This New Race*, 77–78.

9. Anna Sapir Abulafia, *Christians and Jews in the Twelfth-Century Renaissance* (London: Routledge, 1995), 6.

10. Ibid., 7; see also Karl F. Morrison, *Understanding Conversion* (Charlottesville: University of Virginia Press, 1992), 75.

11. Jonathan Elukin, "The Discovery of the Self: Jews and Conversion in the Twelfth Century," in *Jews and Christians in Twelfth-Century Europe*, ed. Michael A. Singer and John van Engen (Notre Dame, IN: Notre Dame University Press, 2001), 72.

12. Georgina Dopico Black, *Perfect Wives, Other Women: Adultery and Inquisition in Early Modern Spain* (Durham, NC: Duke University Press, 2001), 8–9.

13. Quoted in ibid., 2–3.

14. Tzvetan Todorov would hardly dare advance the claim that if the capitulation of Moctezuma to Cortès can be attributed to the cyclical worldview and failure of reflexive consciousness among the Aztecs, as he says in *The Conquest of America*, then the failure of Jews to maintain their place in Christian Spain was due to similar causes. Indeed, once we grant that Todorov has not given the Aztecs their due, we are led to question his account of the "Spaniards" as well, and particularly his assumption that notions of linearity offer a better fit with reality and thus access to greater material power. Todorov's general framework is clearly biased toward a notion of progress: "By his mental structures, which link him to the medieval conception of knowledge, Columbus is closer to those whom he discovered than to some of his own companions: how shocked he would have been to hear it!" Tzvetan Todorov, *The Conquest of America: The Question of the Other* (New York: Harper and Row, 1984), 75.

15. Patricia Seed, "'Are These Not Also Men?': The Indians' Humanity and Capacity for Spanish Civilisation," *Journal of Latin American Studies* 25 (1993): 636–37. Such a distinction between humans and animals would itself have required explanation to the Nahua targets of Spanish missionizing. "The Nahuas did not set humanity off from the rest of nature like Christianity does. Human beings were a part of the world; the world was not something to be rejected or striven against." Louise M. Burckhardt, *The Slippery Earth: Nahua-Christian Moral Dialogue in Sixteenth-Century Mexico* (Tucson: The University of Arizona Press, 1989), 48.

Note also Anthony Pagden's claim that "for the Thomists," neither the Decalogue nor the Gospels had the character of natural law. Anthony Pagden, "The Search for Order: The School of Salamanca and the 'Ius Naturae,'" in *The Uncertainties of*

Empire: Essays in Iberian and Ibero-American Intellectual History, Collected Studies Series (Brookfield, VT: Ashgate Publishing 1994), 158). Jaroslav Pelikan suggests an important distinction in late medieval Catholic thought between knowledge, attainable by nature, of "the existence of God, and even the supreme goodness of God," and knowledge of the Trinity, which according to Aquinas was unattainable by natural reason. Jaroslav Pelikan, *The Growth of Medieval Theology (600–1300)* (Chicago: University of Chicago Press, 1978), 286–88.

16. Beatriz Pastor Bodmer, *The Armature of Conquest: Spanish Accounts of the Discovery of America*, 1492–1589, trans. Lydia Longstreth Hunt (Stanford, CA: Stanford University Press, 1992), 17, 128.

17. "America existed as a legal document before it was physically discovered." Roberto González-Echevarría, "The Law of the Letter: Garcilaso's *Commentaries* and the Origins of Latin American Narrative," *Yale Journal of Criticism* 1:1 (1987), 108.

18. See Myra Jehlen, "History before the Fact; Or, Captain John Smith's Unfinished Symphony," *Critical Inquiry* 19:4 (1993), 677–92.

19. David E. Stannard, *American Holocaust: Columbus and the Conquest of the New World* (New York: Oxford University Press, 1992), 183.

20. Gilbert Dahan, *Les Intellectuels chretiens et les Juifs au Moyen Age* (Paris: Le Cerf, 1990), 519.

21. Dwayne E. Carpenter, "Social Perception and Literary Portrayal: Jews and Muslims in Medieval Spanish Literature," in *Convivencia: Jews, Muslims, and Christians in Medieval Spain*, ed. Vivian B. Mann, Thomas F. Glick, and Jerrilynn D. Dodds (New York: George Braziller, 1992).

22. Kathleen Kulp-Hill, trans., *Songs of Holy Mary of Alfonso X, the Wise: A Translation of the Cantigas de Santa María* (Tempe: Arizona Center for Medieval and Renaissance Studies, 2000), 135.

23. Jeremy Cohen, *The Friars and the Jews: The Evolution of Medieval Anti-Judaism* (Ithaca, NY: Cornell University Press, 1982), 24; see also his *Living Letters of the Law: Ideas of the Jew in Medieval Christianity* (Berkeley: University of California Press, 1999), 259.

24. Brigitte Miriam Bedos-Rezak, "Les Juifs et l'écrit dans la mentalité eschatologique du Moyen Age chrétien occidental (France 1000–1200)," *Annales* 49:5 (1994), 1062–63.

25. Iogna-Prat, *Order and Exclusion*, 301.

26. Ivan G. Marcus, "A Jewish-Christian Symbiosis: The Culture of Early Ashkenaz," in *Cultures of the Jews: A New History*, ed. David Biale (New York: Schocken Books, 2002), 478–84; Israel Jacob Yuval, *Two Nations in Your Womb: Perceptions of Jews and Christians in Late Antiquity and the Middle Ages* (Berkeley: University of California Press, 2006).

27. Michael Taussig, *The Devil and Commodity Fetishism in Latin America* (Chapel Hill: University of North Carolina Press, 1980), and *Shamanism, Colonialism, and*

the Wild Man: A Study in Terror and Healing (Chicago: University of Chicago Press, 1987).

28. See, for example, Frank Manuel, *The Broken Staff: Judaism through Christian Eyes* (Cambridge, MA: Harvard University Press, 1992), 24–25.

29. John Tolan, *Petrus Alfonsí and His Medieval Readers* (Gainesville: University Press of Florida, 1993).

30. Discussed in Inga Clendinnen, *Ambivalent Conquests: Maya and Spaniard in Yucatan, 1517–1560* (New York: Cambridge University Press, 1987).

31. Alan Dundes, ed., *The Blood Libel Legend: A Casebook in Anti-Semitic Folklore* (Madison: University of Wisconsin Press, 1991); Clendinnen, Ambivalent Conquests, 191. For a signal contribution to the explication of this logic—one drawing heavily on structural anthropology and psychoanalysis, rather than on literary analysis—see Claudine Fabre-Vassas, *The Singular Beast: Jews, Christians, and the Pig*, trans. Carol Volk (New York: Columbia University Press, 1997).

32. José Alcina Franch, "Introduccion," in *Diego Andres Rocha, el prigen de los Indios* (Madrid: Historia 16, 1988), 14.

33. Joshua Trachtenberg, *The Devil and the Jews: The Medieval Conception of the Jew and Its Relation to Modern Antisemitism* (Cleveland: World Publishing Company, 1961; first published 1943).

34. Caroline Walker Bynum, *The Resurrection of the Body in Western Christianity, 200–1336* (New York: Columbia University Press, 1995), 56.

35. J.H. Elliot, *The Old World and the New, 1492–1650* (Cambridge: Cambridge University Press, 1970), 42–43.

36. Bodmer, *The Armature of Conquest*, 208.

37. Cited in Michael Palencia-Roth, "The Cannibal Law of 1503," in *Early Images of the Americas: Transfer and Invention*, ed. Jerry M. Williams and Robert E. Lewis (Tucson: University of Arizona Press, 1993), 28.

38. Barbara Fuchs, *Mimesis and Empire: The New World, Islam, and European Identities* (Cambridge: Cambridge University Press, 2001), 44.

39. Gustavo Gutiérrez, *Las Casas: In Search of the Poor of Jesus Christ*, trans. Robert E. Barr (Maryknoll, NY: Orbis Books, 1993).

40. William E. Connolly, "Identity and Difference in Global Politics," in *Intertextual/International Relations: Postmodern Readings of World Politics*, ed. James Der Derian and Michael Shapiro (Lexington, MA: D.C. Heath and Company, 1989), 330.

41. Walden Browne, *Sahagún and the Transition to Modernity* (Norman: University of Oklahoma Press, 2000), 72–73.

42. Seed, " 'Are These Not Also Men?' "

43. Osvaldo F. Pardo, *The Origins of Mexican Catholicism: Nahua Rituals and Christian Sacraments in Sixteenth-Century Mexico* (Ann Arbor: University of Michigan Press, 2004), 50, 51.

44. Ibid., 28.

45. Luis N. Rivera, *A Violent Evangelism: The Political and Religious Conquest of the Americas* (Louisville, KY: Westminster/John Knox Press, 1992), 289n.22.

46. Alcina Franch, "Introduccion," 11; John Leddy Phelan, *The Millennial Kingdom of the Franciscans in the New World*, 2nd ed. (Berkeley: University of California Press, 1970).

47. See Robert F. Berkhofer, *The White Man's Indian* (New York: Alfred A. Knopf, 1978).

48. Fuchs, *Mimesis and Empire*, 78.

49. John Edwards, "La prehistoria de los estatutos de 'limpieza de sangre,'" in *Xudeus e conversos na historia*, ed. Carlos Barros (Santiago de Compostela: La Editorial de la Historia, 1994), 355.

50. Kenneth Stow, *Jewish Dogs: An Image and its Interpreters: Continuity in the Catholic-Jewish Encounter* (Stanford, CA; Stanford University Press, 2006).

51. Marc Shell, "Marranos (Pigs), or from Coexistence to Toleration," *Critical Inquiry* 17 (1991), 306–35. The classification of certain kinds of people as bestial, especially for juridical purposes, came more fully into vogue toward the end of the period covered in this book. "More alarming still is the burning of a Parisian together with his Jewish mistress on a charge of bestiality recorded by Nicholas Boër in his *Decisiones aureae Parlamenti Burdegalensis* (Lyon, 1620). Evans cites another seventeenth-century authority which justified such actions on the grounds that 'coition with a Jewess is precisely the same as if a man should copulate with a dog.' In a discussion of crimes against nature ('Vuylle faycten iegens der nature'), the distinguished Belgian jurist, Joos de Damhoudere, described the crime of bestiality as the worst of these crimes, for which the punishment was burning. What is remarkable is that he included intercourse with Turks, Saracens or Jews in the same category 'inasmuch as such persons in the eye of the law and our holy faith differ in no wise from beasts because of their hostility to the Christian faith.'" Peter Mason, "The Excommunication of Caterpillars: Ethno-Anthropological Remarks on the Trial and Punishment of Animals," *Social Science Information* 27 (1988), 268. Here the identification of Christianity with humanity could not be any more exact.

52. Cited in *Dahan, Les intellectuels chrétiens et les Juifs*, 150.

53. Of course, Spanish writers could make arguments that were at the same time humanitarian and paternalistic. One such was Gerónimo de Mendieta, who referred to the Indians as "children" in need of "fathers." Phelan, *The Millennial Kingdom of the Franciscans*, 8, 25.

54. *Dahan, Les intellectuels chrétiens et les Juifs*, 151. Dahan cites *Quodl.* II, q. 4, a. 2, "Utrum parvuli Iudaeorum sint baptizandi initis parentibus," ed. R. Spiazzi, *Questiones quodlibetales* (Turin, 1956), 28–29.

55. Stephen Greenblatt, *Marvelous Possessions: The Wonder of the New World* (Chicago: University of Chicago Press, 1991), 138.

56. William L. Merrill, "Conversion and Colonialism in Northern Mexico: The Tarahumara Response to the Jesuit Mission Program, 1601–1767," in *Conversion to*

Christianity: Historical and Anthropological Perspectives on a Great Transformation, ed. Robert W. Hefner (Berkeley: University of California Press, 1993), 140.

57. J. H. Elliott, "The Spanish Conquest and Settlement of America," in *The Cambridge History of Latin America*, vol. 1 (Cambridge: Cambridge University Press, 1984), 174.

58. Anthony Pagden, "The Humanism of Vasco de Quiroga's 'Información en Derecho,'" in *The Uncertainties of Empire: Essays in Iberian and Ibero-American Intellectual History*, Collected Studies Series (Brookfield, VT: Ashgate Publishing, 1994), 165, citing Gonzalo de las Casas (1587–88).

59. Judith Laikin Elkin, "Imagining Idolatry: Missionaries, Indians, and Jews," in *Religion and the Authority of the Past*, ed. Tobin Siebers (Ann Arbor: University of Michigan Press, 1993), 97.

60. Ibid.

61. Quoted in Lewis Hanke, *The Spanish Struggle for Justice in the Conquest of America* (Boston: Little, Brown and Company, 1965), 175. Compare the rhetoric of Jerome: "'He whom we look down upon, whom we cannot bear to see, the very sight of whom causes us to vomit, is the same as we, formed with us from the self-same clay, compacted of the same elements. Whatever he suffers, we also suffer.'" Quoted in Peter Brown, *Power and Persuasion in Late Antiquity: Towards a Christian Empire* (Madison: University of Wisconsin Press, 1992), 153.

62. Dahan, *Les intellectuels chrétiens et les Juifs*, 528; Jeffrey Cohen, *Medieval Identity Machines* (Minneapolis: University of Minnesota Press, 2002), 201.

63. Cohen, *Medieval Identity Machines*, 193.

64. Albert A. Sicroff, *Les controverses des statuts de 'pureté de sang' en Espagne du 15e au 17e siècle* (Paris: Didier, 1960), 27, citing Henry Charles Lea, *A History of the Inquisition of Spain*, vol. 1 (New York: AMS Press, 1988; originally published 1906), 75–76.

65. However, one leading scholar strenuously cautions against "any idea of a *limpieza* mania sweeping the country" and insists that it never became "a national obsession." Henry Kamen, *The Spanish Inquisition: A Historical Revision* (New Haven: Yale University Press, 1997), 239, 252.

66. Perez Zagorin, *Ways of Lying: Dissimulation, Persecution, and Conformity in Early Modern Europe* (Cambridge, MA: Harvard University Press, 1990); Shell, "Marranos (Pigs)"; Henry Kamen, *Inquisition and Society in Spain in the Sixteenth and Seventeenth Centuries* (Bloomington: Indiana University Press, 1982).

67. David Nirenberg, "Conversion, Sex, and Segregation: Jews and Christians in Medieval Spain," *American Historical Review* 107 (October 2002): 1069.

68. David Nirenberg, "Mass Conversion and Genealogical Mentalities: Jews and Christians in Fifteenth-Century Spain," *Past and Present* 174 (February 2002): 6–7.

69. Kamen, *The Spanish Inquisition*, 34.

70. Sicroff, *Les controverses des statuts de 'pureté de sang*,' 65.

71. Kamen, *The Spanish Inquisition*, 35.

72. See esp. Homi K. Bhabha, *The Location of Culture* (New York: Routledge, 1994).

73. Sicroff, *Les controverses des statuts de 'pureté de sang,'* 69.

74. Ibid., 79. John W. O'Malley stresses that, following the example of Ignatius, the Jesuits for their part refused at least in principle to discriminate on the basis of blood "until 1593, when the Fifth General Congregation, in the wake of a severe internal crisis, absolutely excluded from entrance persons of Jewish or Muslim descent." John W. O'Malley, *The First Jesuits* (Cambridge, MA: Harvard University Press, 1993), 189.

75. Sicroff, *Les controverses des statuts de 'pureté de sang,'* 74.

76. David Nirenberg, "Race and the Middle Ages: The Case of Spain and Its Jews," in *Rereading the Black Legend: The Discourses of Religions and Racial Difference in the Renaissance Empires*, ed. Margaret R. Greer, Walter D. Mignolo, and Maureen Quilligan (Chicago: University of Chicago Press, 2007), 82.

77. Ibid., 77.

78. Maurice Kriegel points to a divergence of interests in the period leading up to the Expulsion, as well, between the institution of the Inquisition in general and the monarchy: "In reality, the Inquisitorial milieux were motivated by a generalized antisemitism, which demanded the expulsion of Jews on the one hand, and repressive politics against the conversos on the other; while the sovereigns could claim on their own behalf the Inquisitorial discourse without any manipulative intention conditioning their usage of it, because they hoped indeed that the disappearance of the Jewish presence as a counter-acculturating factor would make it possible to envisage full integration of the conversos into global society: the agreement on the decision hides a disagreement over the reasons for the decision." Maurice Kriegel, "De la 'question' des 'nouveaux-chrétiens' á l'expulsion des juifs: la double modernité des procès d'exclusion dans l'Espagne du quinzième siècle," in *Le Nouveau Monde, mondes nouveaux,* ed. Serge Gruzinski and Natan Wachtel (Paris: Éditions Recherche sur les Civilisations; Éditions de l'École des Hautes Études en Sciences Sociales, 1996), 487.

79. Sicroff, *Les controverses des statuts de 'pureté de sang,'* 85.

80. Elliott, "The Spanish Conquest and Settlement of America," 201.

81. Charles H. Lippy, Robert Choquette, and Stafford Poole, *Christianity Comes to the Americas* (New York: Paragon House, 1992), 14.

82. María Elena Martínez, "Interrogating Blood Lines: 'Purity of Blood,' the Inquisition, and *Casta* Categories," in *Religion in New Spain*, ed. Susan Schroder and Stafford Poole (Albuquerque: University of New Mexico Press, 2007), 196–217. The standards that were eventually declared hardly constituted a "one drop" rule for barring those with native ancestry, but permitted rather as much as one native grandparent (210). Also, "it is clear that by the late sixteenth century the discourse of limpieza de sangre was being extended to blacks" (209).

83. María Elena Martínez, "The Black Blood of New Spain: *Limpieza de Sangre*, Racial Violence, and Gendered Power in Early Colonial Mexico," *William and Mary Quarterly* LXI:3 (2004), 481–520, at 494.

84. Luis Pericot, *América Indígena: El hombre americano: Los pueblos de América*, 2nd ed. (Barcelona: Salvat Pericot, 1962), cited in Alcina Franch, "Introduccion," 31. Rocha's book can be found in a 2004 facsimile reprint of an 1891 edition. Unflattering comparisons to Indians could also be made between rival groups among the Spaniards. Thus Bernal Díaz del Castillo, on the expeditionary force under Pánfilo de Narváez that came to Mexico in May 1520 to challenge Cortés: "We come from Old Castile and are called Castilians, and that captain . . . and his men come from another province, called Vizcaya. They are called vizcaínos, and they speak like Otomi Indians." Quoted in Elliott, "The Spanish Conquest and Settlement of America," 178. By contrast, the trope of Spanish bravery extends even to the characterization of medieval Spanish Jewry by a twentieth-century Jewish historian: "Whereas the Jews in most lands in the Moslem East and Christian Europe were a minority, tolerated, persecuted, and helpless, the Jews of the Iberian peninsula were proud and courageous, ready to draw the sword and seize the spear, to be on close terms with kings and nobles of the land. Such were the Jews of Spain for hundreds of years, and such were they when the Moslems invaded this land and conquered it." Eliyahu Ashtor, *The Jews of Moslem Spain*, vol. 1, trans. Aaron Klein and Jenny Machlowitz Klein (Philadelphia: Jewish Publication Society, 1973), 25.

85. See Dahan, *Les intellectuels chrétiens et les Juifs*, 529; Peter Biller, "Views of Jews from Paris around 1300," *Studies in Church History* 29 (1992). Willis Johnson provides an extended analysis of what he calls "the myth of Jewish male menses," pointing out that in its antecedent versions "there is no evidence . . . that this infirmity was thought to indicate that Jewish men were feminine." Willis Johnson, "The Myth of Jewish Male Menses," *Journal of Medieval History* 24, no. 1 (1998): 287.

86. Todorov, *The Conquest of America*, 210.

87. Andrée Collard, Introduction to *History of the Indies: Bartolomé de Las Casas* (New York: Harper & Row, 1971), ix.

88. Bartolomé de Las Casas, *History of the Indies*, trans. and ed. Andrée Collard (New York: Harper & Row, 1971), 3–4; see also Anthony Pagden, "*Ius et Factum*: Text and Experience in the Writings of Bartolomé de Las Casas," *Representations* 33 (1991), 155.

89. Pagden, "*Ius et Factum*," 152.

90. Fernando Cervantes, *The Devil in the New World: The Impact of Diabolism in New Spain* (New Haven: Yale University Press, 1994), 39.

91. Ibid.

92. Cervantes does not cite Joshua Trachtenberg's *The Devil and the Jews*, first published in 1943. This is unfortunate for a book that claims "it is difficult to think of any recent studies that deal seriously with the subject of diabolism" (1), especially since Trachtenberg confronted precisely the same problem of taking diabolism seriously and eloquently insisted that understanding the Middle Ages was relevant at a time of contemporary disaster. See also Neil Forsyth, *The Old Enemy: Satan and the Combat Myth* (Princeton, NJ: Princeton University Press, 1989), and several books by Jeffrey

Burton Russell, such as *Lucifer, The Devil in the Middle Ages* (Ithaca, NY: Cornell University Press, 1984).

93. Each instance of such identification or confusion is, in the words of Cynthia Robinson and Leyla Rouhi, a "prooftruth"—"the word, the line, the motif, the monument, the *exemplum*, which was passed as-was (and left that way for easy future identification) across perceived cultural lines and which remains intact as testimony to such exchange." But, as they also imply, to focus overmuch on the documentation of such prooftruths almost inevitably reinforces the perception of the cultural "lines" whose very reification is under question. Editors' introduction to *Under the Influence: Questioning the Comparative in Medieval Castile* (Leiden: Brill, 2005), 1–18.

94. Merrill, "Conversion and Colonialism in Northern Mexico," 149–50.

95. See Shlomo Simonson, *The Apostolic See and the Jews: Vol. 1, Documents: 492–1404* (Toronto: Pontifical Institute of Mediaeval Studies, 1988), 183.

96. Pardo, *The Origins of Mexican Catholicism.*

CHAPTER FIVE

1. Nirenberg, David 2006. "Figures of Thought and Figures of Flesh: 'Jews' and 'Judaism' in Late-Medieval Spanish Poetry and Politics." *Speculum* 81 (2006), 398–426.

2. Norman Lewis, *The Missionaries: God Against the Indians* (London: Arena, 1988), 210.

3. Ibid. As Norman Lewis adds, "It seems common practice among the missionaries to accuse Indians of killing Christ."

4. David Lawton, *Blasphemy* (Philadelphia: University of Pennsylvania Press, 1993), 83.

5. My thanks to Jennifer Ottman for this point and for its wording.

6. Louise M. Burckhardt, *The Slippery Earth: Nahua-Christian Moral Dialogue in Sixteenth-Century Mexico* (Tucson: The University of Arizona Press, 1989), 53–54.

7. Osvaldo F. Pardo, *The Origins of Mexican Catholicism: Nahua Rituals and Christian Sacraments in Sixteenth-Century Mexico* (Ann Arbor: University of Michigan Press, 2004), 5.

8. Walter D. Mignolo, *The Darker Side of the Renaissance: Literacy, Territoriality and Colonization* (Ann Arbor: University of Michigan Press, 1995).

9. Ibid., 82.

10. Ibid., 17–18.

11. Brian Stock, *The Implications of Literacy* (Princeton, NJ: Princeton University Press, 1983), 7.

12. Patricia Seed, "Taking Possession and Reading Texts: Establishing the Authority of Overseas Empires," in *Early Images of the Americas: Transfer and Invention*, ed. Jerry M. Williams and Robert E. Lewis (Tucson: University of Arizona Press), 112.

13. Obviously, military conquest also was necessary in order to make the claim a "good" one. By contrast, at one moment on Columbus's second voyage he compelled his entire crew to declare that the southern coast of Cuba could not possibly be an island (and therefore had to be the Asian mainland); that claim was not a good one. Edmundo O'Gorman, *The Invention of America: An Inquiry Into the Historical Nature of the New World and the Meaning of Its History* (Bloomington: Indiana University Press, 1961), 89.

14. Cited in Gustavo Gutiérrez, *Las Casas: In Search of the Poor of Jesus Christ*, trans. Robert E. Barr (Maryknoll, NY: Orbis Books, 1993), 114.

15. Ibid., 115. The outcome of the process begun centuries earlier and farther north in Europe by which many of the literate and legal functions of priests began to be carried out by secular clerks is evident here. Certainly a priest *could* have carried out this function, yet there were in fact no priests along on Columbus's first voyage. Not until the second voyage, when "emphasis was laid on the conversion of the islanders," were missionary priests sent along. J.H. Elliott, "The Spanish Conquest and Settlement of America," in *The Cambridge History of Latin America*, vol. 1 (Cambridge: Cambridge University Press, 1984), 201. For thumbnail sketches of the accountants and notaries active in the original conquest of Peru, none of them evidently clerics, see James Lockhart, *The Men of Cajamarca: A Social and Biographical Study of the First Conquerors of Peru* (Austin: University of Texas Press, 1972), 258–86. Lockhart captures much of the cultural arsenal of Spanish conquest by stating of one of these men, "Aliaga was a conqueror by the book." Ibid., 259.

16. See Nirenberg, "Figures of Flesh," 416.

17. See W.D. Phillips, Jr., "Transatlantic Encounters: Eyewitness Testimony and Spain's First American Possession, 1492–1536," *Medieval Encounters* 13 (2007), 145–57, at 153.

18. Tomaž Mastnak, *Crusading Peace: Christendom, the Muslim World, and Western Political Order* (Berkeley: University of California Press, 2002), 52. In a rather different field of conflict, allusions to the early history of Christianity were rhetorically tempting to monastic polemicists. During debates between the Cluniacs and the Cistercians in the mid-twelfth century, the Cluniac "black-monk position was in part a sheer defence of the authority of accepted custom. As Matthew of Albano demanded to know, 'What is this new law? What is this new teaching?' They found particularly offensive the Cistercian claim to a monopoly of the Rule of Benedict, which they alone observed literally: 'a new race of Pharisees comes back to the world, who set themselves apart and prefer themselves to others.'" Colin Morris, *The Papal Monarchy: The Western Church from 1050 to 1250* (Oxford: Clarendon Press, 1989), 253. We expect such rhetoric in early modern English Protestant rhetoric of exploration and conquest, and indeed we find it there as well. The archives of colonial ideology are replete with such Biblical justifications as Hakluyt's dedication to Walter Raleigh of a translation of an exploration account published in 1587: "'Be you of a valiant courage and faint not, as the

Lord said unto Joshua, in the conquest of the land of promise.'" Quoted in Robert A. Williams, *The American Indian in Western Legal Thought: The Discourses of Conquest* (New York: Oxford University Press, 1990), 183; see also Jonathan Boyarin, "Reading Exodus Into History," *New Literary History* 23 (1992), and Benjamin Z. Kedar, "*De Iudeis et Sarracensis*: On the Categorization of Muslims in Medieval Canon Law," in *Studia in Honorem Eminentissimi Cardinalis Alphonsi M. Stickler*, Studia et Textus Historiae Iuris Canonici 7 (Rome: LAS, 1992), 125–26.

19. Lewis Hanke, *The Spanish Struggle for Justice in the Conquest of America* (Boston: Little, Brown and Company, 1965), 31.

20. See Donald Harmon Akenson, *God's Peoples: Covenant and Land in South Africa, Israel, and Ulster* (Ithaca, NY: Cornell University Press, 1992).

21. John Leddy Phelan, *The Millennial Kingdom of the Franciscans in the New World*, 2nd ed. (Berkeley: University of California Press, 1970), 131 n19.

22. Christian writers were presumably freer with the text when their (fictive or actual) audience did not include Jews. See, for example, Lieu, *Christian Identity in the Jewish and Graeco-Roman World*, 38. Yet even quotes from the "Hebrew Bible" by such polemicists were not always what Jews would have found in their own texts. Anna Sapir Abulafia, *Christians and Jews in the Twelfth-Century Renaissance* (London: Routledge, 1995), 95–96.

23. Phelan, *The Millennial Kingdom of the Franciscans*, 103.

24. Sabine MacCormack, *Religion in the Andes: Vision and Imagination in Early Colonial Peru* (Princeton, NJ: Princeton University Press, 1991), 214.

25. Ibid.

26. Cited in ibid., 218.

27. Ibid., 221.

28. Doris Heyden, "Translator's Introduction," *The History of the Indies of New Spain: Fray Diego Durán* (Norman: University of Oklahoma Press, 1994), xxviii. "Born in Seville in 1537, and still a child when he arrived in Mexico around 1542, the Dominican Fray Diego Durán took on from 1565 to 1581 the elaboration of a vast ethnographic chronicle, the *Historia de las Indias de Nueva España, e Islas de la Tierra Firme*, which stands out among the works of the first chroniclers for its attempt to explain and rehabilitate the pre-Columbian past." Georges Baudot, *Utopia and History in Mexico: The First Chroniclers of Mexican Civilization (1520–1569)*, trans. Bernard R. Ortiz de Montellano and Thelma Ortiz de Montellano (Niwot: University Press of Colorado, 1995), 72 n.1.

29. Fray Diego Durán, *The History of the Indies of New Spain*, trans. and ed. Doris Heyden (Norman: University of Oklahoma Press, 1994), 3–11; cf. the summary in Tzvetan Todorov, *The Conquest of America: The Question of the Other* (New York: Harper and Row, 1984), 210.

30. *Saint Augustine: The City of God, Books VIII–XVI*, trans. Gerald G. Walsh and Grace Monahan (Washington, DC: Catholic University of America Press, 1952), 489.

31. Durán asserted, as a key part of the "proof" of the Indians' Jewishness, that their state at the time of his writing not only conformed typologically to the exile and wandering of the Jews, but exemplified the punishments and degradation promised by the Bible as a divine retribution for their straying "from belief in the true God." Durán, *The History of the Indies*, 5. Furthermore, this comes after the first, generalized likening of the Indians' characteristics to those of the "Jews and Hebrews"—perhaps intended here to include those of Durán's day. As were Jews in the sixteenth century, the Indians are described by Durán as having "cowardly, pusillanimous, and fearful hearts," which he uses to build his explanation that Cortés's astonishing victory, in which millions fled before three hundred, was a fulfillment of scriptural augury. Ibid., 6.

32. Karl F. Morrison, *I Am You: The Hermeneutics of Empathy in Western Literature, Theology, and Art* (Princeton, NJ: Princeton University Press, 1988); Gilbert Dahan, *Les intellectuels chrétiens et les Juifs au Moyen Âge* (Paris: Le Cerf, 1990), 9.

33. Jeremy Cohen, *The Friars and the Jews: The Evolution of Medieval Anti-Judaism* (Ithaca, NY: Cornell University Press, 1982), 92.

34. Robert Chazan, *Fashioning Jewish Identity in Medieval Christendom* (Cambridge: Cambridge University Press, 2004), 182.

35. Robert Chazen, *Barcelona and Beyond: The Disputation of 1263 and Its Aftermath* (Berkeley: University of California Press, 1992); see also his *Daggers of Faith: Thirteenth-Century Christian Missionizing and Jewish Response* (Berkeley: University of California Press, 1989).

36. Walter D. Mignolo, "When Speaking Was Not Good Enough: Illiterates, Barbarians, Savages, and Cannibals," in *Amerindian Images and the Legacy of Columbus*, ed. Rene Jara and Nicholas Spadaccini (Minneapolis: University of Minnesota Press, 1992).

37. Walter D. Mignolo, "Literacy and Colonization: The New World Experience," in *1492–1992: Re/discovering Colonial Writing*, ed. Rene Jara and Nicholas Spadaccini (Minneapolis: University of Minnesota Press), 53; Inga Clendinnen, *Ambivalent Conquests: Maya and Spaniard in Yucatan, 1517–1560* (New York: Cambridge University Press, 1987).

38. Walter D. Mignolo, "Signs and Their Transmission: The Question of the Book in the New World," in *Writing without Words: Alternative Literacies in Mesoamerica and the Andes*, ed. Elizabeth Hill Boone and Walter D. Mignolo (Durham, NC: Duke University Press, 1994), 226.

39. Walter D. Mignolo, *The Darker Side of the Renaissance.*

40. Mignolo, "Signs and Their Transmission," 226.

41. Barbara Fuchs, *Mimesis and Empire: The New World, Islam, and European Identities* (Cambridge: Cambridge University Press, 2001), 23.

42. Baudot, *Utopia and History in Mexico*, 86–89.

43. Burckhardt, *The Slippery Earth*, 3.

44. Walden Browne, *Sahagún and the Transition to Modernity* (Norman: University of Oklahoma Press, 2000), 73, 34.

45. Quoted in Heyden, "Translator's Introduction," *The History of the Indies of New Spain*, xxx, xxxii.

46. *Pace* those studies of oral discourse and even of non-Western textual forms that are still sometimes marred by a caricature of Western scriptural reading as "monologic alphabetism." See Dennis Tedlock, *The Spoken Word and the Work of Interpretation* (Philadelphia: University of Pennsylvania Press, 1983).

47. Brigitte Miriam Bedos-Rezak, "Les Juifs et l'écrit dans la mentalité eschatologique du Moyen Âge chrétien occidental (France 1000–1200)," *Annales* 49:5 (1994), 1051.

48. Abulafia, *Christians and Jews in the Twelfth-Century Renaissance*, 26.

49. Jaroslav Pelikan, *The Growth of Medieval Theology (600–1300)* (Chicago: University of Chicago Press, 1978), 246; Chazan, *Fashioning Jewish Identity in Medieval Christendom*, 8. It is worth bearing in mind that even if "nearly all 'anti-Jewish' polemic has a more immediate goal in shaping Christian identity," the "literary works composed by Jewish authors—in Hebrew at that—were obviously intended for Jewish eyes and ears only." Lieu, *Christian Identity*, 81; Chazan, *Fashioning Jewish Identity in Medieval Christendom*, 14.

50. MacCormack, *Religion in the Andes*, 35.

51. Ibid., 37.

52. Ibid., 38.

53. Jeremy Cohen, *Living Letters of the Law: Ideas of the Jew in Medieval Christianity* (Berkeley: University of California Press, 1999), 214.

54. Georgina Dopico Black, *Perfect Wives, Other Women: Adultery and Inquisition in Early Modern Spain* (Durham, NC: Duke University Press, 2001), 65. The identification of literalism with "Jewish" reading practices was especially wide of the mark with regard to the Song of Songs. As Daniel Boyarin suggests, the Rabbis of the Talmud "read the Song of Songs as a mashal [parable] written by Solomon to be the hermeneutic key to the unlocking of the book of Exodus." Daniel Boyarin, *Intertextuality and the Reading of Midrash* (Bloomington: Indiana University Press, 1990), 107.

55. Brigitte Miriam Bedos-Rezak, "The Confrontation of Orality and Textuality: Jewish and Christian Literacy in Eleventh- and Twelfth-Century Northern France," in *Rashi, 1040–1990: Hommage à Ephraïm E. Urbach*, ed. Gabrielle Sed-Rajna (Paris: Le Cerf, 1993), 551.

56. Bedos-Rezak, "Les Juifs et l'écrit," 1052.

57. Ibid., 1054.

58. Ibid., 1055.

59. It might be supposed that literacy (and in the first instance, Biblical literacy) as a common cultural competence among Jews would threaten the stable authority of the biblical text within Jewish communities as well. In effect, however, Bedos-Rezak goes so far as nearly to reverse the charge of Jewish literalism and turn it against the

monks. She claims that "the monks manipulate the letter (sign) and not the word (language), expanding the use of writing precisely because they conceive it as a mode of signification, not as a system of communication." Ibid., 1061. It is hard not to suppose this is an overstatement: The distinction between signifying and communicating cannot be so absolute. Monastic scholars often had goals other than the expansion of their authority. Some of them communicated with Jewish readers as well. The particular letters (signs) used in a given text/context were never entirely arbitrary.

60. These charters are strikingly reminiscent of the role of texts in the contemporary native highland community of Cumbal, Columbia, whose leaders are engaged in an ongoing struggle to regain ancestral lands. In pursuit of that struggle, the Cumbales resort to colonial titles drawn up by Spanish *letrados* in the eighteenth century. For the native people of Cumbal, the colonial titles "have symbolic importance much like reclaimed lands and other symbols of political power, such as the staffs of office carried by council members." Diane Digges and Joanne Rappaport, "Literacy, Orality, and Ritual Practice in Highland Colombia," in *The Ethnography of Reading*, ed. Jonathan Boyarin (Berkeley: University of California Press, 1993), 144; see also Joanne Rappaport, *The Politics of Memory* (New York: Cambridge University Press, 1990). They freely appropriate, select, recombine, and reinvent the substance of these treaties. The Colombian state officials whom they confront read the texts of the treaties in a "strict constructionist" and highly officious manner. Clearly for the Cumbales, the *textuality* of those treaties is more important than exactly what they said, yet the Cumbales' free reworking of documents seems no more arbitrary than the bureaucrats' refusal to deal with their appeal on technical jurisdictional grounds.

61. Peter Brown, *The Rise of Western Christendom: Triumph and Diversity, A.D. 200–1000*, 2nd ed. (Malden, MA: Blackwell, 2003), 63. Here as elsewhere, the specificity of Christian expansion should be kept in mind. Otherwise, it is too easy to simply reify the book as an instrument of mystification.

62. Fray Bernardino de Sahagún, "The Aztec-Spanish Dialogues of 1524," trans J. Jorge Klor de Alva, *Journal of Ethnopoetics* 4:2 (1980), 64–65.

63. Ibid., 130.

64. Angel Rama, *La ciudad letrada* (Hanover, NH: Ediciones del Norte, 1984), discussed in Rolena Adorno, "La ciudad letrada y los discursos coloniales," *Hispamerica* 48 (December 1987); see also the English edition of this work, *The Lettered City* (Durham, NC: Duke University Press, 1996).

65. Ibid.

66. See Benedict Anderson, *Imagined Communities: Reflections on the Spread of Nationalism*, 2nd ed. (London: Verso, 1991).

67. Anthony Pagden, "The Humanism of Vasco de Quiroga's 'Información en Derecho,'" in *The Uncertainties of Empire: Essays in Iberian and Ibero-American Intellectual History*, Collected Studies Series (Brookfield, VT: Ashgate Publishing, 1994), 138. Other Spanish visitors were sufficiently impressed by the social organization of the Aztecs that this claim appears almost meretricious.

68. Miri Rubin, *Gentile Tales: The Narrative Assault on Late Medieval Jews* (New Haven: Yale University Press, 1999), 90; see also Kathleen Biddick, *The Typological Imaginary: Circumcision, Technology, History* (Philadelphia: University of Pennsylvania Press, 2003), ch. 3.

CONCLUSION

1. Dominique Iogna-Prat, *Order and Exclusion: Cluny and Christendom Face Heresy, Judaism, and Islam (1000–1150)*, trans. Graham Edward Roberts (Ithaca, NY: Cornell University Press, 2002), 23.

2. See, for example, Jaroslav Pelikan, *The Growth of Medieval Theology (600–1300)* (Chicago: University of Chicago Press, 1978), 248–49.

3. Walden Browne, *Sahagún and the Transition to Modernity* (Norman: University of Oklahoma Press, 2000), 117.

4. Ibid., 85, 205.

5. "Converted" or not, the Nahua did not accede to the consignment of their ancestors to an unredeemed past. In the *Cantares mexicanos*, a collection of indigenous texts recorded around 1580, "[p]agan past is united with Christian present; the discontinuity represented by the Conquest is denied." Louise M. Burckhardt, *The Slippery Earth: Nahua-Christian Moral Dialogue in Sixteenth-Century Mexico* (Tucson: University of Arizona Press, 1989), 57.

6. Jeremy Cohen, *The Friars and the Jews: The Evolution of Medieval Anti-Judaism* (Ithaca, NY: Cornell University Press, 1982), 246.

7. Browne, *Sahagún and the Transition to Modernity*, 111; see also Osvaldo F. Pardo, *The Origins of Mexican Catholicism: Nahua Rituals and Christian Sacraments in Sixteenth-Century Mexico* (Ann Arbor: University of Michigan Press), 156.

8. Edmundo O'Gorman, *The Invention of America: An Inquiry into the Historical Nature of the New World and the Meaning of Its History* (Bloomington: Indiana University Press, 1961), 20.

9. Significantly, Gustavo Gutiérrez's scholarly hagiography of Las Casas is subtitled *In Search of the Poor of Jesus Christ*. Peter Brown has articulated how in the first Christian centuries, the rhetoric of the masses of the poor as belonging to Jesus underlay the roots of Christian universalism: "For the poor stood for the width of the bishop's range of concern. On the social map of the city, they marked the outermost boundary of the 'universal way' associated with the Christian church, just as the bookless wisdom of the monks indicated a cultural desert that stretched far beyond the narrow confines of Greek *paideia*. A mystical link was held to bind the bishop to the poor of the city." Peter Brown, *Power and Persuasion in Late Antiquity: Towards a Christian Empire* (Madison: University of Wisconsin Press, 1992), 94. The pope is, of course, the bishop of Rome, and here we see one underlying aspect of the notion—nuanced and disputed, to be sure—that Christianity justified the universal dominion of Christians

over those who had not yet accepted the Gospel. Here already the Christian dimension is simultaneously spiritual ("a mystical link") and spatially expansive ("the outermost boundary"). For Las Casas, too, the realm of the church's concern and the realm of its jurisdiction were one and the same question.

10. This is a rather different statement from the assertion that "Las Casas posed the problem, so relevant today, of the attitude of a 'cultured' or 'developed' people toward an 'underdeveloped' people and masterfully defined the philosophy of aid to underdeveloped people." Angel Losada, "The Controversy Between Sepúlveda and Las Casas in the Junta of Valladolid," in *Bartolomé de Las Casas in History*, ed. Juan Friede and Benjamin Keen (DeKalb, IL: Northern Illinois University Press, 1971), 296.

11. Cited in Cohen, *The Friars and the Jews*, 147.

12. W. D. Davies, *The Gospel and the Land: Early Christianity and Jewish Territorial Doctrine* (Berkeley: University of California Press, 1974), 371.

13. Krister Stendahl, *Paul among Jews and Gentiles* (Philadelphia: Fortress Press, 1976), 5.

14. Iogna-Prat, *Order and Exclusion*, 361.

15. Ibid., 316–17; Jeremy Cohen, *Living Letters of the Law: Ideas of the Jew in Medieval Christianity* (Berkeley: University of California Press, 1999), 357.

16. Cited in Cohen, *The Friars and the Jews*, 247.

17. Bernard of Clairvaux, *On the Song of Songs IV*, trans. Irene Edmonds, intro. Jean Leclercq (Kalamazoo, MI: Cistercian Publications, 1980), 141–42; see also Cohen, *Living Letters of the Law*, 233.

18. Beatriz Pastor Bodmer, *The Armature of Conquest: Spanish Accounts of the Discovery of America, 1492–1589*, trans. Lydia Longstreth Hunt (Stanford, CA: Stanford University Press, 1992), 210. Here, as throughout this book, the argument is not that Jews were the *only* available model for thinking about how to think about Indians. Las Casas used the same kind of paternalistic, developmental rhetoric to argue that just as the ancient Spaniards had been Christianized and civilized, so could the natives. Bartolomé de Las Casas, *History of the Indies*, trans. and ed. Andrée Collard (New York: Harper and Row, 1971), 4.

19. Elisa Marie Narin van Court, "Critical Apertures: Medieval Anti-Judaisms and Middle English Narrative," Ph.D. diss., University of California, Berkeley, 1995, 54.

20. I use this term intentionally here to refer to that aspect of Christian thought that is focused on integrating aspects of Jewish textuality and doctrine.

21. Albert A. Sicroff, *Les controverses des statuts de "pureté de sang" en Espagne du 15e au 17e siècle* (Paris: Didier, 1960), 44.

22. Rolena Adorno, *Guaman Poma: Writing and Resistance in Colonial Peru* (Austin: University of Texas Press, 1986), 21, citing Felipe Guaman Poma de Ayala, *El nueva corónica y buen gobierno*, 3 vols., critical ed. by John V. Murra and Rolena Adorno, trans. and textual analysis of Quechua by Jorge L. Urioste (Mexico City: Siglo Veintiuno, 1980).

23. Sabine MacCormack, *Religion in the Andes: Vision and Imagination in Early Colonial Peru* (Princeton: Princeton University Press, 1991),145.

24. Cohen, *The Friars and the Jews*, 242. This declaration was followed by efforts on the part of Gregory and later popes to have Jewish books confiscated and burned. See, for example, Shlomo Simonson, *The Apostolic See and the Jews. Vol. 1: Documents, 492–1404* (Toronto: Pontifical Institute of Mediaeval Studies, 1988), 170–74, and *The Apostolic See and the Jews. Vol. 2, 1394–1464* (Toronto: Pontifical Institute of Mediaeval Studies, 1989), 593.

25. Gilbert Dahan, *Les intellectuels chrétiens et les Juifs au Moyen Âge* (Paris: Le Cerf, 1990), 515–16.

26. Ibid., 517. Early in the twelfth century, the traditional Benedictines were busy reproaching Jews for legalism and lack of spirituality while they themselves were being attacked for indulging in worldly pleasures. Brigitte Miriam Bedos-Rezak, "Les Juifs et l'écrit dans la mentalité eschatologique du Moyen Âge chrétien occidental (France 1000–1200)," *Annales* 49, no. 5 (1994): 1054, citing John Van Engen, "The 'Crisis of Cenobitism' Reconsidered: Benedictine Monasticism in the Years 1050–1150," *Speculum* 61 (1986), 269–304.

27. Dahan, *Les intellectuels chrétiens et les Juifs*, 512–13.

28. Lewis Hanke, *The Spanish Struggle for Justice in the Conquest of America* (Boston: Little, Brown and Company, 1965), 31.

29. William L. Merrill, "Conversion and Colonialism in Northern Mexico: The Tarahumara Response to the Jesuit Mission Program, 1601–1767," in *Conversion to Christianity: Historical and Anthropological Perspectives on a Great Transformation*, ed. Robert W. Hefner (Berkeley: University of California Press, 1993). For the case of the Philippines see Vicente Rafael, *Contracting Colonialism: Translation and Christian Conversion in Tagalog Society Under Early Spanish Rule* (Durham, NC: Duke University Press, 1993).

30. Inga Clendinnen, *Ambivalent Conquests: Maya and Spaniard in Yucatan, 1517–1560* (New York: Cambridge University Press, 1987), 52.

31. Aamir Mufti, in *Enlightenment in the Colony: The Jewish Question and the Crisis of Post-Colonial Culture* (Princeton, NJ: Princeton University Press, 2007), has begun the necessary articulation of at least some ways that discourses on Jewish difference in nineteenth-century Europe informed and constrained discourses on religion, modernity, and nationalism in twentieth-century south Asia. My effort here has been to open similar questions for another time and space of Christian European empire and self-making.

32. Bernardino Vérastique, *Michoacán and Eden: Vasco de Quiroga and the Evangelization of Western Mexico* (Austin: University of Texas Press, 2000), 124.

33. Robert A. Williams, *The American Indian in Western Legal Thought: The Discourses of Conquest* (Oxford: Oxford University Press, 1990), Part 1: The Medieval and Renaissance Origins of the Status of the American Indian in Western Legal Thought, 13–118.

BIBLIOGRAPHY

Abulafia, Anna Sapir. *Christians and Jews in the Twelfth-Century Renaissance*. London: Routledge, 1995.

———. "The Intellectual and Spiritual Quest for Christ and Central Medieval Persecution of Jews." In *Religious Violence between Christians and Jews: Medieval Roots, Modern Perspectives*, edited by Anna Sapir Abulafia, 61–85. New York: Palgrave, 2002.

Adorno, Rolena. *Guaman Poma: Writing and Resistance in Colonial Peru*. Austin: University of Texas Press, 1986.

———. "La *Ciudad Letrada* y los Discursos Coloniales." *Hispamerica* 48 (December 1987): 3–24.

———. "The Negotiation of Fear in Cabeza de Vaca's *Naufragios.*" *Representations* 33 (1991): 163–99.

———. "Reconsidering Colonial Discourse for Sixteenth- and Seventeenth-Century America." *Latin American Research Review* 28 (1993): 135–45.

Akenson, Donald Harmon. *God's Peoples: Covenant and Land in South Africa, Israel, and Ulster*. Ithaca: Cornell University Press, 1992.

Alcina Franch, José. "Introduccion." In *Diego Andres Rocha, El Origen de los Indios*. Madrid: Historia 16, 1988.

Anderson, Benedict. *Imagined Communities: Reflections on the Origin and Spread of Nationalism*. Second ed. London: Verso, 1991.

Anidjar, Gil. *The Jew, the Arab: A History of the Enemy*. Stanford, CA: Stanford University Press, 2003.

———. *Our Place in al-Andalus: Kabbalah, Philosophy, Literature in Arab Jewish Letters*. Stanford: Stanford University Press, 2002.

———. "Postscript: Futures of Al-Andalus." In *In the Light of Medieval Spain: Islam, the West, and the Relevance of the Past*, edited by Simon R. Doubleday and David Coleman. New York: Palgrave Macmillan, 2008, 189–208.

Aranda, Antonio Garrido. *Moriscos e Indios: Precedentes Hispanicos de la Evangelización en México*. Mexico: Universidad Nacional Autónoma de México, 1980.

Asad, Talal. *The Idea of an Anthropology of Islam*. Occasional Papers Series. Center for Contemporary Arab Studies, Georgetown University, 1986.

———. *Genealogies of Religion: Discipline and Reasons of Power in Christianity and Islam*. Baltimore: Johns Hopkins University Press, 1993.

———. *Formations of the Secular: Christianity, Islam, Modernity*. Stanford, CA: Stanford University Press, 2003.

Ashtor, Eliyahu. *The Jews of Moslem Spain*. Vol. 1. Translated by Aaron Klein and Jenny Machlowitz Klein. Philadelphia: Jewish Publication Society, 1973.

Baker, James N. "The Presence of the Name: Reading Scripture in an Indonesian Village." In *The Ethnography of Reading*, edited by Jonathan Boyarin, 98–138. Berkeley: University of California Press, 1993.

Barker, Frances, ed. *Europe and Its Others: Proceedings of the Essex Conference on the Sociology of Literature, July 1984*. 2 vols. Colchester: University of Essex Press, 1985.

Bartlett, Robert. *The Making of Europe: Conquest, Colonization and Cultural Change, 950–1350*. Princeton, NJ: Princeton University Press, 1993.

Battaglia, Debbora, ed. *Rhetorics of Self-Making*. Berkeley: University of California Press, 1995.

Baudet, Henri. *Paradise on Earth: Some Thoughts on European Images of Non-European Man*. New Haven: Yale University Press, 1965.

Baudot, Georges. *Utopia and History in Mexico: The First Chroniclers of Mexican Civilization (1520–1569)*. Translated by Bernard R. Ortiz de Montellano and Thelma Ortiz de Montellano. Niwot: University Press of Colorado, 1995.

Beckwith, Sarah. *Christ's Body: Identity, Culture and Society in Late Medieval Writings*. New York: Routledge, 1993.

Bedos-Rezak, Brigitte Miriam. "The Confrontation of Orality and Textuality: Jewish and Christian Literacy in Eleventh- and Twelfth-century Northern France." In *Rashi, 1040–1990: Hommage à Ephraïm E. Urbach*, edited by Gabrielle Sed-Rajna, 541–58. Paris: Le Cerf, 1993.

———. "Les Juifs et l'écrit dans la mentalité eschatologique du Moyen Âge chrétien occidental (France 1000–1200)." *Annales* 49, no. 5 (1994): 1049–64.

Benbassa, Esther, and Jean-Christophe Attias. *The Jew and the Other*. Translated by G. M. Goshgarian. Ithaca, NY: Cornell University Press, 2004.

Pope Benedict XVI, "Prepolitical Moral Foundations of a Free Republic." In *Political Theologies*, edited by Hent de Vries and Lawrence E. Sullivan. New York: Fordham University Press, 2006.

Benton, John E. "Consciousness of Self and Perceptions of Individuality." In *Culture, Power and Personality in Medieval France*, edited by Thomas N. Bisson, 327–56. London: Hambildon Press, 1991.

Berger, David. *The Jewish-Christian Debate in the High Middle Ages*. Philadelphia: Jewish Publication Society, 1979.

Berkhofer, Robert F. *The White Man's Indian*. New York: Alfred A. Knopf, 1978.

Bernard of Clairvaux, *On the Song of Songs IV*. Translated by Irene Edmonds, with introduction by Jean LeClercq. Kalamazoo, MI: Cistercian Publications, 1980.

Bernstein, Michael André. *Foregone Conclusions: Against Apocalyptic History*. Berkeley: University of California Press, 1994.

Bhabha, Homi K. Introduction to *Nation and Narration*, edited by Homi K. Bhabha, 1–7. New York: Routledge, 1990.

———. Call for Proposals: Frontlines/Borderposts. *Critical Inquiry* 19, no. 3 (1993): 595–98.

———. *The Location of Culture*. New York: Routledge, 1994.

Biddick, Kathleen. *The Typological Imaginary: Circumcision, Technology, History*. Philadelphia: University of Pennsylvania Press, 2003.

Biller, Peter. "Views of Jews from Paris around 1300." *Studies in Church History* 29 (1992).

Black, Georgina Dopico. *Perfect Wives, Other Women: Adultery and Inquisition in Early Modern Spain*. Durham, NC: Duke University Press, 2001.

Bodian, Miriam. *Hebrews of the Portuguese Nation: Conversos and Community in Early Modern Amsterdam*. Bloomington: Indiana University Press, 1997.

Bodmer, Beatriz Pastor. *The Armature of Conquest: Spanish Accounts of the Discovery of America, 1492–1589*. Translated by Lydia Longstreth Hunt. Stanford, CA: Stanford University Press, 1992.

Bolton, Herbert Eugene. *Rim of Christendom: A Biography of Eusebio Francisco Kino, Pacific Coast Pioneer*. Tucson: University of Arizona Press 1974. First edition 1936.

Boyarin, Daniel. *Intertextuality and the Reading of Midrash*. Bloomington: Indiana University Press, 1990.

———. *Carnal Israel: Reading Sex in Talmudic Culture*. Berkeley: University of California Press, 1993.

———. *A Radical Jew: Paul and the Politics of Identity*. Berkeley: University of California Press, 1994.

———. "Freud's Baby, Fliess's Maybe: Male Hysteria, Homophobia, and the Invention of Oedipus." *GLQ* 2, no. 1 (1995): 1–33.

———. *Border Lines: The Partition of Judaeo-Christianity*. Philadelphia: University of Pennsylvania Press, 2004.

Boyarin, Daniel, and Jonathan Boyarin. "Diaspora: Generation and the Ground of Jewish Identity." *Critical Inquiry* 19, no. 4 (1993): 693–725.

Boyarin, Jonathan. "Reading Exodus into History." *New Literary History* 23, no. 3 (1992): 523–54.

———. ed. *The Ethnography of Reading*. Berkeley: University of California Press, 1993.

Brown, Peter. *Power and Persuasion in Late Antiquity: Towards a Christian Empire*. Madison: University of Wisconsin Press, 1992.

———. *Authority and the Sacred: Aspects of the Christianization of the Roman World*. Cambridge: Cambridge University Press, 1995.

———. *The Rise of Western Christendom: Triumph and Diversity, A.D. 200–1000*. 2nd ed. Malden, MA: Blackwell, 2003.

Browne, Walden. *Sahagún and the Transition to Modernity*. Norman: University of Oklahoma Press, 2000.

Bruns, Gerald. "What is Tradition?" *New Literary History* 22, no. 1 (1991): 3–21.

Buell, Denise Kimber. *Making Christians: Clement of Alexandria and the Rhetoric of Legitimacy*. Princeton, NJ: Princeton University Press, 1999.

———. "Race and Universalism in Early Christianity." *Journal of Early Christian Studies* 1, no. (4 (2002): 429–68.

———. *Why This New Race: Ethnic Reasoning in Early Christianity*. New York: Columbia University Press, 2005.

Burckhardt, Louise M. *The Slippery Earth: Nahua-Christian Moral Dialogue in Sixteenth-Century Mexico*. Tucson: The University of Arizona Press, 1989.

Burman, Thomas E. *Religious Polemic and the Intellectual History of the Mozarabs, c. 1050–1200*. Leiden: Brill, 1994.

———. *Reading the Qur'an in Western Christendom, 1140–1560*. Philadelphia: University of Pennsylvania Press, 2007.

Burns, J. H., ed. *The Cambridge History of Medieval Political Thought: C. 350–C. 1450*. New York: Cambridge University Press, 1988.

Bynum, Caroline Walker. *Jesus as Mother: Studies in the Spirituality of the High Middle Ages*. Berkeley: University of California Press, 1982.

———. *The Resurrection of the Body in Western Christianity, 200–1336*. New York: Columbia University Press, 1995.

Cameron, Averil. *Christianity and the Rhetoric of Empire*. Berkeley: University of California Press, 1991.

Carpenter, Dwayne E. "Social Perception and Literary Portrayal: Jews and Muslims in Medieval Spanish Literature." In *Convivencia: Jews, Muslims, and Christians in Medieval Spain*, edited by Vivian B. Mann, Thomas F. Glick, and Jerrilynn D. Dodds, 61–82. New York: George Braziller, 1992.

Cervantes, Fernando. *The Devil in the New World: The Impact of Diabolism in New Spain*. New Haven: Yale University Press, 1994.

Chazan, Robert. *European Jewry and the First Crusade*. Berkeley: University of California Press, 1987.

———. *Daggers of Faith: Thirteenth-Century Christian Missionizing and Jewish Response.* Berkeley: University of California Press, 1989.

———. *Barcelona and Beyond: The Disputation of 1263 and Its Aftermath.* Berkeley: University of California Press, 1992.

———. *Fashioning Jewish Identity in Medieval Christendom.* Cambridge: Cambridge University Press, 2004.

Chejne, Anwar G., *Islam and the West: The Moriscos, a Cultural and Social History.* Albany: State University of New York Press, 1983.

Clanchy, M.T. *From Memory to Written Record: England 1066–1307.* Cambridge, MA: Harvard University Press, 1979.

Clendinnen, Inga. " 'Fierce and Unnatural Cruelty': Cortés and the Conquest of Mexico." *Representations* 33 (1991): 65–100.

———. *Ambivalent Conquests: Maya and Spaniard in Yucatan, 1517–1560.* New York: Cambridge University Press, 1987.

Cohen, Jeffrey, ed. *The Postcolonial Middle Ages.* New York: St. Martin's Press, 2002.

———. *Medieval Identity Machines.* Minneapolis: University of Minnesota Press, 2003.

Cohen, Jeremy. *The Friars and the Jews: The Evolution of Medieval Anti-Judaism.* Ithaca, NY: Cornell University Press, 1982.

———. *Living Letters of the Law: Ideas of the Jew in Medieval Christianity.* Berkeley: University of California Press, 1999.

Colbert, Edward P. *The Martyrs of Córdoba (850–859): A Study of the Sources.* Washington, D.C.: Catholic University of America Press, 1962.

Collard, Andrée. "Introduction." In *History of the Indies: Bartolomé de Las Casas.* New York: Harper & Row, 1971, ix–xxiv.

Connolly, William E. "Identity and Difference in Global Politics." In *Intertextual/ International Relations: Postmodern Readings of World Politics*, edited by James Der Derian and Michael Shapiro, 323–42. Lexington, MA: D.C. Heath and Company, 1989.

Cortés, Hernan, *Conquest: Dispatches from the New World*, edited by Harry M. Rosen with introduction and commentaries by Irwin R. Blacker. New York: Grosset & Dunlap, 1962.

Costen, Michael. *The Cathars and the Albigensian Crusade.* Manchester, UK: Manchester University Press, 1997.

Cutler, A. "The Ninth-Century Spanish Martyrs' Movement and the Origins of Western Christian Missions to the Muslims." *Muslim World* 58 (1968): 57–71, 155–64.

Dahan, Gilbert. *Les intellectuels chrétiens et les Juifs au Moyen Âge.* Paris: Le Cerf, 1990.

Daniel, E. Randolph. *The Franciscan Concept of Mission in the High Middle Ages.* Lexington: University Press of Kentucky, 1975.

Daniel, Norman. *Islam and the West: The Making of an Image*. Edinburgh: The University Press, 1960.

Davies, W.D. *The Gospel and the Land: Early Christianity and Jewish Territorial Doctrine*. Berkeley: University of California Press, 1974.

Davis, Kathleen. "Time Behind the Veil: The Media, the Middle Ages, and Orientalism Now," in *The Postcolonial Middle Ages*, edited by Jeffrey Jerome Cohen. New York: St. Martin's Press, 2000, 105–122.

de Epalza, Mikel. "Principes chrétiens et principes musulmans face au problème morisque." In *Les Morisques et l'Inquisition*, edited by Louis Cardaillac, 37–50. Paris: Publisud, 1990.

del Castillo, Bernal Díaz. *The Conquest of New Spain*, translated with introduction by J.M. Cohen. Baltimore: Penguin, 1963.

Derrida, Jacques. *The Other Heading: Reflections on Today's Europe*. Bloomington: Indiana University Press, 1992.

———. *Specters of Marx : The State of the Debt, the Work of Mourning, and the New International*. Translated by Peggy Kamuf, with introduction by Bernd Magnus and Stephen Cullenberg. New York: Routledge, 1994.

Djait, Hichem. *Europe and Islam*. Berkeley: University of California Press, 1985.

Digges, Diane, and Joanne Rappaport. "Literacy, Orality, and Ritual Practice in Highland Colombia." In *The Ethnography of Reading*, edited by Jonathan Boyarin, 139–57. Berkeley: University of California Press, 1993.

Duggan, Lawrence G. " 'For Force is not of God?' Compulsion and Conversion from Yahweh to Charlemagne." In *Varieties of Religious Conversion in the Middle Ages*, edited by James Muldoon, 49–62. Gainesville: University of Florida Press, 1991.

Dundes, Alan, ed. *The Blood Libel Legend: A Casebook in Anti-Semitic Folklore*. Madison: University of Wisconsin Press, 1991.

Durán, Fray Diego. *The History of the Indies of New Spain*. Translated and edited by Doris Heyden. Norman: University of Oklahoma Press, 1994.

Dussel, Enrique. "Beyond Eurocentrism: The World-System and the Limits of Modernity," in *The Cultures of Globalization*, edited by Fredric Jameson and Masao Miyoshi. Durham, NC, and London: Duke University Press, 1998, 3–31.

Echevarria, Ana. *The Fortress of Faith: The Attitude towards Muslims in Fifteenth-Century Spain*. Leiden: Brill, 1999.

Edwards, John. *The Jews in Christian Europe, 1400–1700*. New York: Routledge, 1991.

———. "La prehistoria de los estatutos de 'limpieza de sangre.' " In *Xudeus e conversos na historia*, edited by Carlos Barros, 351–58. Santiago de Compostela: La Editorial de la historia, 1994.

Eilberg-Schwartz, Howard. *The Savage in Judaism*. Bloomington: Indiana University Press, 1990.

Elkin, Judith Laikin. "Imagining Idolatry: Missionaries, Indians, and Jews." In *Reli-*

gion and the Authority of the Past, edited by Tobin Siebers, 75–99. Ann Arbor: University of Michigan Press, 1993.

Elliott, J. H. *The Old World and the New, 1492–1650*. Cambridge: Cambridge University Press, 1970.

———. "The Spanish Conquest and Settlement of America." In *The Cambridge History of Latin America*, vol. 1., 149–206. Cambridge: Cambridge University Press, 1984.

———. "A Europe of Composite Monarchies," Past and Present 137 (1992): 48–71.

Elukin, Jonathan. "From Jew to Christian? Conversion and Immutability in Medieval Europe." In *Varieties of Religious Conversion in the Middle Ages*, edited by James Muldoon, 171–89. Gainesville: University Press of Florida, 1997.

———. "The Discovery of the Self: Jews and Conversion in the Twelfth Century." In *Jews and Christians in Twelfth-Century Europe*, edited by Michael A. Singer and John van Engen. Notre Dame, IN: Notre Dame University Press, 2001, 63–76.

———. *Living Together, Living Apart: Rethinking Jewish-Christian Relations in the Middle Ages*. Princeton, NJ, and Oxford: Princeton University Press, 2007.

Encyclopedia Britannica. Fifteenth Edition, vol. 16, 1992.

Epstein, Steven. *Genoa and the Genoese, 958–1528*. Chapel Hill: University of North Carolina Press, 1996.

Fabian, Johannes. *Time and the Other*. New York: Columbia University Press, 1983.

Fabre-Vassas, Claudine. *The Singular Beast: Jews, Christians, and the Pig*. Translated by Carol Volk. New York: Columbia University Press, 1997.

Farriss, Nancy M. *Maya Society under Colonial Rule: The Collective Enterprise of Survival*. Princeton, NJ: Princeton University Press, 1984.

Faur, José. *In the Shadow of History: Jews and Conversos at the Dawn of Modernity*. Albany: State University of New York Press, 1992.

Feliciano, Maria Judith, and Cynthia Robinson, eds. "Interrogating Medieval Encounters," special issue of *Medieval Encounters* 12:3, 2006.

Foreville, Raymonde. *Latran I, II, III et Latran IV*. Paris: Éditions de L'Orante, 1965.

Forsyth, Neil. *The Old Enemy: Satan and the Combat Myth*. Princeton, NJ: Princeton University Press, 1989.

Foucault, Michel. "Questions on Geography." In *Power/Knowledge*, edited by Colin Gordon, 63–77. New York: Pantheon, 1980.

Fraher, Richard M. "IV Lateran's Revolution in Criminal Procedure: The Birth of *Inquisitio*, the End of Ordeals, and Innocent III's Vision of Ecclesiastical Politics." In *Studia in Honorem Eminentissimi Cardinalis Alphonsi M. Stickler*, 97–113. Studia et Textus Historiae Iuris Canonici 7. Rome: LAS, 1992.

Frassetto, Michael, "The Image of the Saracen as Heretic in Sermons of Ademar of Chabannes," in *Western Views of Islam in Medieval and Early Modern Europe: Perception of Other*, edited by David R. Blanks and Michael Frassetto. New York: St. Martin's Press, 1999, 83–96.

Fredriksen, Paula, *Augustine and the Jews: A Christian Defense of Judaism*. New York: Doubleday, 2008.

Fuchs, Barbara. *Mimesis and Empire: The New World, Islam, and European Identities*. Cambridge: Cambridge University Press, 2001.

———. "Imperium Studies: Theorizing Early Modern Expansion," in *Postcolonial Moves: Medieval through Modern*, edited by Patricia Clare Ingham and Michelle R. Warren. New York: Palgrave MacMillan, 2003, 71–90.

———. "The Spanish Race," in *Rereading the Black Legend: The Discourses of Religions and Racial Difference in the Renaissance Empires*, edited by Margaret R. Greer, Walter D. Mignolo, and Maureen Quilligan. Chicago: University of Chicago Press, 2007, 88–98.

Fuchs, Barbara, and David J. Baker, eds. "Postcolonialism and the Past," special issue of *Modern Language Quarterly* 65:3 (2004).

Gerber, Jane. *The Jews of Spain: A History of the Sephardic Experience*. New York: The Free Press, 1992.

Glei, Reinhold, ed. *Petrus Venerabilis Schriften zum Islam*. Corpus Islamico-Christianum, Series Latina 1, 30–225. Altenberge: Oros, 1985.

Goldsmith, Steven. *Unbuilding Jerusalem: Apocalypse and Romantic Representation*. Ithaca, NY: Cornell University Press, 1993.

González-Echevarría, Roberto. "The Law of the Letter: Garcilaso's *Commentaries* and the Origins of Latin American Narrative." *Yale Journal of Criticism* 1, no. 1 (1987): 107–32.

Greenblatt, Stephen. *Renaissance Self-Fashioning*. Chicago: University of Chicago Press, 1980.

———. *Shakespearean Negotiations: The Circulation of Social Energy in Renaissance England*. Berkeley: University of California Press, 1988.

———. *Marvelous Possessions: The Wonder of the New World*. Chicago: University of Chicago Press, 1991.

———. "Kindly Visions." *The New Yorker*, October 11, 1993, 112–20.

Greenberg, Gershon. "American Indians, Ten Lost Tribes and Christian Eschatology." In *Religion in the Age of Exploration: The Case of Spain and New Spain*, edited by Bryan F. LeBeau and Menachem Mor. Omaha: Creighton University Press, 1996.

Greenleaf, Richard E. *The Mexican Inquisition of the Sixteenth Century*. Albuquerque: University of New Mexico Press, 1969.

Greer, Margaret R., Walter D. Mignolo, and Maureen Quilligan, eds.. *Rereading the Black Legend: The Discourses of Religions and Racial Difference in the Renaissance Empires*. Chicago: University of Chicago Press, 2007, 1–24.

Guaman Poma de Ayala, Felipe. *El nueva corónica y buen gobierno*. 3 vols. Critical Edition by John V. Murra and Rolena Adorno, with translation and Textual Analysis of Quechua by Jorge L. Urioste. Mexico City: Siglo Veintiuno, 1980.

Guicciardi, Jean-Pierre. Introduction to *Abrégé du manuel des inquisiteurs*, edited by André Morellete, 7–54. Grenoble: Jérôme Millon, 1990.

Gutiérrez, Gustavo. *Las Casas: In Search of the Poor of Jesus Christ*. Translated by Robert E. Barr. Maryknoll, NY: Orbis Books, 1993.

Hanke, Lewis. *The Spanish Struggle for Justice in the Conquest of America*. Boston: Little, Brown and Company, 1965.

———. *Aristotle and the American Indians: A Study in Race Prejudice*. Bloomington: Indiana University Press, 1975.

Harpham, Geoffrey Galt. "So . . . What *Is* Enlightenment? An Inquisition into Modernity." *Critical Inquiry* 20, no. 3 (1994): 524–56.

Harris, Max. Aztecs, Moors, and Christians: Festivals of Reconquest in Mexico and Spain. Austin: University of Texas Press, 2000.

Harvey, L.P. *Islamic Spain, 1250–1500*. Chicago: University of Chicago Press, 1990.

———. *Muslims in Spain, 1500 to 1614*. Chicago: University of Chicago Press, 2005.

Hartog, François. *The Mirror of Herodotus: The Representation of the Other in the Writing of History*. Berkeley: University of California Press, 1988.

Hassig, Ross. *Time, History, and Belief in Aztec and Colonial Mexico*. Austin: University of Texas Press, 2000.

Hay, Denys. *Europe: The Emergence of an Idea*. Edinburgh: Edinburgh University Press, 1957.

Herrin, Judith. *The Formation of Christendom*. Princeton, NJ: Princeton University Press, 1987.

Heng, Geraldine. "The Romance of England: *Richard Coeur de Lyon*, Saracens, Jews, and the Politics of Race and Nation." In *The Postcolonial Middle Ages*, edited by Jeffrey Jerome Cohen. New York: St. Martin's Press, 2000, 135–171.

Heyden, Doris. Translator's introduction to *The History of the Indies of New Spain: Fray Diego Durán*, xxv–xxxvi. Norman: University of Oklahoma Press, 1994.

Hiatt, Alfred. "Mapping the Ends of Empire." In, *Postcolonial Approaches to the European Middle Ages: Translating Cultures*, edited by Ananya Jahanara Kabir and Deanne Williams. Cambridge: Cambridge University Press, 2005, 48–76.

Hillenbrand, Hans J. *The Division of Christendom: Christianity in the Sixteenth Century*. Louisville, KY: Westminster/John Knox Press, 2007.

Himerich y Valencia, Robert. *The Encomenderos of New Spain, 1521–1555*. Austin: University of Texas Press, 1991.

Hood, John Y. B. *Aquinas and the Jews*. Philadelphia: University of Pennsylvania Press, 1995.

Horkheimer, Max, and Theodor Adorno. *Dialectic of Enlightenment*. New York: Seabury Press, 1972.

Howe, John. "The Nobility's Reform of the Medieval Church." *The American Historical Review* 93 (1988): 317–39.

Hulme, Peter. *Colonial Encounters: Europe and the Native Caribbean, 1492–1797.*
London: Methuen, 1986.

———. "European Ethnography and the Caribbean." In *Implicit Understandings: Observing, Reporting, and Reflecting on the Encounters between Europeans and Other Peoples in the Early Modern Era*, edited by Stuart B. Schwartz, 157–97. New York: Cambridge University Press, 1994.

Huygens, R.B.C., ed. *Guibert de Nogent: Dei Gesta per Francos et cinq autres textes.* Corpus Christianorum: Continuatis Medievalis 12A. Turnholt: Brepols, 1996.

Iogna-Prat, Dominique. *Order and Exclusion: Cluny and Christendom Face Heresy, Judaism, and Islam (1000–1150).* Translated by Graham Edward Roberts, with foreword by Barbara H. Rosenwein. Ithaca, NY: Cornell University Press, 2002.

Jehlen, Myra. *American Incarnation: The Individual, the Nation and the Continent.* Cambridge, MA: Harvard University Press, 1986.

Kabir, Jahanara, and Deanne Williams, *Postcolonial Approaches to the European Middle Ages: Translating Cultures.* Cambridge: Cambridge University Press, 2005.

Kadafar, Cemal. *Between Two Worlds: The Construction of the Ottoman State.* Berkeley: University of California Press, 1995.

Kadir, Djelal. *Columbus and the Ends of the Earth.* Berkeley: University of California Press, 1992.

Kamen, Henry. *Inquisition and Society in Spain in the Sixteenth and Seventeenth Centuries.* Bloomington: Indiana University Press, 1982.

———. *The Spanish Inquisition: A Historical Revision.* New Haven: Yale University Press, 1997.

Kaplan, Yosef, ed. *Jews and Conversos.* Jerusalem: Magnes Press, 1985.

Kedar, Benjamin Z. *Crusade and Mission: European Approaches toward the Muslims.* Princeton, NJ: Princeton University Press, 1984.

———. "*De Iudeis et Sarracensis*: On the Categorization of Muslims in Medieval Canon Law." In *Studia in Honorem Eminentissimi Cardinalis Alphonsi M. Stickler*, 207–13. Studia et Textus Historiae Iuris Canonici 7. Rome: LAS, 1992.

Keely, Avril. "Arians and Jews in the *Histories* of Gregory of Tours." *Journal of Medieval History* 23, no. 2 (1997):103–15.

Kilgour, Maggie. *From Communion to Cannibalism: An Anatomy of Metaphors of Incorporation.* Princeton, NJ: Princeton University Press, 1990.

Klor de Alva, J. Jorge. "Colonizing Souls: The Failure of the Indian Inquisition and the Rise of Penitential Discipline." In *Cultural Encounters: The Impact of the Inquisition in Spain and the New World*, edited by Mary Elizabeth Parry and Anne J. Cruz, 3–22. Berkeley: University of California Press, 1991.

Kriegel, Maurice. "De la 'question' des 'nouveaux-chrétiens' á l'expulsion des juifs: La double modernité des proces d'exclusion dans l'Espagne du quinzième siècle." In *Le Nouveau Monde, Mondes nouveaux*, edited by Serge Gruzinski and Natan Wachtel, 469–90. Paris: Éditions Recherche sur les Civilisations; Éditions de l'École des Hautes Études en Sciences Sociales, 1996.

Kruger, Steven F. *The Spectral Jew: Conversion and Embodiment in Medieval Europe*. Minneapolis: University of Minnesota Press, 2006.

Kulp-Hill, Kathleen, trans. *Songs of Holy Mary of Alfonso X, the Wise: A Translation of the Cantigas de Santa María*. Introduction by Connie L. Scarborough. Tempe, AZ: Arizona Center for Medieval and Renaissance Studies, 2000.

Ladero Quesada, Miguel. "Spain, Circa 1492: Social Values and Structures." In *Implicit Understandings: Observing, Reporting, and Reflecting on the Encounters between Europeans and Other Peoples in the Early Modern Era*, edited by Stuart B. Schwartz, 96–133. New York: Cambridge University Press, 1994.

Lamana, Gonazol. "Of Books, Popes, and *Huacas*: Or, the Dilemmas of Being Christian." In *Rereading the Black Legend: The Discourses of Religions and Racial Difference in the Renaissance Empires*, edited by Margaret R. Greer, Walter D. Mignolo, and Maureen Quilligan, 117–50. Chicago: University of Chicago Press, 2007.

Lambropoulos, Vassilis. *The Rise of Eurocentrism: Anatomy of Interpretation*. Princeton, NJ: Princeton University Press, 1992.

Langmuir, Gavin. *History, Religion, and Antisemitism*. Berkeley: University of California Press, 1990.

Las Casas, Bartolomé de. *History of the Indies*. Translated and edited by Andrée Collard. New York: Harper and Row, 1971.

Lawton, David. *Blasphemy*. Philadelphia: University of Pennsylvania Press, 1993.

Lea, Henry Charles. *A History of the Inquisition of Spain*. New York: AMS Press, 1988. First edition 1906.

Le Goff, Jacques. *Intellectuals in the Middle Ages*. Cambridge, MA: Blackwell, 1993.

Léon-Portilla, Miguel. *Vision de los Vencidos: Cronicas Indigenas*. Madrid: Historia, 1985.

Levine, Robert. *The Deeds of God through the Franks: A Translation of Guibert de Nogent's Gesta Dei per Francos*. Rochester, NY: Bordell and Brewer, 1997.

Lewis, Norman. *The Missionaries: God against the Indians*. London: Arena, 1988.

Leyser, K.J., "Concepts of Europe in the Early and High Middle Ages," *Past and Present* 137 (1992), 25–47.

Lieu, Judith. *Christian Identity in the Jewish and Graeco Roman World*. Oxford: Oxford University Press, 2004.

Lincoln, Bruce. *Discourse and the Construction of Society*. New York: Oxford University Press, 1989.

Lippy, Charles H., Robert Choquette, and Stafford Poole. *Christianity Comes to the Americas*. New York: Paragon House, 1992.

Lieu, Judith M. *Christian Identity in the Jewish and Graeco-Roman World*. New York: Oxford University Press, 2004.

Little, Lester K. *Benedictine Maledictions: Liturgical Cursing in Romanesque France*. Ithaca, NY: Cornell University Press, 1993.

Lockhart, James. *The Men of Cajamarca: A Social and Biographical Study of the First Conquerors of Peru.* Austin: University of Texas Press, 1972.

Losada, Angel. "The Controversy between Sepúlveda and Las Casas in the Junta of Valladolid." In *Bartolomé de Las Casas in History,* edited by Juan Friede and Benjamin Keen, 279–308. DeKalb, IL: Northern Illinois University Press, 1971.

Luscombe, D.E., and G.R. Evans. "The Twelfth-Century Renaissance." In *The Cambridge History of Medieval Political Thought: C. 350–C.1450,* edited by J.H. Burns, 306–40. New York: Cambridge University Press, 1988.

Luxon, Thomas H. *Literal Figures: Puritan Allegory and the Reformation Crisis in Representation.* Chicago and London: The University of Chicago Press, 1993.

MacCormack, Sabine. *Religion in the Andes: Vision and Imagination in Early Colonial Peru.* Princeton, NJ: Princeton University Press, 1991.

———. "Demons, Imagination, and the Incas." *Representations* 33 (1991):147–62.

Malkiel, Yakov, and María-Rosa Lida Malkiel. "The Jew and the Indian: Traces of a Confusion in the Hispanic Tradition." In *For Max Weinreich on His Seventieth Birthday: Studies in Jewish Languages, Literature, and Society,* 203–8. The Hague: Mouton, 1964.

Manasseh ben Israel. *The Hope of Israel.* Edited with an introduction by Henry Méchoulan and Gérard Nahon. Oxford: Oxford University Press, 1987.

Manuel, Frank. *The Broken Staff: Judaism through Christian Eyes.* Cambridge, MA: Harvard University Press, 1992.

Marcus, Ivan G. "A Jewish-Christian Symbiosis: The Culture of Early Ashkenaz." In *Cultures of the Jews: A New History,* edited by David Biale, 449–516. New York: Schocken Books, 2002.

Martínez, María Elena, "Interrogating Blood Lines: 'Purity of Blood,' the Inquisition, and *Casta* Categories." In *Religion in New Spain,* edited by Susan Schroder and Stafford Poole, 196–217. Albuquerque: University of New Mexico Press, 2007.

———. "The Black Blood of New Spain: *Limpieza de Sangre,* Racial Violence, and Gendered Power in Early Colonial Mexico." *William and Mary Quarterly* LXI:3 (2004), 481–520.

Mason, Peter. "The Excommunication of Caterpillars: Ethno-Anthropological Remarks on the Trial and Punishment of Animals." *Social Science Information* 27, no. 2 (1988):265–73.

Mastnak, Tomaž. *Crusading Peace: Christendom, the Muslim World, and Western Political Order.* Berkeley: University of California Press, 2002.

McLean, Ian. " 'The Circumference Is Everywhere and the Centre Nowhere': Modernity and the Diasporic Discovery of Columbus as Told by Tzvetan Todorov." *Third Text* 24 (1992–93): 5–10.

Menocal, María Rosa. *Shards of Love: Exile and the Origins of the Lyric.* Durham, NC: Duke University Press, 1994.

Merrill, William L. "Conversion and Colonialism in Northern Mexico: The Tara-humara Response to the Jesuit Mission Program, 1601–1767." In *Conversion to Christianity: Historical and Anthropological Perspectives on a Great Transformation*, edited by Robert W. Hefner, 129–63. Berkeley: University of California Press, 1993.

Migne, J.-P., ed. *Burchardi Vormatiensis Episcopi Opera Omnia*. Patrologiae Cursus Completus ... Series Latina, v. 140. Paris: Garnier, 1880.

Mignolo, Walter D. "Literacy and Colonization: The New World Experience." In *1492–1992: Re/discovering Colonial Writing*, edited by Rene Jara and Nicholas Spadaccini, 51–96. Minneapolis: University of Minnesota Press, 1989.

———. When Speaking Was Not Good Enough: Illiterates, Barbarians, Savages, and Cannibals." In *Amerindian Images and the Legacy of Columbus*, edited by Rene Jara and Nicholas Spadaccini, 312–45. Minneapolis: University of Minnesota Press, 1992.

———. "Signs and Their Transmission: The Question of the Book in the New World." In *Writing without Words: Alternative Literacies in Mesoamerica and the Andes*, edited by Elizabeth Hill Boone and Walter D. Mignolo, 220–70. Durham, NC: Duke University Press, 1994.

———. *The Darker Side of the Renaissance: Literacy, Territoriality, and Colonization*. Ann Arbor: University of Michigan Press, 1995.

———. "Globalization, Civilizing Processes, and the Relocation of Languages and Cultures." In *The Cultures of Globalization*, edited by Fredric Jameson and Masao Miyoshi, 32–53. Durham and London: Duke University Press, 1998.

———. "The Many Faces of Cosmo-Polis: Border Thinking and Critical Cosmopolitanism," Public Culture 12:3 (2000), 721–48.

———. "Afterword: What Does the Black Legend Have to Do With Race?" In *Rereading the Black Legend: The Discourses of Religions and Racial Difference in the Renaissance Empires*, edited by Margaret R. Greer, Walter D. Mignolo, and Maureen Quilligan, 312–24. Chicago: University of Chicago Press, 2007.

Milbank, John. *Theology and Social Theory: Beyond Secular Reason*. New York: Blackwell, 1990.

Miller, Perry. *Errand Into the Wilderness*. Cambridge, MA: Belknap Press of Harvard University Press, 1956.

Mirrer, Louise. *Women, Jews and Muslims in the Texts of Reconquest Castile*. Ann Arbor: University of Michigan Press, 1996.

Moore, R.I. *The Formation of a Persecuting Society: Power and Deviance in Western Europe, 950–1250*. New York: Basil Blackwell, 1987.

———. *The First European Revolution, c. 970–1215*. Oxford and Malden, MA: Blackwells, 2000.

———. *The Formation of a Persecuting Society: Power and Deviance in Western Europe, 950–1250* (2nd edition). Malden, MA: Blackwells, 2007.

Moraña, Mabel, Enrique Dussel, and Carlos A. Jáuregui, eds., *Coloniality at Large: Latin America and the Postcolonial Debate*. Durham, NC: Duke University Press, 2008.

Moreno de los Arcos, Roberto. "New Spain's Inquisition for Indians from the Sixteenth to the Nineteenth Century." In *Cultural Encounters: The Impact of the Inquisition in Spain and the New World*, edited by Mary Elizabeth Perry and Anne J. Cruz, 23–36. Berkeley: University of California Press, 1991.

Morris, Colin. *The Papal Monarchy: The Western Church from 1050 to 1250*. Oxford: Clarendon Press, 1989.

Morrison, Karl F. *I Am You: The Hermeneutics of Empathy in Western Literature, Theology, and Art*. Princeton, NJ: Princeton University Press, 1988.

———. *Understanding Conversion*. Charlottesville: University of Virginia Press, 1992.

Mufti, Aamir. *Enlightenment in the Colony: The Jewish Question and the Crisis of Post-Colonial Culture*. Princeton, NJ: Princeton University Press, 2007.

Muldoon, James. *Popes, Lawyers, and Infidels: The Church and the Non-Christian World, 1250–1550*. Philadelphia: University of Pennsylvania Press, 1979.

———, ed. *The Expansion of Europe*. Philadelphia: University of Pennsylvania Press, 1977.

Nederman, Cary J., "Introduction: Discourses and Contexts of Tolerance in Medieval Europe." In *Beyond the Persecuting Society: Religious Toleration Before the Enlightenment*, edited by John Christian Laursen and Cary J. Nederman. Philadelphia: University of Pennsylvania Press, 1998.

Netanyahu, Benzion. *The Origins of the Inquisition in Fifteenth-Century Spain*. New York: Random House, 1995.

Nirenberg, David. *Communities of Violence: Persecution of Minorities in the Middle Ages*. Princeton, NJ: Princeton University Press, 1996.

———. "Conversion, Sex, and Segregation: Jews and Christians in Medieval Spain." *American Historical Review* 107 (October 2002): 1065–93.

———. "Mass Conversion and Genealogical Mentalities: Jews and Christians in Fifteenth-Century Spain." *Past and Present* 174 (February 2002): 3–41.

———. "Race and the Middle Ages: The Case of Spain and Its Jews." In *Rereading the Black Legend: The Discourses of Religions and Racial Difference in the Renaissance Empires*, edited by Margaret R. Greer, Walter D. Mignolo, and Maureen Quilligan. Chicago: University of Chicago Press, 2007, 71–88.

———. "Figures of Thought and Figures of Flesh: 'Jews' and 'Judaism' in Late-Medieval Spanish Poetry and Politics." *Speculum* 81 (2006): 398–426.

Obeyesekere, Gananath. *The Apotheosis of Captain Cook*. Princeton, NJ: Princeton University Press, 1992.

———. "'British Cannibals': Contemplation of an Event in the Death and Resurrection of James Cook, Explorer." *Critical Inquiry* 18 (Summer 1992): 630–54.

O'Callaghan, Joseph F. *Reconquest and Crusade in Medieval Spain*. Philadelphia: University of Pennsylvania Press, 2003.

O'Gorman, Edmundo. *The Invention of America: An Inquiry into the Historical Nature of the New World and the Meaning of Its History*. Bloomington: Indiana University Press, 1961.

O'Malley, John W. *The First Jesuits*. Cambridge: Harvard University Press, 1993.

Pagden, Anthony. *The Fall of Natural Man*. New York: Columbia University Press, 1986.

———. *Spanish Imperialism and the Political Imagination*. New Haven: Yale University Press, 1990.

———. "*Ius et Factum*: Text and Experience in the Writings of Bartolomé de Las Casas." *Representations* 33 (1991): 147–62.

———. "The Humanism of Vasco de Quiroga's 'Información en Derecho.'" In *The Uncertainties of Empire: Essays in Iberian and Ibero-American Intellectual History*, Collected Studies Series, 133–42. Brookfield, VT: Ashgate Publishing, 1994.

———. "The Search for Order: The School of Salamanca and the 'Ius Naturae.'" In *The Uncertainties of Empire: Essays in Iberian and Ibero-American Intellectual History*, Collected Studies Series, 155–56. Brookfield, VT: Ashgate Publishing, 1994.

Palencia-Roth, Michael. "The Cannibal Law of 1503." In *Early Images of the Americas: Transfer and Invention*, edited by Jerry M. Williams and Robert E. Lewis, 21–63. Tucson: University of Arizona Press, 1993.

Pardo, Osvaldo F. *The Origins of Mexican Catholicism: Nahua Rituals and Christian Sacraments in Sixteenth-Century Mexico*. Ann Arbor: University of Michigan Press, 2004.

Pearce, Roy Harvey. *Savagism and Civilization: The Indian and the American Mind*. 1953. Berkeley: University of California Press, 1988. First edition 1953.

Pelikan, Jaroslav. *The Growth of Medieval Theology (600–1300)*. Chicago: University of Chicago Press, 1978.

Pericot, Luis. *América indígena: El hombre americano. Los pueblos de América*. 2nd ed. Barcelona: Salvat, 1962.

Perry, Mary Elizabeth. *The Handless Maiden: Moriscos and the Politics of Religion in Early Modern Spain*. Princeton, NJ: Princeton University Press, 2005.

———. "Memory and Mutilation: The Case of the Moriscos." In *In the Light of Medieval Spain: Islam, the West, and the Relevance of the Past*, edited by Simon R. Doubleday and David Coleman. New York: Palgrave MacMillan, 2008.

Peterson, Willard J. "What to Wear? Observation and Participation by Jesuit Missionaries in Late Ming Society." In *Implicit Understandings: Observing, Reporting, and Reflection on the Encounters between Europeans and Other Peoples in the Early Modern Era*, edited by Stuart B. Schwartz. New York: Cambridge University Press, 1994.

Phelan, John Leddy. *The Millennial Kingdom of the Fransciscans in the New World*. 2nd ed. Berkeley: University of California Press, 1970.

Phillips, W.D., Jr.. "Transatlantic Encounters: Eyewitness Testimony and Spain's First American Possession, 1492–1536." *Medieval Encounters* 13 (2007), 145–57.

Pick, Lucy. *Conflict and Coexistence: Archbishop Rodrigo and the Muslims and Jews of Medieval Spain*. Ann Arbor: University of Michigan Press, 2004.

Pollock, Donald K. "Conversion and 'Community' in Amazonia." In *Conversion to Christianity: Historical and Anthropological Perspectives on a Great Tradition*, edited by Robert W. Hefner, 165–97. Berkeley: University of California Press, 1993.

Poole, Stafford, C.M. "The Declining Image of the Indian among Churchmen in Sixteenth-Century Spain." In *Indian-Religious Relations in Colonial Spanish America*, edited by Susan E. Ramírez, 11–19. Syracuse, NY: Maxwell School of Citizenship and Public Affairs, 1989.

Popkin, Richard H. "The Rise and Fall of the Jewish Indian Theory." In *Menasseh Ben Israel and His World*, edited by Yosef Kaplan, Henry Mèchoulan, and Richard H. Popkin. Leiden: Brill, 1989.

Rabasa, José. "Dialogue as Conquest: Mapping Spaces for Counter-Discourse." In *The Nature and Context of Minority Discourse*, edited by Abdul R. JanMohamed and David Lloyd, 187–215. New York: Oxford University Press, 1990.

———. *Inventing America: Spanish Historiography and the Formation of Eurocentrism*. Norman: University of Oklahoma Press, 1993.

Rafael, Vicente. *Contracting Colonialism: Translation and Christian Conversion in Tagalog Society under Early Spanish Rule*. Durham, NC: Duke University Press, 1993.

Ragussis, Michael. "The Birth of a Nation in Victorian Culture: The Spanish Inquisition, the Converted Daughter, and the 'Secret Race.'" *Critical Inquiry* 20, no. 3 (1994): 477–509.

Rama, Angel. *La ciudad letrada*. Hanover, NH: Ediciones del Norte, 1984.

———. *The Lettered City*. Edited and translated by John Charles Chasteen. Durham, NC: Duke University Press, 1996.

Rappaport, Joanne. *The Politics of Memory*. New York: Cambridge University Press, 1990.

Reff, Daniel T., "Making the Land Holy: The Mission Frontier in Early Medieval Europe and Colonial Mexico," in *The Spiritual Conversion of the Americas*, edited by James Muldoon. Gainesville: University Press of Florida, 2004, 17–35.

Reilly, Bernard F. *The Medieval Spains*. Cambridge: Cambridge University Press, 1993.

Ricard, Robert. *The Spiritual Conquest of Mexico: An Essay on the Apostolate and the Evangelizing Methods of the Mendicant Orders in New Spain: 1523–1572*. Translated by Lesley B. Simpson. Berkeley: University of California Press, 1966.

Rivera, Luis N. *A Violent Evangelism: The Political and Religious Conquest of the Americas*. Louisville, KY: Westminster/John Knox Press, 1992.

Robinson, Cynthia. "Trees of Love, Trees of Knowledge: Toward the Definition of a Cross-Confessional Current in Late Medieval Spirituality." *Medieval Encounters* 12, no. 3 (2006): 388–43.

Robinson, Cynthia, and Leila Rouhi, eds. *Under the Influence: Questioning the Comparative in Medieval Castile*. Leiden: Brill, 2005.

Rocha, Diego Andres. *Tratado único y singular del origen de los indios del Perú, Méjico, Santa Fé y Chile*. Alicante: Biblioteca Virtual Miguel de Cervantes, 2004.

Rosenwein, Barbara H., and Lester K. Little. "Social Meaning in the Monastic and Mendicant Spirituality." *Past and Present* 63 (1974): 21–32.

Rosman, Moshe. *How Jewish Is Jewish History?* Oxford: The Littman Library of Jewish Civilization, 2007.

Rothberg, Michael. *Multidirectional Memory: Remembering the Holocaust in the Age of Decolonization*. Stanford, CA: Stanford University Press, 2009.

Rubert de Ventós, Xavier. *The Hispanic Labyrinth: Tradition and Modernity in the Colonization of the Americas*. Translated by Mary Ann Newman. New Brunswick, NJ: Transaction Books, 1991.

Rubin, Miri. *Corpus Christi: The Eucharist in Late Medieval Culture*. Cambridge: Cambridge University Press, 1991.

———. *Gentile Tales: The Narrative Assault on Late Medieval Jews*. New Haven: Yale University Press, 1999.

Ruiz, Teofilo. *Spanish Society, 1400–1600*. Harlow, UK: Longmans, 2001.

Russell, Jeffrey Burton. *Lucifer, The Devil in the Middle Ages*. Ithaca, NY: Cornell University Press, 1984.

Sahagún, Fray Bernardino de. "The Aztec-Spanish Dialogues of 1524." Translated by J. Jorge Klor de Alva. *Alcheringa: Journal of Ethnopoetics* 4, no. 2 (1980): 52–193.

Said, Edward W. "Representing the Colonized: Anthropology's Interlocutors." *Critical Inquiry* 15, no. 2 (1989): 205–25.

———. *Culture and Imperialism*. New York: Alfred A. Knopf, 1993.

Seed, Patricia. " 'Are These Not Also Men?': The Indians' Humanity and Capacity for Spanish Civilisation." *Journal of Latin American Studies* 25 (1993): 629–52.

———. "Taking Possession and Reading Texts: Establishing the Authority of Overseas Empires." In *Early Images of the Americas: Transfer and Invention*, edited by Jerry M. Williams and Robert E. Lewis, 111–47. Tucson: University of Arizona Press, 1993.

———. *Ceremonies of Possession in the New World, 1492–1640*. Cambridge: Cambridge University Press, 1995.

———. *American Pentimento: The Invention of Indians and the Pursuit of Riches*. Minneapolis: University of Minnesota Press, 2001.

Shell, Marc. "Marranos (Pigs), or From Coexistence to Toleration." *Critical Inquiry* 17 (1991): 306–35.

Sicroff, Albert A. *Les controverses des statuts de "pureté de sang" en Espagne du 15e au 17e siècle*. Paris: Didier, 1960.

Silverblatt, Irene. "The Black Legend and Global Conspiracies: Spain, the Inquisition, and the Emerging Modern World." In *Rereading the Black Legend: The Discourses of Religions and Racial Difference in the Renaissance Empires*, edited by Margaret R. Greer, Walter D. Mignolo, and Maureen Quilligan, 99–116. Chicago: University of Chicago Press, 2007.

Simonson, Shlomo. *The Apostolic See and the Jews. Vol. 1, Documents: 492–1404*. Toronto: Pontifical Institute of Mediaeval Studies, 1988.

———. *The Apostolic See and the Jews. Vol. 2, 1394–1464*. Toronto: Pontifical Institute of Mediaeval Studies, 1989.

Simpson, Lesley Bird. "Translator's Preface." In *The Spiritual Conquest of Mexico*, by Robert Ricard, vii–viii. Berkeley: University of California Press, 1966.

Smith, Henry Nash. *Virgin Land*. Cambridge, MA: Harvard University Press, 1970. First edition 1950.

Southern, R.W. *Scholastic Humanism and the Unification of Europe. Vol. 1: Foundations*. Oxford: Blackwells, 1995.

Spivak, Gayatri Chakravorti. "Can the Subaltern Speak?" *In Marxism and the Interpretation of Culture*, edited by Cary Nelson and Lawrence Grossberg, 271–313. Urbana: University of Illinois Press, 1988.

Stannard, David E. *American Holocaust: Columbus and the Conquest of the New World*. New York: Oxford University Press, 1992.

Stendahl, Krister. *Paul among Jews and Gentiles*. Philadelphia: Fortress Press, 1976.

Stock, Brian. *The Implications of Literacy*. Princeton, NJ: Princeton University Press, 1983.

———. Afterword to *The Ethnography of Reading*, edited by Jonathan Boyarin, 170–75. Berkeley: University of California Press, 1993.

Stow, Kenneth R. *Alienated Minority: The Jews of Medieval Latin Europe*. Cambridge, MA: Harvard University Press, 1992.

———. *Jewish Dogs: An Image and Its Interpreters: Continuity in the Catholic-Jewish Encounter*. Stanford, CA: Stanford University Press, 2006.

Strickland, Debra. *Saracens, Demons, and Jews: Making Monsters in Medieval Art*. Princeton, NJ: Princeton University Press, 2003.

Summit, Jennifer, and David Wallace, eds. "Medieval/Renaissance: After Periodization," special issue of *The Journal of Medieval and Early Modern Studies*, 37(3): 2007.

Taussig, Michael. *The Devil and Commodity Fetishism in Latin America*. Chapel Hill: University of North Carolina Press, 1980.

———. *Shamanism, Colonialism, and the Wild Man: A Study in Terror and Healing*. Chicago: University of Chicago Press, 1987.

Taylor, Charles. *Sources of the Self: The Making of the Modern Identity*. Cambridge, MA: Harvard University Press, 1989.

———. "Modes of Civil Society." *Public Culture* 3 (Fall 1990): 95–118.

Tedlock, Dennis. *The Spoken Word and the Work of Interpretation.* Philadelphia: University of Pennsylvania Press, 1983.

Tellenbach, G. *Church, State, and Christian Society at the Time of the Investiture Contest.* Translated by R.F. Bennett. Toronto: University of Toronto Press, 1991.

Tilly, Charles. *Coercion, Capital and European States, 990–1992.* Cambridge, MA: Basil Blackwell, 1992.

Todorov, Tzvetan. *The Conquest of America: The Question of the Other.* New York: Harper and Row, 1984.

Tolan, John. *Petrus Alfonsí and His Medieval Readers.* Gainesville: University Press of Florida, 1993.

———. *Saracens: Islam in the Medieval European Imagination.* New York: Columbia University Press, 2002.

———. *Sons of Ishmael: Muslims through European Eyes in the Middle Ages.* Gainesville: University Press of Florida, 2008.

Trachtenberg, Joshua. *The Devil and the Jews: The Medieval Conception of the Jew and Its Relation to Modern Antisemitism.* Cleveland: World Publishing Company, 1961. First edition 1943.

Trevor-Roper, Hugh. *The Rise of Christian Europe.* New York: Harcourt Brace and World, 1965.

Tueller, James B. *Good and Faithful Christians: Moriscos and Catholicism in Early Modern Spain.* New Orleans: University Press of the South, 2002.

Turner, Frederick W. *Beyond Geography.* New Brunswick, NJ: Rutgers University Press, 1980.

Valk, Heiki. "Christianisation in Estonia: A Proces of Dual-Faith in Syncretism." In *The Cross Goes North: Processes of Conversion in Northern Europe, AD 300–1300.* York, UK: York Medieval Press, 2003, 571–79.

van Court, Elisa Marie Narin. "Critical Apertures: Medieval Anti-Judaisms and Middle English Narrative." Ph.D. diss., University of California, Berkeley, 1995.

Van Engen, John. "The Christian Middle Ages as an Historiographic Problem." *American Historical Review* 91, no. 3 (1986): 519–52.

———. "The 'Crisis of Cenobitism' Reconsidered: Benedictine Monasticism in the Years 1050–1150." *Speculum* 61 (1986): 269–304.

Veeser, H. Aram, ed. *The New Historicism.* New York: Routledge, 1989.

Vérastique, Bernardino. *Michoacán and Eden: Vasco de Quiroga and the Evangelization of Western Mexico.* Austin: University of Texas Press, 2000.

Vidal-Nacquet, Pierre. "Herodote et l'Atlantide: Entre les Grecs et les Juifs. Reflexions sur l'historiographie du siècle des Lumieres." *Quaderni Di Storia* 16 (1982): 5–74.

Wachtel, Natan. *The Vision of the Vanquished: The Spanish Conquest of Peru through Indian Eyes.* New York: Barnes and Noble, 1977.

———. Introduction to *Le Nouveau Monde, mondes nouveaux,* edited by Serge

Gruzinski and Natan Wachtel. Paris: Éditions Recherche sur les Civilisations; Éditions de l'École des Hautes Études en Sciences Sociales, 1996.

Walsh, Gerald G., and Grace Monahan, trans. *Saint Augustine: The City of God, Books VIII–XVI*. Washington, DC: Catholic University of America Press, 1952.

Weinreich, Max. "The Reality of Jewishness versus the Ghetto Myth: The Sociolinguistic Roots of Yiddish." In *To Honor Roman Jakobson*, vol. 3, 2199–2212. The Hague: Mouton, 1967.

Williams, Jerry M., and Robert E. Lewis. Introduction to *Early Images of the Americas: Transfer and Invention*, edited by Jerry M. Williams and Robert E. Lewis, xix–xxxiii. Tucson: University of Arizona Press, 1993.

———. Preface to *Early Images of the Americas: Transfer and Invention*, edited by Jerry M. Williams and Robert E. Lewis, xiii–xviii. Tucson: University of Arizona Press, 1993.

Williams, Robert A. *The American Indian in Western Legal Thought: The Discourses of Conquest*. New York: Oxford University Press, 1990.

Wood, Diana. "Infidels and Jews: Clement VI's Attitude to Persecution and Toleration." In *Persecution and Toleration*, edited by W. J. Sheils, 115–24. Studies in Church History 21. London: Basil Blackwell, 1984.

Wright, Robin. *Stolen Continents: The "New World" Through Indian Eyes*. Boston: Houghton Mifflin, 1992.

Yovel, Yermiyahu. *Spinoza and Other Heretics: The Marrano of Reason*. Princeton, NJ: Princeton University Press, 1992.

Yuval, Israel Jacob. "'They Tell Lies: You Ate the Man': Jewish Reactions to Ritual Murder Accusations." In *Religious Violence between Christians and Jews: Medieval Roots, Modern Perspectives*, edited by Anna Sapir Abulafia, 86–106. New York: Palgrave, 2002.

———. *Two Nations in Your Womb: Perceptions of Jews and Christians in Late Antiquity and the Middle Ages*. Berkeley: University of California Press, 2006.

Zagorin, Perez. *Ways of Lying: Dissimulation, Persecution, and Conformity in Early Modern Europe*. Cambridge, MA: Harvard University Press, 1990.